On Span and Space

Using materials and structures to form the guiding principles for architectural knowledge, *On Span and Space* offers an understanding of architecture from the consideration of how architectural works are actually put together.

The physical way our houses and buildings are constructed greatly influences their appearance and the way they are experienced. Today, the challenges for architectural engineering come from the new and increasing complexities of architectural concepts of space. With an increasing number of building materials as well as ever more refined manufacturing technologies, architecture can be expected to become more structurally complex, displaying a wider range of forms and geometries.

Formulating and discussing the main requisites for structural form in architecture, *On Span and Space* brings together concepts from both of the disciplines of architecture and engineering. The book is structured in three parts, each presenting a unique approach: it moves from a philosophical consideration of the ways and means of approaching structures in architecture, to discussing mechanical aspects of structural form – structural materials, structural efficiency and structural scale – to a final focus on an aesthetics of the structures of architecture, based on how beams, columns, arches and other structure types act spatially and mechanically in forming features of works of architecture.

An important text for any student, lecturer or researcher in architectural engineering, architectural design, history or theory, architectural or building technology and structural mechanics, this book provides for the first time both architectural and engineering areas of wisdom united in one theory which allows for a thorough understanding and solid knowledge base for one of architecture's most central means of expression.

Bjørn Normann Sandaker is Professor of Architectural Technology at the Oslo School of Architecture and Design in Norway. For over twenty years he has specialised in the crossover discipline of structural design in architecture, teaching undergraduate and postgraduate courses in which structural mechanics are taught alongside studio work for architectural design.

On Span and Space

Exploring structures in architecture

Bjørn Normann Sandaker

Routledge
Taylor & Francis Group

LONDON AND NEW YORK

First published 2008 by Routledge
2 Park Square, Milton Park, Abingdon, OX14 4RN
Simultaneously published in the USA and Canada by Routledge
270 Madison Avenue, New York, NY10016

Routledge is an imprint of the Taylor & Francis Group, an informa business

Typeset in 9/12.5 pt Frutiger by The Running Head Limited, www.therunninghead.com

Printed and bound in Great Britain by The Cromwell Press, Trowbridge, Wiltshire

British Library Cataloguing in Publication Data
A catalogue record for this book is available from the British Library

Library of Congress Cataloging in Publication Data
Sandaker, Bjørn Normann, 1954–
On span and space : exploring structures in architecture / Bjørn Normann Sandaker.
    p.   cm.
Includes bibliographical references and index.
ISBN 978-0-415-35787-6 (hbk: alk. paper) – ISBN 978-0-415-35792-0 (pbk: alk. paper)
1. Architecture and technology. I. Title.
NA2543.T43S23 2007
721—dc22
2007015478

ISBN10: 0-415-35787-X (hbk)
ISBN10: 0-415-35792-6 (pbk)
ISBN10: 0-203-00394-2 (ebk)
ISBN13: 978-0-415-35787-6 (hbk)
ISBN13: 978-0-415-35792-0 (pbk)
ISBN13: 978-0-203-00394-7 (ebk)

Front cover The Nordic Pavilion, Venice (1962). Architect Sverre Fehn, structural
engineer Arne Neegård.

To Wenche, my dear wife,
and Victoria, Nicolay and Sophie,
the loveliest of children

Contents

Illustration credits

The author and publishers would like to thank the following for permission to reproduce illustrations. We have made every effort to contact copyright holders, but if any errors or omissions have been made we would be happy to correct them in a subsequent edition.

The Architectural Archives, University of Pennsylvania 2.57, 2.58
Einar Bangsund 3.53
Birkhäuser Verlag 2.66
Egil Bjerke 3.15
Geir Brendeland 1.2
Buro Happold 3.21
Calatrava Valls SA 3.48
Constrado 2.31
Coop-Himmelb(l)au 3.36, 3.38
Einar Dahle 2.27, 2.28
Dover Publications 2.2, 2.3, 2.53, 2.64
Arne Eggen 2.35
Steinar Eriksrud 2.7, 2.80
G.H. Fisher 3.5
Per Olaf Fjeld 3.24, 3.25, 3.28, 3.33, 3.34
Fossum AS 3.55
Franken Architekten/Friedrich Busam 3.41, 3.42, 3.43
Neven Fuchs-Mikac 2.6
Oskar Graf 3.39
Harvard University Press 2.23
Christian Hermansen 3.7
Herzog und Partner 2.78, 2.79
Mari Hvattum 2.45
Toyo Ito & Associates 3.26, 3.27
Peter Kulka 3.44, 3.45, 3.46, 3.47
Ian Lambot 2.16, 2.18
Jens Lindhe 2.39
Bruno Mancia 2.26

Peter Manning 2.67, 2.68
Nils Mjaaland 3.54
Moelven 3.13, 3.14
Moncalvo/Harvard University Press 2.55
Pearson Education 2.65
Renzo Piano Building Workshop/ Paul Hester 3.29
Renzo Piano Building Workshop/ Richard Bryant 3.30
Renzo Piano Foundation 3.31
Princeton Maillart Archive 2.25
QAPhotos/Jim Byrne 3.20
Mandy Reynolds/Buro Happold 3.23
Bjørn N. Sandaker 1.1, 1.4, 1.6, 1.7, 1.9, 1.10, 2.4, 2.5, 2.8, 2.9, 2.10, 2.11, 2.12, 2.13, 2.15, 2.17, 2.20, 2.21, 2.22, 2.30, 2.32, 2.33, 2.34, 2.40, 2.41, 2.42, 2.44, 2.56, 2.60, 2.61, 2.69, 2.70, 2.72, 2.73, 2.75, 2.76, 2.77, 2.81, 2.82, 3.1, 3.2, 3.4, 3.6, 3.9, 3.10, 3.11, 3.12, 3.22, 3.32, 3.35, 3.49, 3.50, 3.51, 3.52, 3.58
Lars Chr. Sandaker 3.16, 3.17
Søren Sandved 3.57
Stahl-Informations-Zentrum 2.54
Teigen©Knudsens fotosenter 2.50
Von Gerkan u. Marg 3.18, 3.19
Gerald Zugmann 3.37, 3.40

Preface and acknowledgements

Today, the challenges for architectural engineering come from the new and increasing complexity of architectural concepts of space. Technology is rapidly changing and traditional design ideals seem to be losing ground. Now that traditional materials like steel and reinforced concrete can be adapted to virtually any structural form, the current problem is not how to implement the paradigms of structural efficiency and honesty but, rather, how to recognise structural qualities. In this book I shall ask on what basis can we establish a new critique that can appraise structures both as mechanical systems and as expressions of architecturo-spatial intentionality, both as *techne* and *telo*s.

My formulation of problems in this book is the outcome of years of experience teaching structural design at schools of architecture, and of being a consultant to practising architects. My primary objective is to help raise the discussion of the design of structures in architecture to the level of a professional discourse. My main strategy is to try to establish a dialogue between theoretical disciplines and the practical knowledge held by the professions involved, namely engineering and architecture.

I would like to thank the Oslo School of Architecture and Design for their continued encouragement, as well as for giving me the opportunity to reflect on matters which interest me greatly. Of the many people who have helped me, I will mention only very few. For giving me precise advice at a crucial moment during the writing process I would like to thank Dr Bill Addis. He is exceptionally well qualified in the subjects this book deals with; his comments have been invaluable. I want to express my sincere thanks, also, to Caroline Mallinder at Taylor & Francis, whose trust in me has made this book possible. Her support, advice and great patience – and that of her assistant Georgina Johnson – have been hugely important to me. How easy it is to miscalculate the time needed to do all the work in presenting a manuscript! Likewise, I want to thank David Williams of The Running Head, who has made my manuscript into a book. My cooperation with him on both text and pages has been both interesting and stimulating. I am exceptionally pleased with the result. My sincere thanks also go to A. Espen Baerheim, student of the Oslo School of Architecture and Design, for making all the drawings and for producing the electronic images. Without him taking charge of those, I would hardly have been able to concentrate on all the rest.

Lastly, many thanks to my family, who have shown great patience and understanding throughout the long gestation from idea to finished book.

Bjørn Normann Sandaker, Oslo, 23 February 2007

PART 1

PHILOSOPHY

Fundamental aspects of structures

To understand the role and rationale of structures in architecture we need to look at their individual details. This requires some theorising in order to establish a solid footing from which we can develop deeper insights. My intention is to present first a brief but foundational philosophy of structures. My initial attempts to understand, then, will not be restricted to the study of specific empirical evidence but will look at load-bearing structures in general. What are structures? What conditions influence their making, shape and appearance, and why?

Defining structures

In this context, 'structure' means a physical object or a system of material elements necessary for enabling people to cross a river, to lift goods, to enclose a certain space and numerous other functions. These functions always involve the keeping of materials up in the air, resulting in a continuous struggle against gravity. The primary reason, of course, for the existence of structures is the practical purpose they serve. By serving those purposes the logical outcome is that structures have to 'transport' loads from the point of their origin and down to the ground. Structures become load-bearing. This is the natural order of the relationship between the 'why' and the 'how', or reason and consequence: practical purpose comes first, and physical necessity follows.[1]

Offering a definition, however, of the notion of structure solely by stating its purpose does not really answer the question: what is this object that serves a practical function by transporting loads to the ground? Many writers on the subject are content with an operational description, but a notable exception is Daniel Schodek, who suggests a more elaborate but slightly abstract definition. A structure is, he says, 'a physical entity having a unitary character that can be conceived of as an organization of positioned constituent elements in space in which the character of the whole dominates the interrelationship of the parts'.[2]

With the help of this fairly complex definition, Schodek is able to make clear some important points. First, structure in our context is a real physical object, not a kind of abstract organisation. Also, the structure is subjected to gravitational forces as well as to other loads, and will respond to those according to its geometrical configuration and material properties. Furthermore, Schodek's suggestive definition emphasises that a structure functions as a whole: beams, struts, ties, columns or whatever are parts of its constituent elements; they work together and influence each other's physical behaviour. That they should do so is a

1.1 Anthony Caro, *End Game* (1971–4), exhibited at Trajan's Markets, Rome, 1992. The sculpture is readily understood as structural, and can act as a metaphor for architecture.

necessary condition for speaking of a structure at all. A clarification that should be made, however, is that we should think of the word 'character' in terms of physicality and concreteness rather than appearance or aesthetics. The structure does not necessarily have to be designed in a way that its form is *perceived* as having a unitary character, or that the character of the whole dominates the way the parts relate visually to each other. Moreover, in order to keep in mind the operational purpose of the structure, we need to supplement our definition with a reference to the load-bearing function. With these qualifications, however, there should be no problem adopting the definition as offered by Schodek.

What is, then, the purpose or function of a load-bearing structure? 'The function of a structure', Macdonald says, 'is to supply the strength and rigidity which are required to prevent a building from collapsing.'[3] None will disagree with this. Yet if we are considering structures in an architectural context, this statement suggests only the minimum solution to the question of function. That the structure is designed to prevent the collapse of a building is the very least we should expect from it. Engineering is able to solve the most basic requirements, but luckily it leaves the door wide open for making the structure even more momentous. In many cases in architecture, structures are not solely associated with their load-bearing function. In architecture, there is traditionally a very close relationship between structure, architectural space and expression, so that a characterisation in terms of the load-bearing function alone is not enough. Understanding structures will frequently also mean that we see structures as space-defining elements or as devices that control the inflow of daylight; or we may assign them numerous other functions that are required of architectural spaces. Structures serve many purposes; it is important that we keep this in mind, not only for our understanding of structural form in architecture but also for a judicious and illuminating critique of a particular structure.

Generally speaking, we will look at structures that form parts of a work of architecture, as opposed to structures for machines, cranes or aircraft. Since there are obvious difficulties in trying to delimit the field of architecture, we shall keep this part of the definition as open as possible. The main point is that structures in architecture are conceived – and perceived – differently from structures in other contexts. In the integral relationship that exists between structures and architectural spaces certain issues surface which help to characterise those structures, and which differentiate the structures of architecture from structures of other kinds. I will elaborate on those issues in the following chapters.

The relationship between architecture and one of its prime constituent elements, structure, was not always as multifarious or diverse as it is today. In contemporary architecture, structural elements or systems can play a major role as an organiser of the space or as a means for expression – or no role at all, depending on the architect's preferences. It was not always like that: Greek classical architecture depended upon its beams and columns for expression. Proportion, dimension and a refined articulation of form were all related to the structural elements, as was the rich vocabulary of ornamental treatment of primarily structural details and structural connections. This was originally a constructive art where structural elements had both a technological as well as a more abstract and expressive purpose. During the Renaissance this classical inheritance was taken up and looked upon anew. While structural elements were still a prominent part of the architectural vocabulary, they became subordinate to aesthetic and symbolic systems developed from contemporary ideals and theories on universal proportions. Still, expression was linked to construction.

With the advent of modernism, things changed. Auguste Perret and particularly his assistant Le Corbusier made a rhetorical point of separating constructive elements from functional/expressive elements. Even though this was a well-known principle at the time, not least among the architects and engineers of the Chicago School, Le Corbusier advocated it in his role as architectural ideologist. In his Dom-Ino concept the structure has virtually been emptied of any meaning except the purely technical. Architecture could now be seen as two autonomous systems, the purely structural and the purely aesthetic. While the structural system had been reduced to a question of technicalities, the aesthetic system was raised to a kind of abstract, formal composition that included the free plan, the free façade, and a play of surface texture and colour.[4] This ideal inherited from the early modernists is very much present in contemporary architecture too, but is (fortunately) not always the guiding principle. Here we will not pay particular attention to the purely technical aspects of structures. Those are not the kinds of structures I have in mind when we explore the structures of architecture. At least, they are a special case. The skeleton structures of that type have a fairly simple logic: they are products of technical and economic optimisation. *The characteristic feature of the structures I want to look at is that they are somehow part of architectural expression, and influence – or are influenced by – the architectural space.* I would like to see building structures as architecture, or at least as parts of an architectural composition. To be able to understand such structures fully requires the mobilisation not only of scientific and technological knowledge but also architectural competence and sensibility. The concept of technology itself takes on a slightly different meaning in this situation, because existential aspects like 'memory and time are legitimate aspects of an architectural technology that pure engineering technologies do not encompass'.[5] Thus historical references as well as visual representation may both form parts of a structural vocabulary.

Closely linked to the problems of definition is the problem of sorting out the objects of interest (the structures) from the architectural work as a whole. Where does the structure begin and end? The example of a dome is a case where delimitation could prove difficult. Even though a dome is easily identified as a form or *gestalt*, the structure of the dome does not necessarily correspond entirely to this form, but also involves abutment walls and foundations. Such walls are almost certainly also parts of other architectonic configurations. Similarly, a skeletal structure is relatively easy to identify and define as a separable, structural entity, while a solid wall structure defies such a clear-cut and purely structural identification. In the case of a three- or four-storey brick building, the load-bearing structures are also the same objects, or walls, that enclose the interior architectural space. In this case, then, both the physical delimitation of space as well as the support function are aspects of the same objects. From one point of view the walls are enclosures and have spatial properties, while from another the same walls need to be considered as load-bearing devices. Typically, structures in architecture are assigned different functions and take part in complex physical and spatial relationships. We will need to identify those in order to bring the discussion further.

Aspects of structural form

If the purposes of structures are indeed multifarious, their identification and definition really depend on where we direct our attention. If the load-bearing element is the same physical object as the space-enclosing element, we can certainly follow more than one line of reasoning to explain its form properly. Structures in architecture, where they are integral parts of architectural spaces, can only be understood by applying different kinds of knowledge. When we look at a wall we should be able to say whether or not this particular wall is load-bearing – that is, if it is really a part of the structure. If it is, we can comment on the form of the wall – its thickness, the number and size of its openings, its

1.2 Solid timber walls both bear loads and delimit the architectural space. Architects Brendeland and Kristoffersen, engineers Reinertsen AS: low-cost housing (2004), Svartlamoen, Trondheim, Norway.

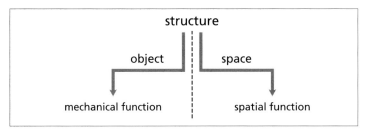

1.3 The main functions of structures in architecture concern mechanics and space.

connections to other building components – on the basis of its function as a supporting element. To do this with any precision we will have to know about the properties of the actual material, its strength and its general behaviour when loaded. We also need to know, at least in general terms, how loads can be transferred through matter. The concepts and laws of the mechanical sciences can help us understand these kinds of problems. The form and proportions of the wall may hence be partly explained by how this wall behaves when subjected to external, physical influences, to loads. We would also expect to find that the particular shape and texture of the wall in some way reflects the making process: the treatment of the raw material, the manufacturing as well as the construction of the wall itself. The latter is the technological aspect. Consequently, the wall may be helpfully – but not fully –interpreted from a technologico-scientific point of view. Such characteristics defined by the natural sciences and technology will be referred to as the mechanical aspects of structures. I will refer to them when addressing the structures' *mechanical functions*.

On the other hand, the same wall may also be intended to close off or visually delimit the architectural space, and thus have a practical purpose other than the role of support. This purpose, referred to here as its *spatial functions*, may easily influence some of the properties of the wall such as thickness, shape and openings. Even if architectural elements have a load-bearing function, their form must also be interpreted with reference to their spatial use. Some might choose not to speak of *structural* elements in such cases, but how is one to distinguish one from the other? As long as an element has several architectural functions, including the support function, then all we can do is to distinguish between aspects of that form according to the different points of view from which they can be studied. If an understanding of structural elements is the aim, we need to look at them in their full, including spatial, context.

We can see how the load-bearing function makes it necessary to consider the structure as an object in its own right, whereas issues concerning utility functions relate structures to questions of the architectural space. We will hence look upon structures as mechanical objects as well as spatial objects that constitute vital elements of architectural spaces. This *object versus space* duality of structures in architecture makes them particularly interesting to design and to study. Any architectural analysis of structural form should therefore take into consideration the two main

1.4 Two extreme structural opposites: one is expressive and relates to the space – a work of art. The other represents pure utility – a crane. Both have to comply with a set of mechanical requirements, enabling them to remain standing. Sculpture in Rotterdam by Coop-Himmelb(l)au and Rotterdam harbour.

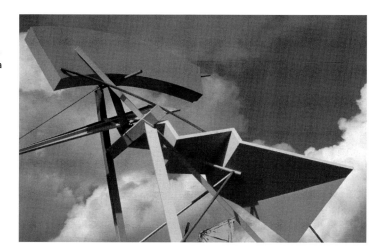

aspects of structures: that structures have both a mechanical as well as a spatial function. By considering structures from both viewpoints we can begin to understand fully the complexity and richness of form and expression that characterises structures in architecture.[6]

To illustrate how an aspect-based approach can be applied to an architectural analysis focusing on structures, we shall take a look at the National Gallery in Parma, Italy. The so-called La Pilotta museum (1986) was designed by the architect Guido Canali.[7] Among many other items, a number of heavy stone sculptures are exhibited, some on a white-painted steel frame. An important *spatial function* of this structure is of course the very simple one of keeping the sculptures in an elevated position so that the public can see them properly; at the same time, the space and the floor area underneath the sculptures are left open. The choice of structural form reflects both functional intentions. However, the deci-

1.5 Heavy stone sculptures raised on a light structural frame. Architect Guido Canali: The National Gallery ('La Pilotta') (1986), Parma, Italy.

sion to support all four stone sculptures by only one structural frame – rather than to bring each one directly and separately down to floor level – must be interpreted in light of the architect's wish to keep the floor space free of obstruction. Both refer to the spatial *utility* aspect of the structure. An interesting feature of the structural detailing, moreover, is that it actually consists of two separate frames. The size of the sculptures' bases are so large that the supporting structure needs to be wide enough for the sculptures to be balanced. The architect secures their stability by splitting the frame into two parallel halves put relatively close together, and makes sure the sculptures are resting on both.

This particular design decision reflects both the structure's practical use and the importance of its relation to architectural space. The introduction of two parallel frames instead of one makes the cross-sections of the frames significantly smaller. Visually, the result is that the structure appears lighter and thus presents an effective contrast to the heavy stone sculptures. In fact, we can recognise an architectural intention if we consider the structure part of the architectural space, heightening our experience of the space itself. This is achieved by the use of contrasting materials and by different forms of visual expressiveness that counterpose lightness and weight. The sculptures and the existing building fabric both visually outweigh the new steel structure and thus appear more perceptually distinct. All three establish a unity of relationship between structure and constructed room with its contents, between span and space. There is a striving here for some sort of spatial coherence where the structure and the space are both meant to form parts of the same context. What we may term *contextuality* (structural form in its architectural and spatial context) is an important aspect of structural design, and one we need to take into consideration if we are to understand the structures of architecture in clarity and depth.

To assert there is a relation between structural form and spatial intentions does not necessarily infer the relationship is harmonious. Indeed, some structures in architecture are best understood by admitting that there are other kinds of relationships than mere 'harmony between the structural system and the architectural form'.[8] Yet 'an important aspect of the art of architecture is to choose a structural strategy that will be in some sort of accord with the intended spatial organisation'.[9] Some sort of coherence between the structure and the space should be identifiable, but it may take many forms.

We may observe that the ability of structures to carry loads is based on the mechanical and geometrical properties of the structural frame, as well as the strength and elasticity of its materials. The frame is able to carry the loads acting on the beam and, through its vertical members, to transport those loads to other more rigid parts of the building. Horizontal stability is secured by the rigidity of the frame (with help from the adjoining walls). The size and shape of the structural members, as well as their strength and elasticity, need (obviously) to be adequate to avoid collapse or undue deformation. The mechanical *sciences* (notably statics and the science of materials) offer some of the available explanations for this particular structural form. By applying theory from these fields, aspects of the structural form become explicable as mechanical features. Those explanations do not point to *a* specific design solution but help to identify one possible candidate among many others. Facts derived from thinking based on mechanics will rule out, in principle, a range of other design proposals, and will help clarify why a particular solution was chosen.[10]

Next, if we direct our attention to Canali's white-painted, scaffolding-like structure spanning the width of the old palace almost at roof level, we will be able to identify more detailed aspects of structural form. This particular structure's main utility functions are obviously to establish

1.6 The National Gallery, Parma. Interior view with the structures of the additional exposition area hovering above.

1.7 The National Gallery, Parma.
Structural details.

elevated floors as additional exposition areas in the generous space
of the converted palace, as well as to provide an adaptable structural
framework which supports (or from which is suspended) a modular panelling system for the display of paintings. We can interpret the
structure even better, however, if we look at aspects of its representation: by employing a structural system normally found on construction
sites, recognisable by its clumsy but effective mechanical detailing, the
structure in some respects looks like tube and clamp scaffolding. This
associative likeness is clearly intentional; by noticing it we are helped
towards a better understanding of this particular structure. In addition
to the many practical functions of structures we may also thus assign a
representational or an *iconographic* function.[11] This makes possible an

understanding of structural form, in some cases, as a representation of an object outside of itself.[12] Although not a 'practical' aspect of structural form, we may still see it as a particular function, a spatial function whose purpose is, in the present case, to enable us to see the structure as an adaptable, impermanent and also, to a certain degree, unfinished work. Thus the structure emphasises, by contrast, the enduring and robust quality of the masonry shell of the surrounding building. Not only do we know the structure to be potentially impermanent, but through its associative likeness to scaffolding we also perceive it as such. In general, then, any serious and thorough critique of structural form must include a possible iconographic reading of it.

When studying this structure from a mechanics point of view we will notice that the multitude of structural members include both vertical and horizontal struts and ties as well as diagonal members, all arranged in a way so that they form a huge spatial truss. The result is a light structure with seemingly quite flexible load transfer possibilities. The concept of impermanence and adaptability has led to a structural design based on a system of components and details which originates in and ostensibly belongs to a construction process rather than to a permanently finished work. The steel tubes, and above all the clamps, stem from a technology developed for speedy and effective erection and subsequent dismantling. From a *technological* point of view, this construction principle is very well suited to the particular building task; the use of small structural components that can easily be brought into the existing building structure and put together *in situ* must definitely be thought of as an advantage. Generally speaking, the structural examples from Parma make explicit that we can, obviously, also expect the structure by its form, its detailing and the surface texture of its materials, to reflect its manufacturing. Technological methods, both regarding the production of materials and components, as well as the actual process of construction, put their mark on the finished result. Hence, reflecting on structures from a technological viewpoint is obviously mandatory for understanding structural form as the result of a working process.

I will at this stage emphasise that it makes perfect sense to distinguish between a technological and a scientific way of understanding structural form. Too often, mechanical aspects relating to load-bearing structures are simply put in a big bag of knowledge labelled 'technology'. There is a big difference, however, between the two approaches. We may on the one hand speak of structural 'forms that are scientific in the sense of being disciplined by the laws of nature'.[13] Certain aspects of those forms are explainable in terms of how nature works; as a result they will suggest a particular framework for exploring structural options. To appreciate structures as mechanical objects requires an ability acquired 'by systematic study of those branches of mechanical science which are concerned with statics, equilibrium and the properties of materials'.[14] On the other hand there is, as Bill Addis says 'something rather worrying

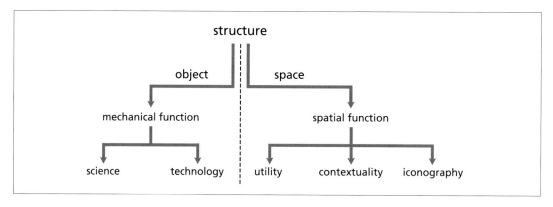

1.8 A taxonomy of aspects of structural form.

about the engineer who believes that all aspects of a design are capable of mathematical formulation according to scientific laws'.[15] The appreciation of structures also requires 'a knowledge of buildings and how they are constructed'.[16] The latter is a kind of technological knowledge that will inform our perspective quite differently from science; it will deal, above all, with material transformation processes. Science and technology are equally relevant bodies of knowledge, and both essential for an understanding of the mechanical aspects of structures. I will elaborate on their differences on pages 16–18.

From our previous discussion, and illustrated by the example of the La Pilotta museum in Parma, we can now identify the aspects of structural form in some detail and from various points of view.

Culture and construction

We have inherited from Vitruvius and Alberti a basic classification of different aspects of a work of architecture. The mechanical/spatial way of seeing structures that I propose here is, however, limited to architectural structures. Still, while such problematisations of the topic seem specifically and delimitedly architectural, at another level of understanding all structures can be seen as products of human culture in the broadest sense. Structures have been built at all times in human history, in all places and under different social conditions, and it is thus to be expected that we might understand certain aspects of structural form by studying the social, cultural and historical conditions under which the structures were conceived and built. Hence it is highly relevant to ask questions like: What was the economic situation that could help explain this or that particular structure? What was the availability of certain materials? What level of scientific and technological knowledge did the structure require of the society that built it? Is a particular structure dependent upon computer-aided design and manufacturing to be financially feasible? What cultural climate was necessary for the general public of the nineteenth century to allow iron to be used as part of their urban structures?

There are three dimensions of structures, Billington says: the scientific, the symbolic and the social. These are thought to correspond with the 'ideals of structural art', namely efficiency, elegance and economy.[17] While the first and the second deal more or less with how structures work and how they are visually perceived, the last is concerned with the social dimension: the demand from society for more utility for less money. Even if cost plays an important part in decisions on structural materials and structural form, it seems to be very difficult if not impossible to link economy directly to the understanding of a particular built form. A low budget does not result in such or such a structure. Contrary to what can be argued for mechanics and the spatial function, economy does not have a shape. This, however, should not prevent us from commenting upon cost, based on general observations of the degree of technological or functional efficiency. A structure made from mass-produced standard parts will probably have lower production costs than one that is custom built, even if new CNC-manufacturing and other technologies are increasingly expected to cut down on the costs of bespoke design. However, the notion of cost varies greatly according to time and place, and from a highly industrialised society to one less so, and is always a question of how societies value labour and how they value materials. Taking into account ever-present technological change, the relative value of labour and materials does not remain constant. Thus while economic considerations clearly play an important part in structural design, it is not equally obvious how the knowledge of the cost of a particular structure can inform its critique, where the idea is to communicate an understanding of built form in a particular spatial context. Because of the multifarious functions that such structures have, economic questions play a most uncertain role. In this book, therefore, the question of cost is not treated explicitly but is considered as part of a social background that (together with a number of other issues) makes up a comprehensive cultural and social context in which a particular structure belongs.

The historical development of structures is another matter. It is quite possible to undertake a historical study of structures, commenting on changes of structural form and structural materials in step with changes in science and culture. This has been done by several authors.[18] On the other hand, a historical approach alone will not help us to see the whole picture when studying a particular work of architecture. Let us settle for a strategy that considers historical aspects as parts of a wider context that may be acknowledged, if relevant, when we try to understand particular structural forms.

Explanation vs. interpretation of structural form

So far, I have suggested some aspects of structures which may act as concepts that can help us recognise characteristic properties of structural form. Those concepts make us see what structures are and why they are designed the way they are. I am following two main lines of

1.9 In terms of mechanics, a structure's shape and size make sense if they prevent the walls from caving in. From a spatial point of view, the purpose of the form of the structural elements might be to provide the right daylight conditions. The two tentative conclusions, however, are reached on very different intellectual grounds. Architect Richard MacCormac, Southwark Station (1999), Jubilee Line, London.

thinking; structures as mechanical objects studied from the point of view of technology and the laws of science, as compared to the study of structures as intimately related to the making of architectural spaces. While the one focuses on structures as objects having their own interior logic dealing with the interrelationship of form, strength, stiffness and process, the other line of thinking sees structures in a wider context where structural forms must be understood by help of certain functional and spatial relationships. Moreover, I have so far avoided commenting on possible *aesthetic* aspects of structures, the fact that we visually experience structures in a more or less pleasurable way. Why is the observation of structures a pleasurable experience in some cases but not in others? What determines whether we experience a certain satisfaction or not when looking at a particular structure? Does the aesthetic experience of structures involve quite different aspects of structures than those we have so far outlined? To answer the last question: that is most unlikely. On the contrary, the aesthetic experience of structures in an architectural context, and the appreciation that may accompany this, is intimately related to both their mechanical and their spatial functions. I will discuss this relationship in precise detail in Part 3 of this book.

Since we are approaching structures from two different methodological viewpoints, we can expect them to seem different according to the selectivities and blindspots of each. Imagine we are considering the shape and height of a structural element. We might conclude, but not necessarily from mere observation, that its dimensions are adequate to prevent it failing or being inappropriately deformed. To get to this point we go through a very different intellectual process than if we imagine that the structural element is such and such particular height because it makes the element reflect light better. In the first case we can argue our point by referring to general laws on how materials react to loads, and then by applying those laws to the element or component in question. This will help explain the particularities of its form. The other way of seeing the element's height means we look at it in a wider context. What are the relevant spatial intentions, if any, of the shape? We interpret the beam in its broader setting, studying how it interacts with other physical conditions. This kind of interpretation, however, is a different matter than any argument based on physics or mechanics. We seek clarification of the architect's intentions for the work; we approach the structure with its context in mind, and light might well be a relevant part of that context. The aim here – a kind of hermeneutical praxis – is to reach an understanding of rather than to offer explanations for structural form.

Hence, depending upon what formal feature of a given structure we study, we draw upon different kinds of explanations or different modes of understanding. After an initial interpretation of a material element as part of a structural system, for example, some aspects of that element are scientifically explainable according to the laws of physics.[19] But what *is* a scientific explanation? According to the philosophy of science, an explanation seeks to make clear why things are as they are and not otherwise; this includes theorisations of origins and causation. This means in our case that there is a *causal* relationship between various physical influences and their effect. When subjected to a particular load configuration, the particular form of a structure will react *by necessity* in a specific and predictable way. This knowledge helps us explain structural form as a design strategy to avoid structural failure. The kinds of explanations that are relevant here are of the deductive-nomological (DN) type – that is, explanations based on deductions from general or natural laws. According to von Wright, these kinds of explanations are typically applied to natural phenomena and, hence, the physical aspects of man-made objects. After all, limestone does not stop expanding with a rise in temperature after it has been transformed through technology into a reinforced concrete beam.[20] When materials, structural strength and stiffness are discussed in the forthcoming chapters, the underlying explanations for structural form are of this type. Awareness of the assumptions and premises of DN explanations will help clarify the effects of natural phenomena on structural form.

What about the technological aspects of structures, namely the knowledge and practices relating to their processing, manufacturing and erection? What kind of thought process clarifies the relationship between actual production and resulting form? Technology, in our context, deals with both the transformation of materials into structural elements and the transformation of those elements into works of architecture. We shall try to grasp what is happening when matter is restructured from one state into another, seeking to understand the relationship between how 'things' are made, and how those 'things' are designed, put to use, and also visually experienced. In short, it is a question of the relationship between process and product.

There is a fundamental cognitive difference, well pointed out by David Billington, between the science and technology of structural form. Science is concerned with describing natural processes and is thus able to establish causal relationships between various physical influences and their effects. We may say that certain shapes are created because they are necessary, taking their load-bearing function into account. Technology, on the other hand, deals with intentional acts, whose products are 'forms that exist only because people want to make them'[21]. As human beings, we are free to choose the technological ways and methods we think appropriate in a particular situation; when we choose a particular technological process or mode, however, the resulting form may suggest a kind of inevitability. This makes the technological aspect an aspect that in addition to intentionality also has elements of causality. Technology, like science, is also bound by certain rules, not the laws of nature, but by a set of methods that must operate within existing and available practical possibilities.[22] A technological approach to structural form implies technological thinking; this, according to Tom Peters, is a combination of analytical and contextual thinking. Analytical thought is 'linear and hierarchical and aims to be independent of the thinker's personal and cultural value system so that results can be repeated by anyone'. Contextual thinking, however, 'is nonlinear. It moves from track to track, from level to level through associative leaps in logic'. It is 'subjective and always depends on the thinker's own value system'.[23]

How, then, do we usually refer to form that results from technological processes? The church of Notre-Dame du Travail was finished in 1902 with a main inner structure of re-used wrought iron elements. The columns are formed from an assemblage of various iron angles and plates instead of ready-made rolled I-sections. This assembled or constructed look is further underlined by additional stiffeners that maintain the local

1.10 Column in the central nave. Architect Jules Astric: Église Notre-Dame du Travail (1902), Paris.

stability of the structure. Because welding in 1902 was still a technology that belonged to the future, rivets articulate all the surfaces in an orderly and almost ornamental pattern, while also guaranteeing the cooperation of the parts and the structural integrity of the whole. The mechanical properties of iron allow curved members to be either bent into shape or cut from flat wrought-iron plates. When trying to understand the relationship between structural form and technology, therefore, it is not enough to invoke causal explanations of scientific relationships – we also need to interpret the conditions governing the manufacturing processes and their consequences. To grasp structural form from the view of technology we need to employ both scientific (or 'analytical') thinking involving causal relationships, as well as interpretations that reveal human intention and agency. We seek to grasp not just the cause but the *reason* for this or that technological choice.

Summing up, when we explain mechanical aspects of structural form in terms of the natural sciences, our explanations are causal and based upon deductions from general laws. When technology is involved, we must not only explain how the actual processes work or function but also interpret the underlying meaning or purpose. More than this, technology seeks to find a practical solution, by way of process and form, to the spatial purposes that are the structure's primary aim. In my previous comments on the National Gallery in Parma I suggested that the double frame of the support for the sculptures expresses a need to provide a firm base of sufficient width; the white-painted scaffolding-like roof structure works both as a device from which paintings can be suspended, as well as having an iconographic function. While obviously not offering causal explanations, I was trying – to the best of my ability and by considering the context – to interpret the meaning, purpose or intention behind the physical structures. In this kind of hermeneutical practice we typically make inferences from something that is observable (the physical form of the structure) to imagine something that is not (suspended pictures, or the scaffolding of a building).[24] We cannot say that we fully understand structural form without also having formed an opinion of the structure's spatial purposes, be those purely practical, contextual or, in some cases, iconographic. When trying to understand structures in an architectural context, there are practical as well as representational matters to observe. There are laws to abide by and relationships to recognise. When we reflect on or reason about structures we need to study form from the point of view of both causality and intentionality.

1.11 An extended taxonomy of aspects of structural form, including conceptions of causality and intentionality.

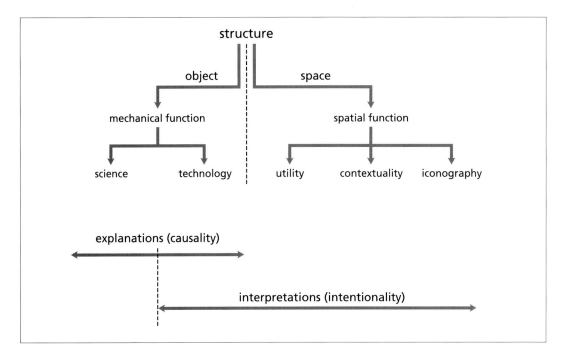

PART 2

PRAGMATICS

Structural form and some mechanical problems

In this part of the book I will discuss structural form from a structural mechanics point of view. We will look at how structures work in terms of loads and load paths, structural actions, and the strength and stiffness of materials; we will also see the implications of choices of technological processes. The discussion will cover the most important mechanical aspects of structural design that inform design decisions and which are thus instrumental for ensuring structural safety and efficiency. The analysis is a necessary preparation for the development of an aesthetics of structures which will follow in Part 3. The discussion here will take the form of practical or pragmatic analysis of how technology and science influence structural form.

Three basic concepts

The parameters of strength, stiffness and stability are clearly crucial for any discussion involving structural mechanics. Yet, fundamental as they are, on their own they seem too broad or open-ended to offer the kinds of theoretical tools we need. We have to take the analysis one step further to explain *how* mechanical issues influence the form of structures in architecture. We will therefore look at questions of form by studying structures from three different design perspectives. We will focus on the concepts of *material* characteristics, structural *efficiency* and structural *scale*. These categories are by no means wholly independent from each other, as will become clear when we look at them more closely. They are all, however, sufficiently distinct, and each has its own particular explanatory power. They also implicitly encompass the fundamental parameters of strength, stiffness and stability.

2.1 Structural form from the point of view of structural mechanics.

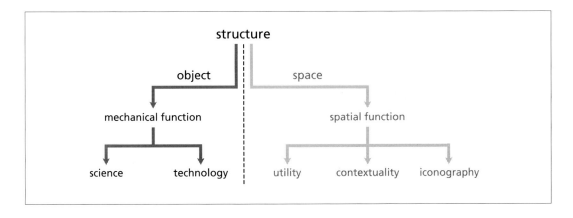

At the heart of most discussions of structures and structural behaviour are questions of the characteristics of different materials. For a long time the implicit relationship between the strength and elastic properties of materials and the 'resultant' structural form has been the subject of a great deal of theoretical attention; it continues to generate much debate. However, contemporary discussions of form should place equal emphasis on the technological characteristics of materials. These characteristics influence form by the specific nature of the processing and manufacturing of structural elements and structural systems. Those aspects are visible, above all, in the detailing and the articulation of structures.

The second key issue is concerned with the set of problems dealing with questions of efficiency. Does a structure respond to loads efficiently? How much material is necessary to resist the loads acting on the structure? Can the manufacturing and construction of a structure be said to be efficient? To achieve as much as possible in terms of load-bearing capacity while using as few resources as possible is – for good or ill – one of the first principles of building construction. As we shall see, the question of mechanical efficiency also plays an important role in the aesthetic appraisal of structures.

Lastly, the final parameter considers the scale of the structure. There is a relationship between the scale of a structure and the level of stresses involved in resisting the loads. Large-scale structures may require the application of different structural principles than smaller-scale ones, even if the basic structural types are essentially the same.

We will start with a discussion of materials, and then go on to the issues of structural efficiency and scale in the following sections.

Structural materials and form

The relationship of matter and form has been the subject of philosophical inquiries since Plato and before. Plato's thinking on the notion of form reflects his theory of ideas. Form is for him quite different from our customary understanding of its meaning, namely the bodily shape or appearance of things. Plato speaks about form as the underlying essence of things, arguing that what we see is merely a pale reflection of that real form. Form exists independently from particular objects, according to him, and is an idea/ideal. Aristotle, on the other hand, is more physical: form, he says, is always linked with a particular material.[1] Rather than engage in a philosophical debate, we will try to pursue these questions by asking: what are the connections between the various characteristics of structural materials and their predispositions or biases towards form?

A brief historical overview

To start off, let us take a brief look at some architects' and engineers' opinions about the relationship between materials and built form. This is by no means a complete historical account but simply a reference to the thoughts of some important past and present writers on architecture and structures. In the rear-view mirror of history some of those writers seem to have been propagating particularly important views on the subject, views that have influenced a great number of people, theorists and designers alike. Their views will naturally influence the direction of our own thoughts.

Not surprisingly, it is quite convenient to start this brief survey by looking at the extensive writings of Eugène-Emmanuel Viollet-le-Duc. He wrote two major works, the 'Dictionnaire raisonné de l'architecture française du XIe au XVIe siècle' (published 1854–68) and the 'Entretiens sur l'architecture' (published between 1863 and 1872). Their influence was enormous, both in Europe and in America. During the 1850s and 1860s a new movement of architectural critique had begun to gather momentum. Contemporary classicist architecture seemed unsuitable for or not interested in engaging with the characteristics and possibilities of new materials and techniques. Viollet-le-Duc quickly became the most prominent spokesman for a 'structural rationalism' in which structural and material considerations became important determinants for architectural form. 'On what could one establish unity in architecture,' he asks, 'if not on the structure, that is, the means of building?'[2] Of particular interest in relation to the use of materials is his declaration 'only by following the order that nature herself observes in her creations can one, in the arts, conceive and produce according to the law of unity'. Viollet-le-Duc invokes *nature* as the model for how to achieve this goal. He understands nature not as a romanticised concept but as an aggregation of phenomena that scientific methods can describe and explain. 'Construction is a science', he says; 'it is also an art.'[3] The practice of architecture means adapting 'both art and science to *the nature of the materials* employed'.[4] The line of reasoning that Viollet-le-Duc follows has, not surprisingly, led many to name him a materially orientated positivist, and his methodology is much inspired by the natural sciences. In some instances he makes a direct comparison between architecture and natural phenomena: 'Thus, just as in viewing a single leaf it is possible to reconstruct the entire plant, and in viewing an animal bone, the animal itself, it is also possible to deduce the members of an architecture from the view of an architectural profile. Similarly the nature of the finished construction can be derived from an architectural member.'[5] Interestingly, by implying an inductive connection between parts and the whole Viollet-le-Duc is suggesting that the diverse elements of an architectural hierarchy are related by a system of logic. According to his theory, a particularity (say, the form of a structural member of a certain

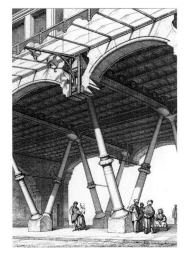

2.2 Viollet-le-Duc: project featuring vaults combining iron and masonry.[6]

2.3 Viollet-le-Duc: project for a covered market-hall.[11]

material) directly reflects the general properties of that material, and that we should be able to deduce the former from the latter.

The central idea in Viollet-le-Duc's thinking on materials is that each material has certain qualities and characteristics that logically 'produce' certain forms, or which imply specific ways of building with them. 'To build, for the architect, is to make use of materials in accordance with their qualities or their own nature.' Also 'the methods of the builder must accordingly vary by reason of the nature of the materials he is working with.'[7] The builder should not only make visible the characteristics of the materials, but also choose technologies that are congruent with the nature of those materials. Moreover, Viollet-le-Duc relates this idea to the notion of truth. One of his most famous statements reads: 'There are in architecture . . . two indispensable modes in which truth must be adhered to. We must be true in respect of the programme, and true in respect of the constructive processes . . . To be true in respect of the constructive processes is to employ the materials according to their qualities and properties.'[8]

There can be no doubt also that the idea of truth to the nature of materials very strongly implies a design whereby the materials are used as efficiently as possible. Thus he recommends that raw materials are employed 'in accordance with their form and their qualities', and states that we 'can force them into assuming certain arbitrary forms. Nevertheless, we are finally obliged to accept wood and stone for what they are and as nature has fashioned them already; certain laws dictated the formation of these natural materials. We are therefore obliged to conceive of a structure for them that accords with their qualities.'[9] Structural efficiency is naturally the outcome of adherence to the laws laid down by nature. More explicitly, Viollet-le-Duc states as being true that 'a supporting structure should be proportioned with respect to the load it will carry, and that if you build a stone wall or pier two or three yards in thickness to carry floors that would be easily supported by a wall one yard in thickness, you produce a work that cannot be justified by reason, which satisfies neither my eyes nor my understanding, and wastes costly materials'.[10]

Also touched upon by Viollet-le-Duc is the influence of the scale of the structure: 'Every use of materials must be proportional to the object . . . [the proportions] are relative with respect to the materials employed, to the object, and to what is made out of it. In architecture it is not possible to establish a fixed formula such as that 2 is to 4 as 200 is to 400. Although you can place a lintel 4 m long on posts 2 m high, you cannot do so with one 400 m long on pillars 200 m in height. When the scale changes, the architect must also change his mode of operating.'[12]

We do not, however, do justice to Viollet-le-Duc without pointing out that he also fully recognises other aspects than the purely material ones as contributors to architectural form. He admits that the building should have the 'appearance' of duration – surely not a scientifically based statement – and also that the builder should give it 'appropriate proportions in accordance with the human senses, human reason and human instinct'.[13] Viollet-le-Duc also recognises human needs, as well as the particular civilisation into which the builder is born, as determinants that must be satisfied. As he says, 'it is the characteristic of truth to reach similar consequences by very different paths'. Also 'these similar consequences may be very different in appearance as being the result of a series of inferences deduced from different conditions'.[14] Although the material aspect is strongly influential, Viollet-le-Duc clearly does not see it as the only determinant of form.

Of the 'Entretiens sur l'architecture', Frank Lloyd Wright is reported to have said: 'Here you find everything you need to know of architecture.'[15] Well acquainted with the works of Viollet-le-Duc, Wright's rhetoric on the subject of materials shares many similarities: 'Bring out the nature of the materials, let their nature intimately into your scheme', Wright writes in 1908.[16] 'Reveal the nature of the wood, plaster, brick or stone in your designs . . . they are by nature friendly and beautiful.' That the nature of a material might be friendly and beautiful seems, however, entirely subjective and a far cry from Viollet-le-Duc's more scientifically based notions. During 1928 Wright published a series of articles in the magazine *The Architectural Record*, all with the subtitle 'The Meaning of Materials'. In this series he reflects in turn upon stone, wood, ceramics, glass, concrete and sheet metal. Interestingly, by announcing that materials not only have characteristics but also have 'meaning', Wright

2.4 Interior with concrete columns. Frank Lloyd Wright: the Johnson Wax Company (1939), Racine, Wisconsin.

2.5 Frank Lloyd Wright: Robie
House (1909), Chicago.

expands on the understanding of materials to embrace both the more culturally conditioned aspects of their use and a subjective sensitivity towards their nature and difference. 'Each material has its own message and, to the creative artist, its own song', he states. 'Each material speaks a language of its own just as line and color speak – or perhaps because they do speak.'[17] Metaphors like these may be inspirational for some designers, but it is very difficult to use them as a basis for a more operational understanding of the form–material relationship.

Frank Lloyd Wright also takes into account science and technology, and directly refers in some cases to the properties of materials concerned with strength and construction. He observed that 'the architect is no longer hampered by the stone arch of the Romans or by the stone beam of the Greeks . . . Why then does he cling to the grammatical phrases of those ancient methods of construction.'[18] In other words, structural form should reflect the possibilities of modern materials. The constraints and limitations of stone no longer apply; adjust your vocabulary accordingly. In fact, Wright goes one step further: 'Every new material', he says, 'means a new form, a new use if used according to its nature.'[19] As we shall see, whether or not this statement is strictly correct from a structural point of view depends on what kind of properties a new material introduces compared to those of existing materials, and also on how form is defined.

Louis I. Kahn expresses a fascination for beginnings, for the source of all things, and paid great attention to the nature of materials: 'Realization is Realization in Form, which means a nature. You realize that something has a certain nature. A school has a certain nature, and in making a school the consultation and approval of nature are absolutely necessary. In such a consultation you can discover the Order of water, the Order of wind, the Order of light, the Order of certain materials. If you think of brick, and you're consulting the Orders, you consider the

2.6 Dormitories. Architect Louis I. Kahn: Indian Institute of Management (1974), Ahmedabad, India.

nature of brick. You say to brick, "What do you want, brick?" Brick says to you, "I like an arch." If you say to brick, "Arches are expensive, and I can use a concrete lintel over an opening. What do you think of that, brick?" Brick says, "I like an arch."'[20]

Of Kahn's notion of order, John Lobell says: 'Order is the principle behind all things and is expressed in them as an existence-will, a quality things have in their beginnings outside of time, which Kahn liked to call Volume Zero. We might also say that Order is, not only an underlying principle and a quality of things, but also an active creativity: it is the way things come into being.'[21] Hence we must, according to Kahn, seek the underlying principle, the nature of the materials, and have the approval of Nature for the way materials are used. Resembling in certain passages the rhetoric of Viollet-le-Duc, Kahn's thinking is more in line with that of Frank Lloyd Wright. Both show a respect for 'Nature' that clearly goes beyond a mere rationalistic concept of employing 'the materials according to their qualities and properties'. 'It is important that you honor the material you use', Kahn says; 'the beauty of what you create comes if you honor the material for what it really is.'[22] Kahn suggests that the material not only has an existence but also that this being has a will of its own: '"I like an arch", says brick.' The idea of a consultation with the material, of probing for the ways of the material's own choosing, is an idea that is remarkably similar to that of the German philosopher Arthur Schopenhauer. He wrote of 'the life of the stone and the manifestations of its will'.[23] Both thinkers conceptualise the nature of materials, metaphorically, by lending them a will and therefore a life of their own. According to Kahn's understanding, each kind of material should express its particular characteristics and distinctiveness in the way it is used, because (more complexly) its nature and the matter itself are one inseparable entity: its nature and specific qualities are not something the material *has*, but something it *is*.

What consequences for the material–form relationship result from observations like these? If, according to Kahn, materials and their nature are inseparable – that we cannot by our choosing disregard this dual but unified nature of matter without dishonoring it – then structural design must respond to the moral imperative of an ethics based on material 'purity'. How about putting steel reinforcement into brick masonry? It may change the properties of the material – or, rather, the composite material – substantially. Is this a new material, with its own nature, even if you cannot see the difference between them by looking at its surfaces? Kahn's particular contribution in this field is perhaps that he takes the idea of 'the nature of the material' to its peak, and this raises several interesting questions.

Let us take a look at some reflections on materials and structures made by a prominent engineer, Pier Luigi Nervi. Nervi's philosophy of structures is best articulated in his book *Aesthetics and Technology in Building*.[24] At the beginning of the opening chapter he sets the tone: 'The structure,' he says, 'be it large or small, must be stable and lasting, must satisfy the needs for which it was built, and must achieve the maximum result with the minimum means.'[25] Here Nervi places himself firmly in the same tradition as Viollet-le-Duc and his numerous other modernist followers, who see the efficient use of structural materials as a criterion for good architecture. He sums up those conditions in the phrase 'building correctly', a concept that is discussed from various angles throughout the whole book. *Costruire correttamente* was also the title of Nervi's previous book, published in Italian in 1955, and in English the following year.[26] An important part of this concept is obviously his thinking on materials: 'We all have a tactile sense and subconscious appreciation of the physical qualities of the materials most commonly used, so that seeing them correctly used, according to their natures, influences the general impression produced by a work of architecture.'[27] Why our appreciation of material qualities should be 'subconscious' is not easily grasped, but in this context it is much more important to observe Nervi's replication of statements first formulated by his forerunners. Not surprisingly, the idea of employing the materials 'according to their nature' is also a necessary premise in Nervi's thinking. In discussing the merits of reinforced concrete (Nervi's preferred material par excellence, along with

2.7 The Small Sports Palace (1956), Rome. Engineer Pier Luigi Nervi.

ferrocement) he is even more specific: 'Reinforced concrete beams lose
the rigidity of wooden beams or of metal shapes and *ask* to be molded
according to the line of the bending moments and the shearing stress.
The vertical supports lose the prismatic quality of columns and pillars in
stone (which was statically exact when a beam exerted only axial and
vertical forces on the columns) and *ask* to be adapted to the combination of flexural and axial stresses which are produced in them.'[28]

At least three things can be observed from these sentences. Firstly,
Nervi underlines the importance of designing structural elements in a
way that they conform to the diagrams of forces, thus making the structures as materially efficient as possible. Second, Nervi here confirms
his views on the necessity for design to take account of the particular
qualities of each material. Third, and this is perhaps the most significant: like Kahn, in his rhetoric Nervi attributes to the materials a will
of their own: they *ask* to be moulded or adapted to a particular shape.
The designer has to comply with the needs of the material rather than
the other way around. Likewise, Nervi also links the notion of 'building
correctly' to that of truth, 'a truth dependent on laws which dominate
and will always dominate the will and the tastes of mankind';[29] 'all *true*
solutions, in any field, are also those of maximum efficiency'.[30] Hence,
truth resides in the materials and the materials themselves are also the
judges: mankind cannot but submit to the domination of laws that
ensure true and efficient solutions.

What else, then, can be said about the theories or opinions of Viollet-
le-Duc, Frank Lloyd Wright, Kahn and Nervi, whose views are represent-
ative of the modernist tradition in one way or another? Their rhetoric is
surprisingly similar even if their architectural works are rather different.
With a hundred years between them, the architecture proselytised by
Viollet-le-Duc is radically different from that built by Louis I. Kahn. The
ideals of conforming with Nature perhaps take on many different forms
in actual building design, depending upon time, place and the individual preferences of the designer. Edward Ford says: 'As for those who
sought form in the nature of the materials, what they found there for
the most part was whatever preconceptions they brought with them.'[31]
This discrepancy could be explained in either of two ways. The first possibility is that there is a weak relationship between theory and practice,
and that the architects and engineers built differently from the way they
spoke and wrote. This is a credible explanation; it happens all the time
that practitioners are unable, or unwilling, to follow their own rhetoric when it comes to actual design. A second equally credible possibility is that the ideals concerned with the 'nature' of things are mostly so
vague that they can be fulfilled by almost any design. When Viollet-le-
Duc talked about 'the nature of materials' he wrote in the context of an
ongoing polemic against the formal excesses represented by the eclec-
tic classicism of his day. To argue that structural design using wrought
iron should avoid repeating the formal system of Renaissance architec-

ture seems to be both a reasonable and precise request. When, however, the same basic premise of designing 'according to the qualities of the materials' applies to twentieth and twenty-first century steel and reinforced concrete, it becomes infinitely harder to invest in that ideal a plausible formal logic specific to each material. For what exactly is the 'nature' of steel, and the 'nature' of reinforced concrete, that points to a specific structural design? Do materials *have* a 'nature' or an 'essence' at all? Or do *all* materials have it? From the point of view of structural design, what would the 'nature' of a material consist of? Or is our understanding of the 'nature' of a material based more on ideology and 'looks' than on mechanics?

The processing and manufacture of materials influences, adjusts, improves and sometimes alters the characteristics the materials might be said to have had in their natural state. For many contemporary materials, technology has become an instrument for the manipulation of their properties and qualities, thus making them in some ways characteristic-free – or, rather, with a bewildering proliferation of characteristics.[32] Many materials can take on almost any form, and can also present quite different surface textures. In this way, matter as such struggles between nature and culture, between necessity and possibility, with technology playing the role of mediator. Technology thus makes culture possible. Our capacity to transform raw materials into new products creates materials with very different characteristics. This kind of transformation makes the concept of 'the nature of materials' – and, for that matter,

2.8 Galleries, La Villette (1986), Paris. Architect Bernard Tschumi.

other anthropomorphised metaphors of nature – even more nebulous and difficult to use.

Before looking more closely into these questions, it is necessary to look at the views on structures and materials of those who see architecture very differently from those discussed above. Among contemporary practitioners, architect and theorist Bernard Tschumi, reflecting on the status of structures in the architecture of the early 1980s, has stated that 'those who advocate a return to "honesty of materials" or solid poché walls are often motivated by ideological rather than practical reasons. It should be stressed, however, that any concern over material substance has implications beyond mere structural stability. The materiality of architecture, after all, is in its solids and voids, its spatial sequences, its articulations, its collisions.'[33] Rejecting the notions of truth and honesty, Tschumi still stresses the importance of material substance. Although known for his theoretical approach to architecture, he is no less concerned with 'the one thing that makes the work of architects ultimately different from the work of philosophers: *materiality*.'[34] In fact, Bernard Tschumi goes one step further, and continues: 'Just as there is a logic of words or of drawings, there is a logic of materials, and they are not the same. And however much they are subverted, something ultimately resists.'[35] Seemingly not very far from the rhetoric of the modernists, Tschumi's 'logic' of materials might still be understood somewhat differently than their 'nature'. Although the concept of 'nature' in reality seems to offer surprisingly few specific design criteria, the notion of a 'logic of materials' rather than a 'nature of materials' is slightly less restrictive vis-à-vis materials and their use, at least theoretically. The formalistic reasoning of logic can be deviated from more easily than 'nature', if one should choose to do so. While the bonds of 'nature' cannot be broken, implying certain necessary or indeed inescapable relationships, the *logic* of materials seems as a concept to convey both a more pragmatic and a more precise and adequate formulation of what a material can easily do and what it cannot.

Coop-Himmelb(l)au, represented here by the speeches and writings of Wolf D. Prix, provide slightly more accessible and direct reflections on the question of structures, materials and form. Explaining how their design technique operates in the initial stages, and their reasons for this technique, Prix says: 'One [reason] is certainly that we want to keep this design moment *free of all material constraints*, in order to arrive at a free ground-plan.'[36] The idea is to avoid a thorough discussion of spatial relations, but instead 'try to define the feeling, the emotion that the space is later to radiate. And then suddenly we have a drawing.'[37] Arriving at a design, also involving structures, by intuitive methods and sometimes even blindfolded, is obviously a strategy for disrupting a possible causal relationship between material properties and a 'resulting' form. Following the earliest sketches, a model is usually built, and the 'model does not have scale; like the drawing, it is intended to be a preliminary im-

2.9 Funderwerk 3 (1988), Kärnten, Austria. Architects Coop-Himmelb(l)au.

pression of the emergent building'.[38] This strategy supposedly develops architectural form independent of the form to which actual materials would most easily adapt. The result is 'mutations' of structural form, 'the idea of the twisted and tilted structures'.[39] One of their intentions, according to Prix, is 'to show the forces running through the architecture', where the structure is 'as a metaphor for forces', but 'following another force, not of weight but of energy'.[40] 'In the initial stages', Prix says, 'structural planning is never an immediate priority, but it does become very important when the project is being realized, when the idea is being transposed into reality.'[41] Hence, structural considerations enter the design when the time is ripe for a 'translation of the spatial idea into architecture'.[42] One reason, of course, that this strategy can actually be followed is that materials like steel and reinforced concrete are available, and in reality can be made to function structurally in almost any form. This is particularly true in some of the architecture of Coop-Himmelb(l)au: 'Efficiency', states Wolf Prix, 'should be replaced by complexity.'[43]

Likewise, the architecture of Frank O. Gehry shows structural form to be extraordinarily subordinate to outward architectural form. As in buildings like the Guggenheim Museum in Bilbao (1997) and the Experience Music Project (EMP) in Seattle (2000), the structure follows faithfully the curves and twists of the external envelope, constructing an architecture conceptualised and designed from the 'skin in'.[44] It follows that the structural sections, like splines, have no alternative other than to adapt

2.10 Ray and Maria Stata Center (2004), MIT, Cambridge, MA. Architect Frank O. Gehry.

to the hidden coordinates defining the topography of the architectural volumes. Those structures describe curved lines that ignore the idea of a structural logic or the nature of the material. On the contrary, form is generated with quite different concepts in mind. There is, however, in Gehry's architecture a certain consciousness, not of structural materials and form, but of the relationship between the form of the external envelope and the properties of the cladding material. It is a weak one, though, whose prime function is to ensure the buildability of the façade. 'Help me make sure that when I am going to create those shapes, I can still use this material', Gehry says to the computer experts, famously bringing into his practice from the aerospace industry the advanced CATIA computer program to analyse the shapes of the skin.[45] Mainly concerned with materials that are relevant for the outward appearance, Gehry makes extensive use of paper model studies to work out the shapes of his building volumes. 'Paper', says Gehry, 'is structure. If I can make it out of paper I know I can build it.' He is relying, without saying so, on a separate structure of a material that may well be different from the cladding material, to keep his paper-thin walls standing up.[46]

The ideology of structure, form and material adopted by these architects is certainly in direct opposition to the tradition of the modernists, with Viollet-le-Duc as one of the forefathers.[47] Terms like 'the nature of materials' and 'truth', and their implicit references to a particular structural and architectural form, are no longer thought by Tschumi, Coop-Himmelb(l)au, Gehry and others to have value as basic design criteria. Form is instead generated by approaching the architectural problems independent of any real concern for the characteristics and constraints of the materials. We can thus sum up the reflections so far by extracting two main viewpoints presented on the material–form relationship. Both act as philosophical guidelines for the design of structures in a context of architecture:

Form 'resides' in the material, and is made explicit by respecting the qualities and properties, or the 'nature', of that material.

Form is conceived irrespective of the material, and is as such free to evolve without preconditions for realisation in a specific material.

Both philosophies can obviously be made to function. The architecture of the contemporary practitioners quoted above is proof of that. Of more interest here, though, is whether one more than the other of those philosophies can claim to have a more effective (in terms of mechanics) real-world rationale. To be able to offer any kind of answer to that question, we will have to sort out the mechanical premises for their validity. Let us propose, as a hypothesis, that both philosophies have rational mechanical reasons for being valid. The premises for this being true, however, are somewhat different from one to the other. We will, as a first condition, have to be more precise in defining what aspects of form we are referring to so that we can discriminate between different levels of form. Second, we will need to specify more properly what kind of materials and characteristics we are considering for their potential affects on form.

Categories of structural form

Any discussion of architecture will obviously involve aspects of form on many different levels. The forms and shapes of architecture appear as spatial forms and surface forms (architectural details and their various textures); they also embrace *structural form*. All are some of the many aspects of form that together make up the architectural work as a whole.[48] In order to refer to this with some precision, it is convenient and necessary to discriminate between different levels of form as it applies to the structure. Firstly, we can speak of the overall formal characteristics of the structural system. This refers to the structural type or principle involved; it also describes both what it roughly looks like (its shape), and how it works structurally. A typical example is the arch structure, with perhaps the additional category of a parabolic arch, a catenary or a circular arch. The term I will use for this level will be the structure's *global form.* Other typical examples of the global form of structures or structural systems are the dome, the structural frame, the beam, the column, etc. Hence, the global form may refer to the overall form of a structural element (beam) or to systems of more than one element (frame). To describe the global form more specifically, additional formal characteristics must be considered, such as a tapering beam or a portal frame. I acknowledge that a more specific description of the global structural form may involve a geometric characterisation: a hyperbolic paraboloid shell, a funicular arch, etc. Thus the geometry of a structure is the (abstract) line diagram that follows the contour of the global form.

Moreover, since the global form comprises a layout that also suggests structural behaviour, we can think of the global form of a structural system – its overall geometry – as belonging to one of three possible categories of structure: form-active systems, semi-form-active systems and non-form-active systems.[49] Whether or not a structure belongs to one or the other of those categories will depend on the relationship between the configuration of loads, the structural geometry and the support conditions. Form-active structures are such that their geometries enable the loads to produce only one type of axial internal force (compression or tension). The parabolic arch is hence a form-active structural system for a uniformly distributed load across the length of the span, producing compression forces only. Semi-form-active structures will work by a combination of bending and axial internal forces or by simultaneous axial compression and tension along two axes, while non-form-active structures have no axial component of the internal forces and the load thus produces bending moments only.[50]

Since the global form refers to the form of the structure as a system rather than the particularities of that form, there is a need for a term that characterises form on a lower, more specific level.[51] An arch exemplifying a global structural form may have a trussed elevation, or a solid rectangular or H-shaped cross-section. The geometrical proportions of depth to span may be 1 to 40 or 1 to 80. The structure's formal characteristics on this level will be referred to as the *local form* of the structure or structural element. Typically, structural detailing will address the structure's local form.

I should at this stage add something about the notion of form. In the discussions of material characteristics versus form in the previous section, form is taken to mean architectural form in general in some instances, and more specifically structural form in others. This poses no problem when, to quote Edward Ford, 'structure equals architecture'. Ford shows that this doctrine has been a pillar of architectural theory for the best part of the last two centuries. 'For the most part', he says, 'the ideal constructional principles of the twentieth century conform to the idealized theories of the nineteenth.'[52] Those theories, according

2.11 Form-active, semi- and non-form-active structures, represented by the tent, the circular arch and the straight beam.

(above) Tent structure, Broadgate development (1991), City of London.

(middle) Sports hall, École d'ingénieurs, ESIEE (1987), Marne-la-Vallée, France. Architect Dominique Perrault.

(below) Office building for Åke Larsson Construction (1988), Oslo. Architect Niels Torp.

2.12 Global form: the three-hinged frame of the original slaughter-hall in Lyon (1914). Architect Tony Garnier.

2.13 Local form: the hinged connection between frame and foundation.

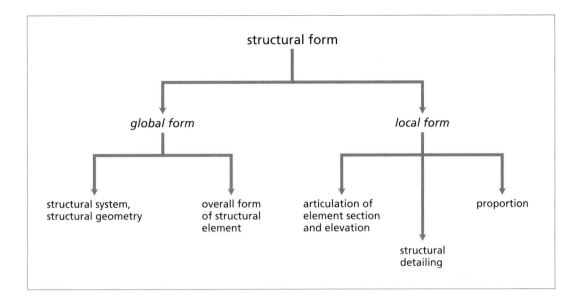

2.14 Levels of structural form.

to Ford, consider form as 'the result of structure'. On the other hand, in a significant number of important architectural works, this is obviously not the case. Architectural and spatial form may evolve quite freely and independently from the form of the primary structure. My main concern is, however, always the form of the structure, and we will look specifically at how structural form relates to the two main viewpoints on the form–materials relationship discussed in the previous section.

Material properties vs. form

When architects Foster Associates and engineers Ove Arup and Partners designed the building structure for the Century Tower in Tokyo, they were quite certainly unaware of a strikingly similar structure built several decades earlier in a remote mountain village in the southern part of Norway. In spite of huge differences in time and space, in climate and functions, in scale, in technological know-how and workmanship, and also in the availability of building materials, the structural frame that keeps the two buildings up is essentially the same. Or, to be more precise, the global forms of the two structures are quite similar. The architecture of the Japanese office building, however, is generally thought of as high-tech, while the Norwegian sawmill is definitely low-tech. The one is constructed from high-grade steel and the other from locally available wood. While the motivation for choosing this particular structural form is very different for the two buildings, the fact remains that the structures of both buildings show essentially the same form resisting vertical and horizontal loads.[53]

How may the similarities of structural form be explained by the properties of the two different materials used? Firstly, both are constructed

2.15 Sawmill at Tunhovd, Norway.

2.16 Structures. Architects Foster Associates, engineers Ove Arup and Partners: the Century Tower (1991), Tokyo.

2.17 Detail. Sawmill at Tunhovd, Norway.

2.18 Detail. The Century Tower, Tokyo.

from materials that have comparable *structural properties*, not in terms of their absolute strength (their relative differences may be in the region of between 1:10 and 1:20), but because both timber and steel are materials that can resist both tension and compression stresses quite well.[54] They can also resist bending moments and shear forces. Second, both materials have similar *geometrical properties*, at least in this case, where both wood and steel appear in a linear and modular form. With all these basic similarities it is not surprising that both materials can work well in this particular global form that involves both bending and compression. As it is, the structures can be classified as semi-form-active, carrying loads by a combination of internal axial stresses and bending stresses.

We can also see differences between the two structures: the technologies involved in the production and assembly of the structural components differ greatly, and mark them distinctly as characteristically wood or steel structures. The materials have different *technological properties*, which result in significant differences on the level of the structures' local form. In the sawmill's case, all members are of solid timber; their joining represents a technology and craftmanship that unmistakably belong to traditional wood construction. The dimensions of the cross-sections correspond to the dimensions of the available trees; when there is a need for more structural material, as is the case with the horizontal beam, two members of equal size are quite simply put one on top of the other. The steel structure, however, is fully welded from box-beam members having internal diaphragm plates to provide for torsional stability.[55] Reflecting the bending moment diagram, the beams are slightly tapered towards the columns, and thus also inform us of their manufacturing process from steel plates: when cut to the right size this deviation from a cross-section with constant height only marginally complicates the manufacturing process, while contributing to a reduction of material and thus weight. In conclusion we can therefore state that the differences of structural form in these two examples are primarily differences of local form, not of overall global form. Both materials show an ability to resist both compression and tension stresses, as well as having similar geometrical properties. This points to the possibility of shaping the two structures globally in a similar way, if there are reasons to do so. Different properties deriving from the two materials' responses to technological processing, however, still yield differences at the level of the structures' local form.

Hence, it seems reasonable to classify materials according to three important characteristics that greatly influence form, namely the materials' *structural*, *technological* and *geometrical* characteristics. The first two categories comprise the parameters concerned with mechanical properties.[56] This taxonomy corresponds to the distinction made between the two different mechanical aspects of structures as proposed in Part 1 (pages 11–12). The first category refers mainly to the strength, stiffness

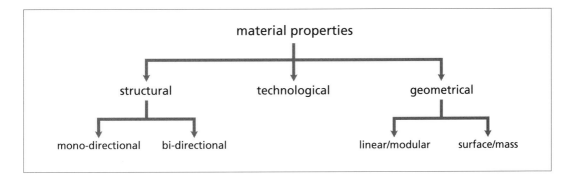

2.19 Structural, technological and geometrical properties of materials.

and weight properties of materials, characteristics that are well understood in classical science. Parameters of this type have been termed 'fundamental'; they are unambiguously measurable and quantitative.[57] In a discussion of overall structural form, however, more important than the actual strength of a material is whether or not the material is able to resist different kinds of stresses. If it can resist both compression *and* tension stresses, it will react differently with respect to form than one capable only of resisting either compression *or* tension. Materials having the ability to resist both compression and tension stresses possess *bi-directional* strength and stiffness properties, while the second group of materials are thought of as being *mono-directional*.[58] The materials in the first group are presupposed, as a consequence, to have also bending strength and shear strength;[59] obvious examples are steel and wood (as discussed above), as well as reinforced concrete. Typical examples of materials having only, or mainly, mono-directional strength are masonry, traditional cast iron and various textiles.[60]

The second category – technological characteristics – is concerned with structural materials in terms of their processing and workability. These characteristics primarily influence the structure's local form; examples include the material's response to being cut, drilled, cast or welded. Parameters of this kind which do not measure single, fundamental properties have been termed 'ranking' parameters because they 'can only be used to rank materials in order of superiority'.[61] Even if technological characteristics are clearly identifiable, they are not always wholly independent of the materials' fundamental parameters. They are, however, nearly entirely different for each group of structural materials and thus elude any attempt at a more detailed classification.

The third category is concerned with the geometrical properties of materials. These characteristics affect what kind of geometrical appearances the structural materials are likely to take. Materials that easily adapt to a skeletal structural type are termed line-forming, or linear/modular materials. Again, steel and wood are clear examples. Materials capable of forming more solid, continuous structures can be described as surface-forming or surface/mass materials.[62] Masonry is a perfect example and so is concrete, even if the latter in the reinforced version also belongs in the first category. Whether or not a material can be said to belong to either of the two categories may also depend on the scale of the structure.

Having established a set of terms that discriminate both between structural form on different levels and between different material properties, we can now return to the problem of making precise observations on the relationship between materials and structural form. Based on those classifications and the few empirical examples already discussed, these are some hypotheses on the relationship between material properties and form:

1   Structures of materials having *mono-directional* strength and stiffness properties have a relationship of necessity between the structural properties of the materials and the global form of the structures. This necessary relationship implies the use of *form-active*, or nearly form-active, structural systems.
2   Structures of materials having *bi-directional* strength and stiffness properties do not have a relationship of necessity between the structural properties of the materials and the global form of the structures. This implies that non-, semi- and form-active structures may all function well as load-bearing systems as long as the global form offers a geometry with structural potential.
3   Structures of materials having *bi-directional* strength and stiffness properties have material-specific form primarily as a *local form* characteristic. This follows partly from the hypothesis above. In other words, the particular properties of such materials are best exposed in the detailing, in the proportions and in the articulation of their structures.

Let us look more closely at the three hypotheses to see how they relate to the two main viewpoints on the material–form relationship in the writings of the architects and engineers discussed earlier (pages 21–33). Those were, in short, that structural form 'resides' in the material, or that structural form may be conceived of irrespective of the material.[63] The first of the three hypotheses deals with materials that are able to resist either compression or tension stresses. The hypothesis suggests that materials of this kind are highly form-sensitive: since such materials are able to resist axial stress along one direction only, excluding bending, it follows that structures relying on those materials have to comply with a global form where stability is achieved by activating only one type of axial force. Such structures are of the form-active type. Hence, it seems that for mono-directional materials, the global form is more descriptive of the material–form relationship than the local form. *Referring to the global form, we can therefore assert that for mono-directional materials, 'form resides in the material'.* For those particular materials at least, it makes sense for a design to be based on 'the nature of the materials' because, unless their own inherent structural capabilities are modified, there is no alternative but to be conscious of their characteristic structural properties and design accordingly. Therefore the 'nature' (if one chooses to employ that term) of those materials, in a load-bearing context, lies precisely in their mono-directional strength and stiffness characteristics.

There is a marvellous work of architecture that happens to show with great clarity the kind of necessity of form referred to here. This applies for both tension and compression types of mono-directional materials. The Mound Stand at Lord's Cricket Ground in London was rebuilt in 1987 by architects Michael Hopkins and Partners and engineers Ove Arup and Partners. Originally built in 1898–9, the Mound Stand comprised a

2.20 Architects Michael Hopkins and Partners: Mound Stand (1987), Lord's Cricket Ground, London.

seven-arched brick colonnade supporting the back of the spectators' terrace. The colonnade was retained in the new building and even extended. Today, this colonnade makes up the base of a layered composition of structural materials, with heavy brick masonry at the bottom and, barely touching the colonnade, a three-storey steel structure above; this is covered with a light tent structure of coated PVC.[64]

The brick masonry at the bottom and the roof membrane on the top are both materials that have mono-directional strength and stiffness characteristics. The global form of the respective structures reflects this by taking on the shape of the wall, the pillar and the arch, as well as the anticlastic surface geometry of the tent as primary structural forms.

2.21 Tent structures. Mound Stand, Lord's.

The arch is particularly well suited to support a distributed load across an opening if employing a material that primarily possesses compression strength. Perhaps for small openings one might also use a beam structure of masonry with an intrados as a straight line, thus falsifying the assumption that such a material requires a form-active shape. However, in that case the active part of the structure would also be an arch created within the beam, leaving the rest of the beam as an inactive lump of material adding only weight to the structure. On a small scale this inactive material could be made to hang in the supporting arch by adhesive stresses in the joints, but on a larger scale we would need steel reinforcement to prevent it from falling out. If using reinforced brick masonry, we would actually have made a different material, a composite with other structural characteristics. Scale is thus very important in any discussion of structural form; an increase in scale will make it even more essential to design for a particular form that is congruent with the properties of the materials.

Likewise, the light PVC membrane requires a very particular structural geometry in order to be supportive: the surface-forming material of high tensile strength is pre-stressed by being point-supported alternately from the interior and the exterior by masts pushing upwards and steel wires pulling from above. This brings about a double curvature surface form, maintaining stiffness by keeping the membrane constantly under tension for all loads. Without this combination of a positive and a negative curvature form, this particular mono-directional material quite simply cannot act structurally and keep rigid along every axis. There are, however, several ways of achieving an anticlastic form, this tent structure representing one of them. Note that we may also include the steel wires in this category of materials and products that have strength and stiffness in one direction only. Accordingly, the form that the wires adapt to is always a form-active geometry carrying loads by means of tension forces only.

The so-called Pavilion of the Future from Expo 92 in Seville is another building that perfectly illustrates the tight bonds between the characteristics of mono-directional materials and the form of the corresponding structures. Peter Rice was leading engineer, in collaboration with architect David Mackay of Martorell Bohigas Mackay. Design of the huge and slender arcade of stone took as its point of departure the similarity between the physical characteristics of stone and glass, adapting the bracing techniques developed for glass in order to use narrow stone elements structurally. In the words of Peter Rice: 'Stone, like glass, is very strong in compression, but fragile and prone to cracking. If we could protect the stone from tension forces and from sudden loads then we could perhaps build the screen using stonework as a primary structural material.'[65] Blocks of granite were accurately cut to size and jointed into modular units resembling pre-cast concrete elements. The stone piers built from a number of those units are braced by a system of steel struts

2.22 Architect David Mackay, engineer Peter Rice: Pavilion of the Future (1992), Seville.

and ties, preventing in-plane and out-of-plane collapse. As is generally the case for masonry, the joints between the granite units have no tensile capacity and can thus be expected to open up if subjected to tensile forces. The series of arches spanning about 15 m between the piers supports the roof load of the pavilion by tension hangers connecting to the suspended girders. Each half-circular arch carries the load of two roof girders. The ingenious way this is done says a lot about the structural properties of the stone material: circular arches made from granite elements having insignificant tension strength are supposed to carry two substantial point loads, obviously without producing bending forces that could lead to the joints opening up. The key to the solution is the introduction of a tie-support system for the roof load of a similar geometry as the stone arches. This is attached to the arches by radial ties, ensuring that 'any change in shape of the stone arches was followed by a corresponding change in shape in the support system. This would guarantee that the loading system would always remain funicular, or of the same form and shape as the stone under geometric change by wind or other non-symmetrical load parallel to the line of the arches.'[66] In short, when the load is symmetrical, the stone arches will support a series of equal point loads that are all radial to their circular form, thus producing only compression forces. The global form of the structure and the geometry of the loads thus constitute a form-active structural system.

The history of architecture is full of overwhelming evidence of the form-sensitivity of mono-directional materials, not least exemplified by the rich stone and brick architecture of previous centuries. A particularly interesting period is the first half of the nineteenth century, which showed a breakthrough for cast-iron building structures. Virtually all larger iron structures from this period are arch types of structures, for example arched bridges, domes or vaults. Or, characteristically, they were suspension bridges made of wrought-iron. Perhaps not until the Crystal Palace in 1851 do we find larger spans in iron based on the trussed beam, in this case with cast-iron in the standardised smaller beams and wrought-iron in the 22 m mid-span. When, however, steel was introduced in the second half of the nineteenth century, a new material became available which, like wood, proved to be of considerable strength both in tension and in compression. Later, reinforced concrete was also to be in common use. In my three hypotheses I claimed that this group of bi-directional materials do not have a relationship of necessity between their structural properties and the global form of their structures. Thus almost any form can be made to stand up, presupposing that the form represents a minimum of geometrical consistency to offer a structural potential. In actual practice, this implies not only that non-, semi- and form-active systems are equally potent contributors to structural form, but also that this freedom may come at the expense of structural efficiency. Hence, the global form is no longer a precise indicator for a specific material. *We will therefore, when it comes to bi-directional materials, be justified in maintaining the possibility that the global form may be conceived independently from any concern for the properties of a particular material.* It is difficult, in this case, to argue for a global design in accordance with 'the nature of the material' because, in a structural context at least, what that 'nature' is that might suggest a particular overall form of the structure is not easily grasped. The global form of the structure does not characterise with any precision a material–form relationship for specific materials of this kind. There is on this level a much looser connection between the structural properties of the materials and actual form. This is clearly shown by the structural system that perhaps is the most commonly employed in architecture today: the multi-storey frame. A common feature in commercial buildings and dwellings alike, the post-and-beam structure may be of the simple type with hinged connections and relying on a separate bracing system for stability, or of the rigid frame type. In practice we find structural frames executed in steel, reinforced concrete, wood and aluminium; as a formal and structural system it belongs to no material in particular. Geometrically, the frame elements are of the linear type, and structurally they are characterised by being subjected to bending or axial forces, or a combination of both.

There are at least two implications of the viewpoint that bi-directional materials do not require a material-specific overall form. One is that almost any global structural form can be made from such a material; we are thus free to explore the structural potential of form in general rather than looking for a specific design applying to a particular

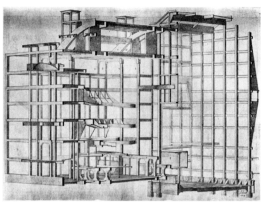

2.23 Structural steel frame. Architect/engineer W. le Baron Jenney: The Fair Building (1891), Chicago.

2.24 Structural reinforced concrete frame. Architect Auguste Perret: Théâtre des Champs Elysées (1910), Paris.

A striking similarity of global structural form is found in these two framed buildings from around the turn of the nineteenth century.

material. The other implication is that in principle global forms can be made from any of those materials. Both implications have a decisive influence on some contemporary architectural trends. Conceptualising, evolving and erecting 'free-form' architecture takes as a necessary premise that structural materials exist which can be made into structural elements that can follow the contours of the folding, twisting or curving geometry, and yet offer adequate strength and stiffness to bring the forces to the ground.

In the case of the Magazzini Generale (Chiasso, Switzerland, 1924) by engineer Robert Maillart, we encounter a structure representing a global structural form that is among the least expected forms in which to execute reinforced concrete (RC) structures. This building features RC in slender, linear and also tensile members. The unlikelihood of encountering this material in such a situation may be taken as a proof of the absence of a relationship of necessity between bi-directional materials and the global form of their structures, as other materials adapt more easily to the design. The thin, sloping roof slabs with eave beam stiffeners are supported by a system of struts connected to a curving lower chord. The distance between the columns is reduced from 25 m to an effective structural span of 20 m by the columns' inward-curving line. The second part of the forked columns reaches out to carry the roof overhang, partly balancing the bending moment created in the columns by the roof loads acting eccentrically.[67] In a similar way as in his deck-stiffened arch bridges, Maillart uses the stiffness in the roof slab and beams to carry the bending that occurs when live-loads act only on the half-span, and thus does away with diagonal truss elements. All the members in the (rather curious) reinforced concrete structure, including those that make up the curving lower chord that Billington refers to as an inverted arch, are made up of straight lines forming a polygon. This greatly simplifies construction, and does not significantly lessen the visual experience of the lower chord as a continuous curve. Later, this geometrical simplification was also to become part of the design for the parabolic arches in some of Maillart's bridges. Interestingly, Maillart introduces a kink in the chord at mid-span, tying the chord up to the gable peak and thus letting the load re-enter the plane of the roof slab, this time resulting in compression forces down both of the sloping sides. One of the consequences of this choice is that the particular mid-span 'colonnette' becomes not a strut, but a hanger that (along with the lower chord) acts in tension. This kink is visually not particularly

2.25 Engineer Robert Maillart: Magazzini Generale (1924), Chiasso, Italy.

2.26 Interior view. Magazzini Generale, Chiasso.

2.27 Architect Álvaro Siza, engineer Cecil Balmond: the Portuguese Pavilion, Expo 98, Lisbon.

pleasing, though, as it interrupts the expected curved continuity of the lower chord and renders the whole structure a little awkward.

The roof structure as a whole, however, poses some interesting questions about the 'nature' of a material like reinforced concrete. Clothed in a global form that might more efficiently be constructed in steel or wood, the monolithic execution is notably characteristic of its material: at the level of *local* form, all the 'connections' show a continuous joining of matter – having been made from one piece – that is undeniably idiomatic of in-situ concrete. The slight widening of the members' cross-sections towards the joints strengthens the structural continuity between the members, and by an appropriate design of the reinforcement contributes to reducing the risk of cracks in the concrete. Some eighty years of performance has certainly proved the structure safe and reliable. The form of the structure is thus mechanically appropriate, and serves its purpose well. But is the design in accordance with what might be thought of as the 'nature' of reinforced concrete? Although the technological properties of RC make possible a continuous casting of joints, it is in this case difficult to understand and accept the choice of material and structural form. Also the complex formwork and the in-situ casting is definitely more difficult than constructing the same in steel or even in timber. The design accords with the material's strength and stiffness characteristics, however: even if pure tension is not the preferred force in reinforced concrete, the material can still be made to cope with it. Maillart was so experienced and comfortable with this particular material that the problems created by the technological processes necessary to carry out the design must have been more easily solved by him than by most others. Moreover, Maillart was not only an engineering designer but a builder whose construction company actually built his designs.

The idea of RC in pure tensile structures is brought to a logical if temporary conclusion in a more recent project: the Portuguese Pavilion for Expo 98 in Lisbon, designed by architect Álvaro Siza with structural collaboration from Cecil Balmond of Ove Arup and Partners.[68] Directly on the waterfront, the design features a ceremonial plaza covered by a huge hanging roof of reinforced concrete. Covering an area that is nearly square, it spans freely about 67 m with a structural thickness of only 200 mm. With a smooth and continuous surface painted white, the curving concrete slab resembles a large piece of hanging cloth or a tent. The tension forces generate large pulling forces at each end that are counteracted by deep porticoes comprising cantilevered shear-walls. Embedded in the concrete is a dense array of steel cables made visible in the last few metres before being hooked up in the system of end walls. This structure is a clear example of a so-called form-active structural form.

2.28 Exposed cables at their point of support. The Portuguese Pavilion, Expo 98, Lisbon.

Taken together, the two projects show the strength capabilities of reinforced concrete in all their aspects, including compression, bending, shear and pure tension. Of those force types, tension is intuitively the

least compatible with the hardness and heaviness of the concrete as 'cast stone'. Tension, of course, renders the concrete itself inactive, relying on the steel reinforcement for strength. Hence, in a cross-section with tension stresses as the only type of stress acting, the concrete will, from a certain point of view, remain inert. Nevertheless, such structural members represent no less truly reinforced concrete structures, with the steel and the concrete both having a function. In the case of the Portuguese Pavilion the concrete lends weight to the structure to keep it from vibrating excessively as a result of wind loads.[69]

The examples show reinforced concrete as a material that can adapt to fit seemingly very unlikely structural forms, including those which depend on pure tension. From a geometrical point of view, RC can make up surface forms like walls, slabs and vaults; in addition to the obvious linear elements of beams and columns, it can also form chords, hangers and ties. In terms of both strength and geometry, this versatile material puts up very few constraints regarding the global structural form. This formal richness is also found in other bi-directional materials like mild steel or laminated timber, except maybe for one thing: on a larger scale, reinforced concrete is probably the only structural material that combines significant compression and bending strength with the ability to form surface forms and mass forms. We might say that reinforced concrete is able to do in a continuous plane what metals and wood do only as lines. The plasticity of RC offers geometrical characteristics that are radically different from those of most other materials, but this does not mean that the overall or global structural forms differ significantly from those achievable with other bi-directional materials. Reinforced concrete makes possible continuous surfaces, whereas materials like metals and wood render the same global forms as skeletons or contours.

If it is true that contemporary bi-directional materials put up very few material constraints for the global design of structures, and that therefore structures made of different materials tend to be somewhat similar to one another, what guidelines for form, if any, exist for their design? In what way are the particularities of each material visible? One possible answer is that there are no mechanical guidelines for the global form of structures other than those ensuring stability and safety, and those are barely material-specific. We will in the next section, however, take a closer look at the local form of structures. According to our third hypothesis, for bi-directional materials the relationship between material properties and form is most precisely expressed by the structures' local form. The material-specific or 'genuine' 'nature' of steel, concrete and wood is more clearly expressed in the way the materials are processed and in how the structural elements are manufactured. Those technological aspects are observed in the details rather than in the overall form of the structure. To understand structures technologically means primarily to study structural detailing or, in broader terms, the local form. 'Le

	mono-directional		bi-directional
	tension	compression	tension + compression
linear/modular materials	steel wires, glass-, aramid and carbon fibres	cast iron	profiles of steel, aluminium, RC, wood, ductile iron, polymer composites
surface/mass materials	fabrics, foils	stone, masonry un-reinforced concrete	plates of steel, aluminium, RC, polymer composites, (glass)
global form	form-active by necessity, material-specific form		non-, semi- or form- active as options, not material-specific form
local form	material-specific form		material-specific form

bon Dieu est dans le detail', Gustave Flaubert said, an expression also attributed to Mies van der Rohe. Whether it is God or the Devil who lives in the detail, the point here is that it is important. In the case of local form we can justifiably claim that form 'resides' in the material. A technological approach to the material–structure relationship becomes for the most common materials of today more valuable than merely observing their multifarious possible applications for overall structural form. Perhaps the advent of a range of strong versatile materials like steel, reinforced concrete and laminated wood has changed the terms of the debate of form versus materials. The discussion no longer primarily concerns overall structural forms or systems, strongly related to the structural constraints of the materials; instead we should more actively involve structural articulation and detailing, drawing on a wide range of technological properties.[70]

2.29 Matrix relating materials' structural and geometrical characteristics to form.

Technology: the importance of structural detailing

In this section we will take a closer look at the formal features of structures previously identified in terms of the 'local form', bearing in mind that structural details in general represent a level of form that specifically expresses the particularities of each design. I will show (with reference to hypothesis 3) that the local form level is truly material-specific. The main clues for identifying a particular material, Bill Addis says, 'are the shapes of the components, how it has been formed and how it is joined to other pieces of material – in other words the way it is manufactured'.[71] Linking the local form level to a technological understanding of structural form, we will focus our discussion on structural connections.

Structural connections become necessary because it is impractical, not to say impossible, to make buildings out of one large piece of material, carving out the architectural spaces (even if this has actually been done in our early history!). Neither is it in most cases possible, for scale reasons, to make one huge mould into which we can pour a liquid material which eventually hardens into a physical substance delimiting an interior space. Since carving and casting are both ruled out, we will have to rely on a third: assembly or construction, where we put together elements of a manageable size. Assembly presents problems of a both practical and aesthetic nature which have to be solved by the structural detail, the meeting point where materials and elements are linked. Frequently we hear architecture described as a kind of poetry. This is an example of enigmatic rhetoric, but is nonetheless a metaphor that helps create a kind of mental attitude when we look at a work of architecture. Continuing the metaphorical language, we might well think of the whole architectural work as a large novel that presents a gallery of participants involved in more or less complex acts. The detail, on the other hand, will (in similar imagery) be like a small poem. In the detail, as in the poem, information and aesthetic experience are completely condensed. The detail is all about giving form to certain functions in a very compressed space, where many different aspects of a building are brought together and resolved by a single idea. Etymologically, the word *detail* consists of two parts: the last -*tail* in this context means 'to cut something to size' in order to delimit something. This is actually what the tailor does. *De-tail* hence means 'to cut off', to separate or isolate something from a larger piece of work.[72] In our context, though, this cutting off must be seen as a mental rather than physical actuality: the detail presents problems that need and deserve special attention, but it is still of course physically as well as conceptually very much part of a larger work.

We will take a look at some trusses and frames manufactured in different materials, observing the structural connections and noting the different approaches to their solutions. The structures themselves, although in different architectural contexts, have many similarities on the level of global form. The differences shown in the detailing, however, result from the diverse technological characteristics of each material, rendering the local form highly material-specific. Each joint presents an appearance that quite distinctly reflects the characteristics or 'mode' of that material.

Comparing steel with reinforced concrete, it is obvious that when RC is applied to make structures in situ, its monolithic technological properties reduce the need for separate structural connections. The joint of different elements, as in the Chiasso warehouse by Maillart, is typically 'erased' by the casting of fresh concrete. In-situ RC thus appears to be significantly poorer than steel on structural detailing. It is interesting, therefore, to observe the structure of the Lloyd's of London building where concrete details have been precast, forming huge joints that

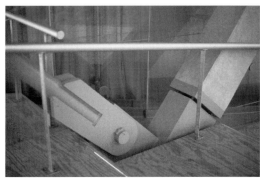

connect RC columns with the diagonal members of the cross-bracing. Although having a certain kinship to steel detailing, the sheer size and solidity of the joints make them entirely 'concrete-ish'. So do the holes, which are imprints of the ties necessary to keep the formwork in place when pouring the concrete.

The Wills Factory near Bristol, England, presents us with a classical steel truss detail. All exposed steelwork is in Cor-Ten weathering steel, and the detailed design for the structural joints is of a particularly high quality. The joint illustrated shows a well-known principle for a bolted connection, with beautifully designed and cut gusset plates. The bolts and nuts are well ordered; they also implicitly demonstrate the strength of the steel and its profiles by the number of bolts necessary to keep them together.

Traditionally, often the dimensions of the members for timber connections need to be enlarged to make room for the necessary number of bolts; in which case the truss members were not fully stressed and were thus uneconomical. A method of making structural joints that overcomes this problem involves hidden steel plates and a large number of thin steel dowels. The steel plates with pre-drilled holes are fitted into sawn cuts in the wood, and the dowels are pressed through both the laminated wooden members as well as the holes in the steel plates that constitute the actual physical connections between the members. The result is a structural detail that is very smooth and appears to be

2.30 Structural detail in reinforced concrete. Architects Richard Rogers Partnership, engineers Ove Arup and Partners: Lloyd's of London (1986).

2.31 Structural detail in Cor-Ten steel. Architects YRM with SOM, engineer Felix Samuely: Wills Factory (1974), Bristol.

2.32 Structural detail in laminated wood. Architects Østgaard: Håkons Hall (1993), Lillehammer, Norway.

2.33 Structural detail showing the character of both reinforced concrete and steel. Architects OMA, structural engineers ABT: Educatorium (1997), Utrecht, the Netherlands.

2.34 Rigid connection in a laminated wooden frame. Architect Sverre Fehn: Storhamarlåven (1976), Storhamar, Norway.

2.35 Rigid connection in a steel frame. Architect Mies van der Rohe: Crown Hall, Illinois Institute of Technology (1956), Chicago.

almost all wood, with the steel parts barely visible. Close scrutiny, however, reveals the thin lines of the plates and the small dots of steel representing the dowels.

In the Educatorium at the University of Utrecht steel members are connected to structural members of concrete to form a composite truss supporting the auditorium. Structural joints of steel adapt to the members of different materials meeting at the same point, showing a characteristic flexibility needed to cope with a hybrid structure.

In the Storhamarlåven project a structural frame in laminated timber is stabilised by bending-stiff connections. In this case, the necessary stiffness is obtained by inserting steel plates in the two corners. The Crown Hall at the Illinois Institute of Technology represents the classical all-steel solution to the same problem by fully welded connections of the beam and column profiles. Stiffeners help to achieve adequate bending stiffness, completing the steel vocabulary in the present situation.

Detail is a precise indicator of material characteristics even if the architectural program wants to diminish its importance in favour of the overall structural form. There is no way of escaping the particular relationship between structural connections and the properties of the structural materials. If not thought architecturally relevant, however, connections might be kept from view, or at least 'not celebrated'. Cecil Balmond links what he calls the celebration of connections to structural elements of 'even distribution', meaning repetitive identical systems where no part has value relative to another, in which case a cultivation of the detail might be seen as a compensation for a dull and uninspiring overall structural design.[73] The choice of where to spend creative energy is, however, always in the hands of the designers and their clients.

To conclude this section, I will briefly sum up our present understanding of the relationship of structures, form and materials. Concentrating on the mechanical aspects of structures, I proposed in Part 1 that science and technology were two different ways, or modes, of explaining and understanding structural form. In Part II, I introduced the idea of the different levels of observable structural form, establishing the two categories of global and local form. Moreover, I addressed the need for a more precise distinction between the different material properties by suggesting the categories of structural properties (fundamental parameters), technological properties (ranking parameters) and geometrical properties. The discussion up to now has shown that an explanation of structural form by way of the stiffness and strength characteristics of the materials, a natural science approach, involves primarily form on the *global* level. More specifically this discussion has shown that materials having mono-directional structural properties by necessity are very form-sensitive on the global level of structural form. Form 'resides' so to speak in the material. On the other hand, materials having bi-directional structural properties lend themselves to a large variety of global structural forms, and we can justifiably claim that global form can be estab-

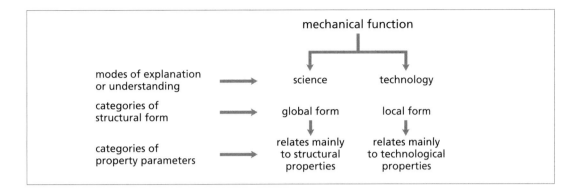

lished irrespective of the material. I will discuss in a later chapter that this point can be somewhat tempered by the structural scale. Finally, bi-directional materials present truly material-specific form primarily on the local level of structural form, involving structural connections as well as the detailed design of structural elements and members.

2.36 The cognitive approaches of science and technology in relation to the issues of material properties and form.

Mechanical efficiency and the economy of means

In buildings, the idea of employing the available resources as efficiently as possible has probably always been a relevant issue, particularly in vernacular architecture. Every period has not therefore aimed at minimalism, but it is reasonable to think that where material, financial and even human resources have been limited, people were forced to consider how materials could be used economically. This involves provision for adequate strength and stability of a building structure while also employing the resources at hand frugally. Numerous stories of buildings that have collapsed suggest that new building types as well as new structural principles have from time to time conceptually and dimensionally approached – or even overstretched – minimal safety limits, for example the structures of Gothic cathedrals.

Structural vs. technological efficiency

There are, however, very significant deviations from this basic observation. The transformation of archaic Greek temple architecture from wooden structures to that of stone resulted in an exactly opposite process. The reasons for this transformation were possibly a wish to use more permanent materials that could withstand the climate over a longer period of time; probably, too, building with more costly and valuable materials was more honouring to the gods. The consequence of this was a replacement of a material well suited for post-and-lintel structures by a material not suited for beam structures at all. The structural properties of wood resist bending forces infinitely better than stone, whether limestone or marble. A beam made of stone is far from being an efficient structure. Moreover, the beam as a structural element is a highly inefficient structural member when it comes to the internal distribution of bending stresses. Regardless of the material, the centre parts around the neutral axis of the cross-section are scarcely stressed while the extreme top and bottom parts may be stressed to the limit. This is particularly true for beams of rectangular, solid cross-sections, like those of the Greek temples. Hence, we may conclude that the pursuit of efficient structures was hardly an issue for the ancient Greek builders; it was overshadowed by human needs of a more profound character, expressed through architectonic style. 'It was the human aspect that the Greeks took as their point of departure, making the trabeated structure an expression of the living forces of carrying and being carried', says Christian Norberg-Schulz.[74] It thus seems quite natural that an emphasis on the vertical and the horizontal should be preferable to that of a possible alternative arch structure. With arches one cannot speak of interaction between an active and a more passive structural element. An arch curves over an opening in a continuous movement, adopting the function of both column and beam. Yet, regardless of obvious examples of structural efficiency being a very low priority, I will argue that the efficient use of materials is a guiding principle for structural design and of the greatest importance when seeking the reasons and explanations for structural forms. There can be no doubt, either, about the increasing importance of weights and loads of materials in the architecture of the very near future, when to a large degree transport and energy consumption will determine the feasibility of a building project in a sustainable world.

Let us be clearer about the actual subject under discussion. The basic topic is the idea of an *economy of means*: maximum output for a minimum of input. This general idea, however, should be broken down into manageable concepts. It implies a search for the least costly structure, or the structure with the highest load-bearing capacity and the lowest weight. It can also mean the structure that is judged to be the most convenient to manufacture. All these aspects are related, but may also be contradictory: the structure with the lowest weight can easily prove to be the most costly. This is wholly dependent on the relative costs of material and labour. However, the involvement of money in a general discussion of structural form complicates matters greatly; it will therefore not be explicitly discussed here. I will mainly address the basic preconditions for *structural efficiency* and comment on the resulting implications for form. Here, the structural efficiency of a system or a member is taken to mean the ratio between the load carried by the structure and its weight, and is thus quantifiable. The higher the strength-to-weight ratio, the more efficient the structure.[75] Clearly, we will see that structural efficiency in many cases may create greater complexity of structural form. By adopting a weight-saving design, the structure may become more difficult to manufacture; its *technological efficiency* may be reduced. In fact, we could speak about a total *mechanical efficiency* of structures,

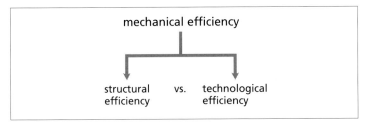

mechanical efficiency

structural   vs.   technological
efficiency   efficiency

2.37 Structural and technological efficiency. While the first is an expression of load capacity relative to weight, the second refers to the efficiency of the manufacturing processes.

defined as the ratio of useful work performed to total work expended.[76] This notion includes not only load-bearing efficiency (high strength/low weight) but also the structure's degree of buildability (efficiency of the manufacturing process). This approach helps us to establish some criteria for critical discussion and hence comparison of structural efficiency against the resulting simplicity/complexity of the actual construction.

From a sustainability point of view, mechanical efficiency is of great importance. Less work means less energy; reduced weight and reduced construction work both point to a reduction in energy consumption. From the life-cycle perspective, however, buildings consume far more operational energy than is embodied in their structure. 'Here there is a dramatic divergence between buildings and civil engineering infrastructure. In buildings it has been found that the operational energy over a typical 60-year design life is ten times the embodied energy during construction.'[77] A strict focus on the efficiency of structures in architecture does not contribute to energy savings as much as the same focus in civil engineering works. This does not mean that reduced weight, work and energy related to the structure is unimportant in architecture; it does, however, put its relevance into perspective.

Structurally efficient materials

We will start with a consideration of the materials. Depending upon the type of load to be resisted (compression, tension, bending, etc.), different materials will perform more or less efficiently.[78] Considering, firstly, a simple *tension* member of cross-sectional area A and length L, we might investigate what material produces the lightest member when a tensile force F is to be carried safely. We seek to maximise the ratio of load to weight, and take the conditions for that as a criterion for the efficiency of different materials when acting in tension. Simple calculations will show that maximum structural efficiency is obtained by the material having the *maximum σ_y/ρ value* – that is, the material with the highest yield strength- (or failure strength-) to-density ratio.[79] If the member with length L is now to support a *compression* force F, we may have a buckling problem. Ideally, a slender strut will support the Euler load $P_E = \pi^2 EI/L^2$. Calculations show that choosing a material which *maximises the ratio of $E^{1/2}/\rho$* will contribute to maximising the structural efficiency for compression members in danger of buckling.

Material	Properties					
	σ_Y (N mm^{-2})	ρ (g mm^{-3})	E (N mm^{-2})	Tension σ_Y/ρ	Bending strength $\sigma_Y^{2/3}/\rho$	Bending stiffness, buckling $E^{1/2}/\rho$
Carbon steel	250–1700	7.8	210,000	32–218	5.1–18.3	58.8
Aluminium alloys	150–500	2.7	70,000	55–185	10.5–23.3	98.0
Titanium alloys	200–1200	4.5	110,000	44–267	7.6–25.1	73.7
Magnesium alloys	70–400	1.85	43,000	37–216	9.2–29.3	112.1
Softwood (spruce, fir)	18–25	0.5	11,000	36–50	13.7–17.1	209.8
Glass	30	2.45	70,000	12	3.9	108.0
GFRP (glass/polymer)	200–500	1.75–1.95	21,000–35,000	102–285	17.5–36.0	74.3–106.9
CFRP (carbon/polymer)	500–1050	1.55–1.60	50,000–60,000	312–677	39.4–66.6	139.8–158.0
KFRP (Kevlar/polymer)	130–150	1.37–1.40	23,000–30,000	93–109	18.3–20.6	108.3–126.4

2.38 A comparison of different materials' abilities to resist tension, buckling and bending efficiently. The higher the number of the given ratio, the more efficient the material.

Similar computations will give us the material efficiency criterion for the *bending strength* of beams. For a cantilever of length L supporting a point load F at the outer end, we will find that *maximising the ratio of $\sigma_Y^{2/3}/\rho$* will contribute to maximising the structural efficiency for bending strength. Lastly, studying the material efficiency related to *bending stiffness*, where the cantilever is as before, we will find that when deflection is the issue, the material having the *highest ratio of $E^{1/2}/\rho$* will be the most weight efficient.

Alloys of magnesium and titanium are not much used in the building industry, despite some interesting strength- and stiffness-to-weight values. The reason for this is obviously that their properties are not really in enough demand to justify their cost.[80] Fibre/polymer composites also have interesting architectural applications, and their efficiency as structural materials suggests that their importance might increase in the future. We notice in particular the very favourable values shown by carbon fibre reinforced composites. However, perhaps the single most revealing result is the remarkably high efficiency displayed in common softwood like spruce and fir. Tension strength properties compared to weight compete with those of medium strength steels, while the bending strength and deflection properties are clearly in favour of wood compared to metals. In other words, sections of solid or laminated wood offer both high strength and stiffness per unit of weight, and ought thus to be considered closely when materials are selected for structural efficiency.

Structural efficiency and structural form

The single most important parameter, however, for the design of efficient, load-bearing structures is without doubt the relationship between structural form and the configuration of the loads. In what way will the structure respond to the imposed loads? What kind of stresses will result? These seem to be the key questions when studying the prerequisites for structural efficiency. Let us start, however, with a general observation: a precondition for achieving efficiency in a structural system is that the loads are transported to the foundations as directly as possible. This (in an ideal world) ensures the shortest and most effective route of forces, and thus contributes to keeping the weight down. However, we know that in any work of architecture the design of spaces will mostly be in conflict with this ideal; the loads must necessarily be spread about in order to establish rooms, and are thus commonly deprived of the most direct course. This play of solids and voids, of span and space – sometimes apparently in conflict with other – is what makes the design of structures in architecture particularly fascinating. The study of this multi-faceted relationship is the central concern of this book.

How is structural efficiency achieved by manipulating structural form? The answers to this question are found by applying the theories of statics and elasticity, which belong to the realm of scientific and mathematical explanation. They analyse the response of structural elements to physical influences in the form of loads, and how those responses change according to the type and direction of the applied loads. The technological issues that arise from this question will be addressed later, by focusing on the manufacturing complexity that very often results from a sophisticated manipulation of form.

Our point of departure is that the efficient use of structural materials entails the search for stiffness and strength through structural form and geometry rather than through mass and dimension. This principle is, however, often not fully exploited in architecture – one is sometimes forced to choose a less favourable system made adequately stiff and strong by increasing the structural dimensions. Yet the principle noted above remains the goal.[81]

Focusing on the concept of structural efficiency, we will firstly consider the structure's global form. The comparison of different structural systems or principles enables us to find the greatest (or least) *global efficiency*. We have already stated that the beam-and-column type of structure is generally not very efficient, i.e. the global efficiency is

2.39 Stiffness through structural geometry. Architect Vilhelm Lauritzen: the roof structure of Copenhagen Airport Terminal Building (1939).

quite low.[82] Secondly, if we change our perspective from the structural system as such to its elements or components, we will realise that when the overall shape of the structural system is given, we can still make a detailed design of its components. Hence, if for whatever reason a structural system is *globally* shaped in a way that acts inefficiently, we may still design each component of that system to act as efficiently as possible. In that case we compensate for an inefficient global system by designing for what might be called the *local efficiency* of the individual members.[83] This is what we do with most structural problems in ordinary design practice. In the case of a steel beam we would design for enhanced efficiency by having the cross-section shaped as an H or an

I, or by replacing a solid cross-section by a truss. Shaping the member along the longitudinal axis – that is, by tapering the form of a compression member or that of a beam – can also naturally achieve higher local efficiency. All beams are not made more locally efficient by a sophisticated cross-section, however, partly because their technological efficiency will be reduced by a higher complexity of form. Besides, both concrete and especially wood are both much lighter materials than steel, and also cheaper, so there is not the same incentive to reduce self-weight. Lastly, the most efficient structure is obviously achieved by striving for both global and local efficiency.

Since structural efficiency is given by the load capacity-to-weight ratio of a structure or a structural member, the geometrical properties of the structure in relation to the configuration of the loads are highly interesting. Structures that are stiff and strong by way of form rather than by mass place material in the space in such a way as to obtain maximum use of that material. Material is placed where it is most needed, and reduced or taken away where not sufficiently employed. Structures that most fully exploit the principle of efficient form are form-active structures. The shape of form-active structures in relation to the configuration of the loads is such that the internal force reactions are axial – that is, they are tension or compression forces. This is the first requirement for the form of a material–efficient structure:

Structures are more efficient when loads cause axial forces in the system rather than bending.

The main reason for this is that the internal stress distribution in axially loaded structures or structural members is more or less constant, and this uniform stress level provides for all of the material to be stressed to the limit. The same is obviously not the case for structures in bending, in which case the stress distribution reaches its maximum in the top and bottom fibres while being zero in the cross-section, where the bending stress changes from compression to tension. Moreover, form-active structures are also more efficient at resisting deformations. Deformations resulting from bending forces are commonly larger by far than those resulting from purely axial forces. The most obvious examples of form-active structures are the hanger, the tension rod, the compression strut, the cable that changes shape in relation to the configuration of the loads, as well as the arch shaped according to the funicular line of compression.

However, axially loaded members become thicker and heavier if they have to cope with instability or buckling. It comes as no surprise, then, that there is a difference between tension members and slender compression members regarding structural efficiency. We can state, as a second requirement for efficiency, that among axially loaded members:

Structures are more efficient when resisting loads by tension forces rather than by compression forces.

Among the most lightweight structures are the cable nets and the soft shells. Those are structures made primarily from steel cables and textiles, elements or materials without any ability to resist compression forces. The shapes of such structures correspond closely with a geometry that is stable by tension forces alone, although they have to interact with compression members for total stability. When high strength/low weight is an issue, it is evident that the necessary compression members in a structure ideally should have a low slenderness ratio. Hence we can postulate a third requirement for efficiency:

Structures are most efficient when compression forces are transported across short distances.

Compression members are thus most efficient when they have a very low slenderness ratio. The risk of buckling means that slender compression members will not be able to carry load according to the strength capacity of the material, but will experience a necessary reduction of the working stress. A theoretical maximum capacity for compression loads is obtained in cases where the slenderness ratio of (for example) a steel column is in the region of 20 or less, which is quite unrealistic in actual practice.

2.40 The slenderness of the arches is a result of the parabolic shape being geometrically close to the form-active structure of the inverted funicular, where self-weight will cause pure compression forces. Architects A. Cruz and A. Ortiz: the Santa Justa Station (1991), Seville.

2.41 A pre-stressed tent structure acting by tension forces in two directions, providing a very light cover for the Buckingham Palace Ticket Office (1995), London. Architect Michael Hopkins, engineers Ove Arup and Partners.

2.42 A light cable net offering protection against the sun at Expo 92, Seville.

2.43 A diagram of theoretical buckling strength versus slenderness ratios for steel.

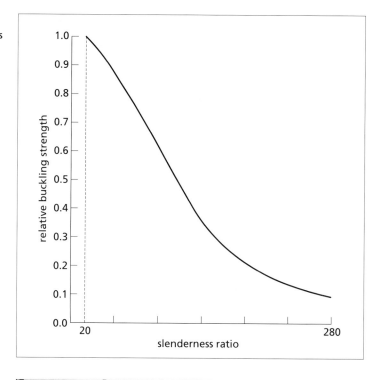

2.44 Short, efficient compression struts with a modest slenderness ratio supporting an efficient and form-active membrane structure. Architect Ron Herron: Imagination Headquarters (1990), London.

For slender compression members there is another effect related to buckling that affects efficiency: a subdivision of a compression force by using more members means increased structural weight. This is because each compression member can only support a portion of the total load restricted by the buckling load of each individual member, and a subdivision increases the slenderness of each member. We can therefore state as a fourth requisite for efficiency that:

Structures are most efficient when a subdivision of compression forces is avoided.

2.45 A group of slender columns with no local bracing. Architect Zaha Hadid, engineers Ove Arup and Partners: the Vitra Fire Station (1993), Weil-am-Rhein, Germany.

The effect of subdivision can easily be calculated. We will find that the use of n slender compression members to resist a certain load leads to a weight increase by √n relative to that of a single member. It should be made clear, however, that this is only correct if the members dividing a force between them are not connected to each other along the length in a way that the buckling stability of the group of members is increased. Likewise it should be pointed out that the relationship noted above only considers the weight of the actual compression members, and does not say anything about the consequences for the structure being supported by one or more compression members.

Up to now, we have looked at form-active structures and structural members subjected to axial forces and comparing them as means of global structural efficiency. Most structures in architecture, however, are not form-active, but semi- or non-form-active. Those are structures that usually work by a combination of axial forces and bending or by bending alone. The extent to which semi-form-active structures are globally efficient will depend on the level of bending stresses in relation to the level of axial stresses in the system. The closer they are to form-active principles, the more efficient they are. However, for all types of semi-form-active or non-form-active structures, and also compressive form-active structures where buckling is of relevance, there is obviously a reservoir of efficiency inherent in the principle of changing the form of the element along the length. We may formulate a fifth requisite for structural efficiency which contributes to local structural efficiency:

Structures are locally most efficient when the members are shaped along the length to follow the variations of the stresses.

The idea is to adapt the structural depth to the varying force intensities in every cross-section. We can show the effect of this by studying some simple cases. If we first take a look at the simply supported beam of length L with a linearly distributed load, we may inquire about the gain in efficiency that results from shaping the beam in accordance with the bending moment diagram. With a constant beam depth corresponding to the maximum bending moment of $qL^2/8$, we may say that the area of the beam profile, and thus the relative weight, is given by $qL^3/8$.[84] On the other hand, for a beam following the contour of the parabolic bending moment diagram we will find the relative beam weight by calculating the area inscribed by that diagram, the result being $qL^3/12$. For simplicity, the beam height is taken to be zero at both ends, allowing for no shear force capacity. Comparing the area of this particular beam to the relative area of the beam having a constant height, we can theoretically observe that a third of the weight is reduced by shaping the beam in accordance with the bending moment diagram instead of keeping the beam height constant. In reality, the gain will be somewhat less because of the necessity to have a certain height at both ends.[85]

A fixed-end beam shaped to follow the contour of its bending moment diagram, having a height at mid-span and at both ends corresponding to the bending moments occurring at those points, will yield a relative weight of $qL^3/18$. Compared to the fixed-end beam of a constant height corresponding to the maximum bending moment of $qL^2/12$, this beam also saves a third of the weight by being shaped to follow the variation in the bending moment diagram.[86]

The effect of tapering compression members is also interesting architecturally. By letting column shapes comply more closely with an idealised shape for resisting buckling, we will achieve a structurally more efficient member. Let us study three different column shapes. All are slender columns with the same effective length and hinged at both ends. The first column has a constant cross-section in the form of a cross, while the next two have the same cross-section, but change dimensions along the column length. The flange thickness t is a constant for all columns. We want to investigate their efficiency as columns where all have the same load-bearing capacity. A column which is tapered towards both ends

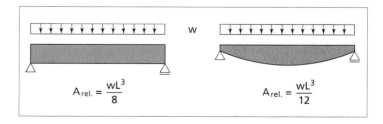

2.46 Simply supported beams.

and having a certain stiffness (governed by I) at mid-span will be weaker than a column having the same cross-sectional stiffness as a constant throughout its length. This means that to make a tapered column with no reduction in axial load capacity implies an enlargement of its mid-span dimensions. We make the simplification that the second moment of area, I_1, is calculated from the flange having extension in the direction of the buckling only, ignoring the contribution of the other flange. In this case we also associate the relative weight of the member with the area of the column's side-elevation, or profile (hL). Furthermore, we take for granted that the columns fail by ideal buckling according to the Euler equation, and that local buckling of the flange in compression does not occur.

Calculations show that the tapered parabolic column with a buckling strength equalling that of the linear column needs an extra width at mid-span resulting in a total cross-sectional dimension of 1.12h, h being the width of the linear column. Implicit in the calculation is a proportional relationship of the minimum and maximum second moments of area of 1:25, yielding a relationship of column widths at top/bottom and at mid-span of 1:2.9 (end widths equal 0.38h). The next step is to find the relative weight of the two columns, based on the area of their profiles. In this case, calculations show that the area of the profile of the tapered column equals 0.87hL, whereas the linear column has an area of hL. Hence, a comparison of the two columns of equal strength shows that the parabolic column of the noted proportions has an area, and thus a relative weight, which amounts to 87% of that of the linear column.

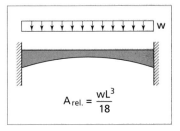

$$A_{rel.} = \frac{wL^3}{18}$$

2.47 Beam with fixed ends shaped according to the bending moment diagram.

2.48 Column 1 with constant width.
2.49 Column 2, a tapered column.

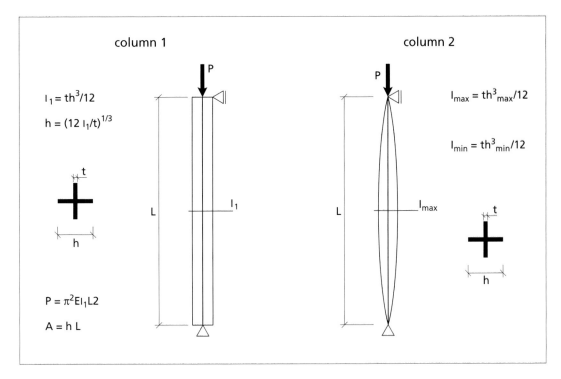

column 1

$I_1 = th^3/12$

$h = (12\, I_1/t)^{1/3}$

$P = \pi^2 EI_1 L2$

$A = h\,L$

column 2

$I_{max} = th^3_{max}/12$

$I_{min} = th^3_{min}/12$

2.50 A tapered column. Architect Arne P. Eggen: National Theatre Underground Station (1998), Oslo.

Computing different proportions between end width and mid-span width yields different column areas and thus weights. We find, however, that the amount of material saved is relatively modest, between 4% and 14% for the calculated columns. Compared to beams with a contour following the bending moment diagram discussed earlier, the columns do not gain much in efficiency by having a variable cross-section. The reason for this difference is obvious: a simply supported beam in bending does not make full use of a constant cross-sectional height, except for the mid-span region; whereas a column, apart from a stability benefit from an enlarged mid-height width, essentially needs its cross-section to carry a more or less constant axial force. A column is essentially always a very efficient structural element; variations of the cross-sections like those studied above are no more than adjustments for coping with the buckling problem. Yet tapered columns attract architectural attention.

A column laterally supported at mid-height by a system of struts and pre-stressed rods or wires is obviously also efficient. The additional material providing stability works in this case by axial forces. If lateral bracing of the column results in a reduction of the effective length to one half of the physical length, then the necessary geometric stiffness of the cross-section can be reduced to one-fourth compared to that of a column of full, unsupported height, resulting in a much smaller cross-section and a significant weight reduction. It must be added, however, that the weight of struts and tensile rods will increase the total weight of the column and thus render the column less material-efficient than suggested here. Still, there can be little doubt this principle makes a contribution to structural efficiency.

Even if self-evident, we may formulate a sixth requisite for efficiency, valid on the local level of structural form:

Structures are locally most efficient when structural members have optimised cross-sections.

In other words, material should be put to best possible effect in the cross-section, giving the highest bending stiffness possible. One way of expressing the local efficiency of a member is to relate the section modulus (Z) to the area of the same section (A). Since a high section modulus will reduce the resulting stresses in a cross-section subjected to bending, it is favourable to have as large a section modulus as possible while using as little material as possible. The idea is therefore to maximise the ratio of Z/A in a cross-section. Let us look at a few examples of steel profiles. If the bending occurs about one axis only, it is obvious that a profile that is symmetrical about the two main axes is unfavourable. Likewise a rectangular hollow section with the same cross-sectional area as that of an I-beam will be less favourable, because the material is less efficiently distributed. We can also observe that for a certain type of beam, say an IPE, the efficiency increases as the profile becomes

cross-section	section area (mm^2)	section modulus (mm^3)	Z_x/A (mm)
CHS d = 114.3 × 6.3 mm	2140	54,700	25.6
RHS 120 × 60 × 6.3 mm	2090	61,000	29.2
IPE 160 h = 160 mm b = 82 mm	2010	109,000	54.2

larger. Large rolled-steel profiles quite simply make better use of the material than smaller ones. This is because the flange and web thicknesses do not increase at the same rate as height, so that the increased weight of the larger profile is put to better use.

Also related to this is the principle of integrating structure and cladding in a so-called stressed-skin structure. This offers another way of optimising the cross-section by putting the cladding to structural use. While used in architecture, the best-known examples are those from the aircraft industry. The strength and stiffness of an aircraft fuselage depend on the outer skin being fixed to the interior stiffening ribs for structural co-operation.

Robert Le Ricolais had a beautiful way of expressing the importance of a carefully considered strategy for the efficient use of materials. He said that 'the art of structure is how and where to put the holes', focusing upon the voids rather than the solid elements.[87] Much can be gained by looking at the *articulation* of form, at how material is distributed locally within a fixed structural shape. A very well-known way of constructing that is well suited to semi- or non-form-active systems is the use of triangulated trusses. The principle of triangulation can transform bending moments to pure axial forces and thus offer high structural efficiency. Hence the seventh requisite for structural efficiency also operates on the local form level. Compared to solid structural members:

Structures are made locally more efficient by triangulated trussing.

Triangulation, however, does not result in quite as high efficiency as obtained in form-active structures, because of the relatively lower efficiency obtained at the joints.[88] We can see triangulation as a technologically efficient adaptation of a yet more efficient basic principle, namely that of distributing material in a structural element according to the law of minimum potential energy. Transforming isostatic stress

	Z_x/A (mm)
IPE 80	26.7
IPE 180	61.6
IPE 300	103.5
IPE 500	166.4
IPE 600	196.8

2.51 Cross-sections of similar weight, but of increasing efficiency.

2.52 Ratio of Z/A for some steel profiles. Larger profiles are more material-efficient in bending.

lines into straight lines will mean using triangulation, if axial forces are to result. The German engineer Karl Culmann published in 1866 a method for finding the principal stresses in a beam graphically, making it relatively easy to draw the trajectories of the principal stresses for a given load. Along the trajectories the principal stress is a constant and the compression stresses are orthogonal to the tension stresses. Pier Luigi Nervi employed the same principle, albeit in a horizontal plane, when he arranged the ribs in the floor slab of the Palace of Labour to follow the trajectories of the principal bending moments. The same strategy obviously inspired architects Michael Hopkins and Partners to do a similar slab in the Schlumberger Phase 2 project in Cambridge.

Lastly, there is the principle of pre-stressing of structural elements or members. The pre-stressing forces are induced in a controlled process, either by pre- or post-tensioning. This causes stresses which oppose those produced by self-weight and live loads, the result being a more efficient internal force distribution and an increase of the structure's capacity for live loads. Alternatively, for a certain live load to be carried, a pre-stressed structure will show a reduction of weight as compared to a structure without pre-stressing. We may hence note the principle of pre-stressing as an eighth requisite for structural efficiency, particularly in structural members made from materials weak in bending:

Structures are locally most efficient when members are pre-stressed.

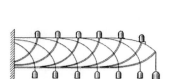

2.53 The principal stresses in a cantilevered beam, after Karl Culmann.

2.54 Triangulation as a practical way of providing for efficient cantilevering of a truss. Architects von Gerkan, Marg and Partners, engineers Krebs and Kiefer, Schlaich Bergermann and Partner: the Olympic Stadium (2004), Berlin.

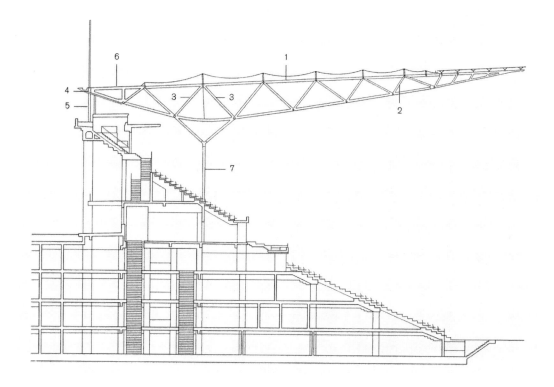

2.55 Isostatic slab structure. The ribs in the floor slab are arranged to follow the trajectories of the principal bending moments. Engineer Pier Luigi Nervi: the Palace of Labour (1961), Milan.

2.56 A more recent example of efficient distribution of concrete in a slab, inspired by Nervi. Architects Michael Hopkins and Partners: Schlumberger Cambridge Research Phase 2 (1992), Cambridge, UK.

2.57 Providing the post-tensioning forces in a beam. Architect Louis I. Kahn, engineer August Kommendant: the Richards Medical Research Laboratories (1960), Philadelphia.

Pre-stressing generally reduces deflection, and may thus save material. The predominant application of pre-stressing is in concrete constructions, where pre-stressed cross-sections have increased stiffness while tension stresses may be totally eliminated. Visually, pre-stressed concrete members appear more slender: depth-to-span ratios for pre-stressed concrete beams are thought to be 25–30% lower than for equivalent non-pre-stressed ones.[89]

In the context of structural efficiency we may also note as being of particular architectural interest the numerous variants of the inverted roof truss, in which a beam is supported not only at each end but at one or more struts or posts along its length. The struts are themselves tied

up to the end supports by a set of tension rods. The pre-stressing of the system that we normally find in such structures is dependent upon the system being statically indeterminate.[90] The efficiency of such structures arises from the combination of two principles: a concentration of the material in discrete axial members, and the shortening of the 'effective' span by creating a continuous beam. The trick of it lies in the struts as mediators between the different principles, or rather that the struts combine them into one principle. In the words of Le Ricolais: 'It's a glorious device, to create fictitious supports, the paradox of columns suspended in the air.'[91]

2.58 Model #1, polyten bridge (1968–9). Structural study of the queen post system. Engineer Robert Le Ricolais.

Efficiency versus complexity

Many of the design strategies for weight reduction can only be achieved through a high degree of technological complexity. The distinction between structural and technological efficiency acknowledges that a weight-saving design might easily conflict with an overall work- or energy-saving design, so that the total work expended on a structure might increase when structural efficiency is the sole objective. A material-saving design often implies a higher complexity of structural forms. On a more fundamental level of structural philosophy, any point of view that counterposes the two aspects of efficiency against one another sees scientific reasoning as antithetical to technological judgement. Hence certain design proposals considered necessary in a strategy for reduced weight come up against a set of practical or technical constraints that must be overcome. An identification of those constraints brings up possible technological solutions, which in turn make it necessary to choose between *levels* of structural efficiency.

An obvious case of conflict between structural and technological efficiency is represented by certain types of shell structures. Double-curved stiff shells, especially those surface forms that are not generated by straight lines, have a geometry that is not easily manufactured on a large scale. Hence, while the resulting forms may offer rich opportunities for a high global efficiency of the finished structure, the amount of work and materials necessary to manufacture those forms can be so substantial that it does not justify the benefit of the structurally efficient design. Numerous variants of concrete formwork systems, as well as the possibilities for precasting shell elements, have not significantly

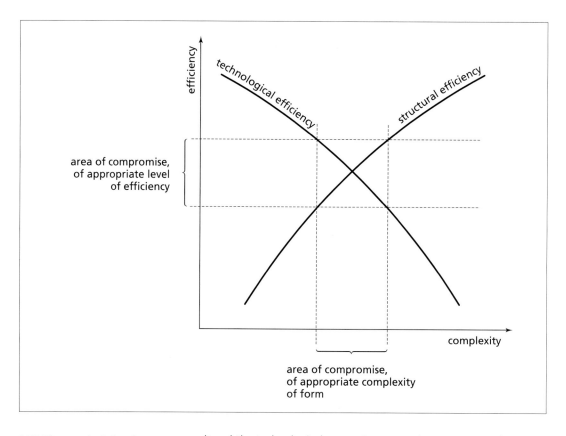

2.59 Diagram depicting the conflict between technological and structural efficiency: a high structural efficiency often implies a high complexity of form, resulting in a low technological efficiency. In actual architectural practice, a balancing or compromise of the two efficiency parameters is often sought.

altered the technological constraints on such structures to the extent that they are beyond doubt practically and economically feasible. This applies in particular to building cultures with high labour costs relative to the cost of materials.

Going back to the tapered columns study of the previous section (pages 68–70), the columns' particular form and proportions meant at the most a 14% reduction of weight compared to a uniformly shaped column of the same strength. From a purely mechanical point of view it is hard to justify the relative complexity of the process necessary to make columns of varying cross-sections unless there are many columns that would all benefit from the same technological operation. When, in spite of this, tapered columns are from time to time represented in architecture, the reason is rather iconographic than mechanical. The image of the bulging column that visually provides resistance is a powerful one, signalling strength.

Both the local and global levels of form tend towards more complexity as structural efficiency increases, gradually leading to more intricate and complex structural geometries where the number of members and joints increases. More work is also necessary for their manufacturing and construction. In actual architectural practice, a balancing of or compromise between structural and technological efficiency is often sought, unless architectural reasons call for a particular design objective. Computer-aided production in the form of CNC manufacturing tools will increasingly make complex structural forms more feasible. This might bring about structures that are material-efficient to a higher degree. Less material combined with less work and energy will undoubtedly contribute to a more sustainable architecture.

Lastly, a striving towards more efficient structural forms is particularly important for structures at a large scale.

Structural scale

Jonathan Swift's Gulliver discovers on his travels that completely new sets of rules apply when as a giant he tries to adapt to a world of dwarfs. In architectural construction, too, as in numerous other matters, the small scale and the large call for quite different analytical and practical solutions – and hence designs.

The scale problem represents one of the fundamental issues in the knowledge of structures. What happens when a certain structural form is scaled up? Or scaled down? What is the relevance of the scale when trying to understand structural form and its relationship to the architectural space? What we *do* know is that there is a certain relationship between the scale of a structure and the level of the stresses involved, which means that the increased weight of a larger structure will tend to leave the structure with less strength to carry other loads. This makes it necessary to apply different structural principles at the larger scale than the smaller. The differences we observe between principles of form at different scales reflect a universal phenomenon by no means restricted to building structures. In the words of d'Arcy Thompson, 'Everywhere Nature works true to scale, and everything has its proper size accordingly. Men and trees, birds and fishes, stars and star-systems, have their appropriate dimensions, and their more or less narrow range of absolute magnitudes.'[92]

Scale and proportion, size and dimension

A sculpture 7 m high and weighing 600 kg takes its shape from a paper clip. Since this is an exact representation of an ordinary paper clip, although on a much larger scale, the form and proportions of this object are precisely the same as in the original. There are some important changes, though: the relationship between the stiffness and the weight of the larger object is different to that of the smaller one, as are the manufacturing processes. The physical structure of its elements is thus different. The large hollow steel tubes substitute for the compact but very thin metal wire – longitudinal welding joints tell us the way the tubes are produced. Moreover, the bending of the curved form is more complicated at the larger scale – the radius of the curvature is almost

2.60 An enlarged paper clip sculpture. At the BI Norwegian School of Management, Oslo.

too small to fit at the new scale. Small wrinkles or folds on the inner side of the curved tubes are the results of this. The enlarged version also needs small steel connectors between the two loops of the paper clip to compensate for the loss of relative stiffness that could lead to flexure or vibrations. As the object became larger, so did the environmental loads from wind and transport, to a point where they no longer could be ignored. It is clear from this example that we would expect not only the stiffness and strength properties to change when the scale changes, but also the technological processes involved in the manufacturing of the structural elements.

What, then, in this context do the terms *scale*, *size*, *dimension*, and *proportion* actually mean? In architectural theory and architectural de-

scriptions in general we frequently meet all four terms. They seem to be
unavoidable when writing or speaking about visual perceptions or interpretations of works of architecture. Scale and proportion imply some
kind of relativity – many studies have looked at the ensuing wide variety
of implications and problems.[93] The same term thus embodies slightly
different meanings, thus making futile a general definition of *scale* valid
for most architectural descriptions. I shall try, however, to be explicit as
to what I mean here. Scale means *size* in relation to other things or to
what we expect. What is the nature of this relation? In the context of
the mechanical characteristics of structures, the most obvious answer is
that we read the size of a structure in terms of (firstly) other structures
and (secondly) our expectations of the size range common for a particular structural type or principle.

Whereas size denotes the degree of bigness or smallness of the whole
object, *dimension* is extension in a single direction, as length, breadth,
and thickness or depth. Hence the size of an object is defined by stating
a number of relevant dimensions. Both size and dimension are therefore absolutes, while scale is relative – one size compared to another.
Likewise, *proportion* simply represents the comparative relation of
one dimension to another. It is important too to point out the distinction here between proportion and scale: proportion mainly denotes the
endogenous relation of the structure's dimensions with itself, whereas
scale refers to the exogenous relation of the size of one structure compared to another. The idea of proportion sometimes also implies a hint of
qualitative evaluation. Expressions like 'out of proportion' mean that an

2.61 A well-known form after
a dramatic change of scale. The
direct transformation creates
technological problems.

object is perceived as representing unsuitable, incorrect or unexpected dimensional relationships. In our case, however, when reflecting upon the mechanical implications of the depth-to-span ratio of a beam, we will let such proportions denote nothing but a numerical relationship between the two dimensions.[94]

It is a well known fact that each structural type as well as each structural material has a certain range of operation outside of which they cannot function mechanically, economically or even aesthetically, even though from a mechanical point of view this range is continuously expanding.[95] To know and pay attention to this is fundamental, even though borderline examples – the structures that strive towards expanding the range – are often the most interesting. Historically, the struggle for ever-greater spans was not without significant setbacks. Structural failures echo through history with the force of legends, although there were probably many reasons for them. One of the most important, however, was a lack of understanding of the 'law of scale' – the need to change the proportions of structural members as the scale increases. A study of scaled-down models quite certainly played a role in deciding on the right structural dimensions for large structures. Before the 'law of scale' was recognised, many buildings were given structural proportions based on such model studies, and were built significantly weaker than they should have been.[96]

The scale problem

There was no clear understanding of the implications of structural proportioning until Galileo Galilei published his treatise *Two New Sciences* in 1638.[97] Before him, Andrea Palladio in *The Four Books of Architecture* states in his third book: 'The bridges, after these four manners, may be inlarged as necessity shall require, making all their parts stronger in proportion.'[98] In his description of four principles of constructing

2.62 Bridge in Bassano by Andrea Palladio (1570), crossing the River Brenta. Model by students of the Oslo School of Architecture and Design.

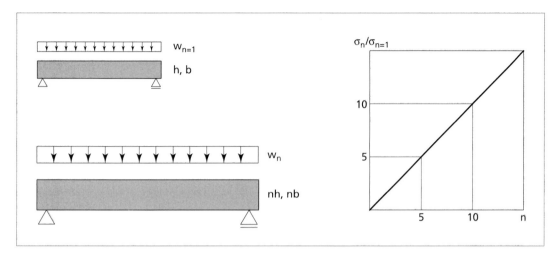

wooden bridges, Palladio envisaged all would be adapted to a larger scale merely by making the structural dimensions proportionally larger. A larger span (compared with the span of Palladio's model bridge) was thought safe if the internal proportions were the same. Later structural insights, starting with Galileo, have proved this to be wrong.

Now consider a beam with a certain width, depth and length. The weight of the beam constitutes the sole loading and the span equals the length of the beam. The resulting maximum bending stress is $\sigma_{n=1}$. Let us try to increase the span by enlarging all dimensions by a factor of n. What happens? The bending stress σ_n also increases by a factor of n, which means that sooner or later the stress will reach the failure strength of the material and the beam will break under its own weight. By increasing all dimensions proportionally, the enlarged volume of the beam will result in a dead load that exceeds the added bearing capacity produced by the increased cross-section.[99] This example shows that it could be dangerous to simply scale up a structure, especially if we are considering structures of a substantial size subjected to relatively low live loads. Examples of such structures are found among roof structures, especially in regions of low or non-existing snow loads where the dead load is by far the most important.

We are obviously not able to increase the structural scale simply by increasing all dimensions proportionally; the proportions of the structural members need to be changed. Hence, one of a number of ways by which the problems of scale can be overcome is

By changing the proportions – that is, to increase the structural depth relatively more than the span.

If the beam with dead weight as the sole load were to span longer, say n times longer than the initial span, then the depth of the beam would have to be increased not in proportion to the increase of the span (n),

2.63 Simply supported beams with self-weight, the larger having a span n times that of the smaller. The relationship between relative stress ($\sigma_n/\sigma_{n=1}$) and scale (n) is such that if the beam is made five times larger in all dimensions, the bending stress will increase by a factor of five.

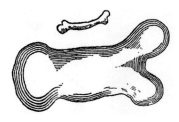

2.64 Animal bone magnified × 3, after Galileo.

but to the square of the increase of the span (n^2), given that the bending stress is not to increase. Galileo illustrated the general nature of this point by referring to the animal world: if an animal is enlarged three times, a certain bone would have to grow so that it changes proportions if it is to perform the same function as in the smaller version. In the words of Galileo: 'Clearly then if one wishes to maintain in a great giant the same proportion of limb as that found in an ordinary man he must either find a harder and stronger material for making the bones, or he must admit a diminution of strength in comparison with men of medium stature; for if his height be increased inordinately he will fall and be crushed under his own weight.'[100]

Galileo speaks of the requirement of changed proportions, but also of the possibility of substituting the structural material. Since every structural material has an ultimate strength, varying from material to material, a second alternative for overcoming the problems that arise when designing larger structures will be to

Change the structural material – that is, to seek a material with a higher strength/stiffness-to-density ratio.

Where the live load is low, the maximum span of a particular structure will to a large extent depend upon the interrelation of the weight, strength and elasticity of the material. The material efficiency criteria for the different types of failures and deflections were discussed in the previous chapter (pages 61–75). There are, however, ways of coping with the problems of scale that work directly on the form of the structural system and the shape of the individual members. These are the most important means we possess in designing for larger structures, and they imply a striving towards more structurally efficient systems. Relating the idea of structural efficiency to the notion of scale, we have acknowledged that the structure's own weight dominates relatively more in the larger scale than in the smaller, resulting in the larger structure having a reduced ability to carry live loads.[101] When designing increasingly larger structures, it will hence be necessary to

Change the structural form, searching for relatively lighter, more efficient structures.

As a general principle this means changing the shape of the structural elements locally by distributing the material more efficiently in order to reduce weight. This embraces the principle of changed proportions. Moreover, it means changing the global form of the structure, allowing larger-scale structures to obtain strength and stiffness by way of efficient form rather than by mass. This was discussed in the previous chapter as a question of structural efficiency (pages 59–77). While the most appropriate materials for large-scale structures have a high

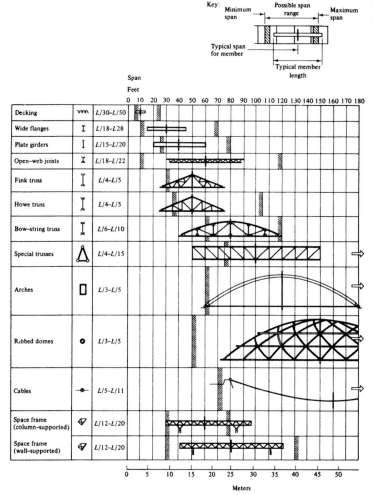

2.65 Span ranges of structural systems of steel, after Schodek.[103]

strength- (and/or stiffness-)to-density ratio, the most appropriate structural elements and systems have a high ratio of live load capacity to that of weight.[102]

Historically, an interesting way of overcoming the scale problem was by overlaying structural principles. Spans in a scale not empirically tested were sometimes designed by a 'melting together' of two or more different load-bearing principles. A trussed beam could be strengthened by an arch partly supporting it, or by supporting the beam on inclined struts from below and hung from above at the same time, or all three principles employed simultaneously. Those structures were not logical in our sense of the word, where logic is seen as promoting a design for clear, computable and efficient structural systems. Instead, they represented a logic based upon the empirical facts that told the builders that two structural principles taken together were stronger and stiffer than one, three such principles stiffer than two, etc. The resulting ambiguous

2.66 Bridges, after Jacob Leupold (1726). The two topmost bridges in particular represent the principle of structural overlay.[105]

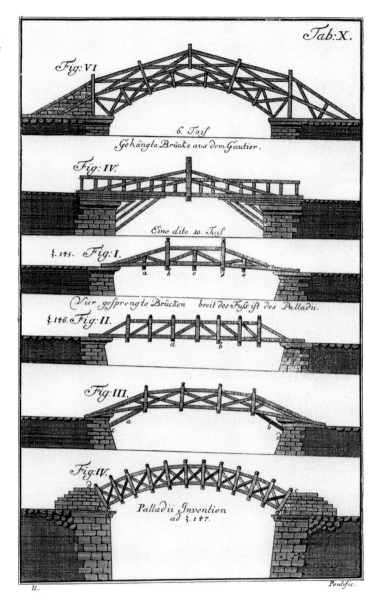

arrangements of overlaying structural principles can hardly be called structural systems. Tom Peters sees them more like forerunners of true systems that work by more unambiguous principles.[104]

The principles for coping with large-scale structures outlined here all refer to the problems arising because the static conditions change when the scale increases. There are also problems related to changed manufacturing requirements which also impact on structural form. Let us consider two pieces of sculpture, both situated in Barcelona. They are both metal sculptures, one made in bronze, the other in steel. The differences of material are not significant, but the differences of scale are.

2.67 *(far right, above)* Sculpture for the Barcelona Pavilion (1929). Sculptor Georg Kolbe.

2.68 *(far right, below)* Peix. Fish sculpture, Barcelona (1992). Architect Frank O. Gehry, engineers SOM.

While the sculpture by Georg Kolbe for Mies van der Rohe's Barcelona Pavilion is about the size of a human being, the fish sculpture by Frank O. Gehry is approximately 54 m long and 35 m tall.[106] The smaller one is made by pouring liquid metal into a mould, by casting, in such a way that the material is just a thin shell that is hollow inside. In this case the form we actually observe is both representational and load-bearing; the sculpture and the 'structure' are a single entity. The same piece of material solves both functions. The enormously larger scale of the other sculpture, however, naturally excludes casting as a technological option, and requires instead a separate structure on to which the skin of woven stainless steel strips is fixed. On the inside a ribbed cage acts as a load-bearing skeleton for the huge fish. It functions as a necessary primary structure that enables the making of a sculpture of its particular size and shape. In this case, then, the structure and the skin are two separate elements, meeting at certain points on the inside where the former is supporting the latter.

The scale, the span and the space

What do the observations made so far mean architecturally? Let us consider the spatial consequences of structural scale, comparing what we (without a specific definition) have called large-scale and small-scale structures. In this context we can see two major ways that scale exerts its influence. An underlying premise for both in the creation of a modern, large-scale building tradition is the historical development of materials like iron, steel and reinforced concrete, and their availability. The large architectural spaces erected in the nineteenth century in the form of railway stations and exhibition halls, uninterrupted by supporting elements, were hardly buildable without materials of a sufficiently high strength-to-density ratio. Now also including laminated wood and textiles, all later developments have been a testimony to the significance of such materials for the construction of really large-spanning structures.

Increasing structural scales influences the relationship between scale and structural efficiency. This has one major architectural consequence. At a larger scale we will be forced to make use of more efficient structural principles that by necessity are relatively lighter. The reason for this is obviously to reduce the influence of the dead-weight of the structure. Strategies for efficiency, like those of triangulation and the designing for axial forces as well as optimised cross-sections, all point to structures that are assembled from a collection of separate members rather than being made as block elements of a dense material. *Hence in most cases the large scale forces structural denseness to become dissolved, solid or opaque elements to become more open.*

A good example of a thinning-out of structural mass is the enlarged baseball bat sculpture by Claes Oldenburg, a familiar object quite differently constructed because of a change of scale. Generally, a larger scale means structures where forces are commonly distributed throughout the structure by a number of discrete and thin elements, or by using an altogether more globally efficient structural principle. We should note that the opposite is also the case: for small-scale structures dead-weight is normally not of particular importance. In the small scale, the manufacturing of a more complex structure in order to increase the structural efficiency will seldom pay off.

However, the tendency towards relative lightness in larger structures is true only on certain conditions. To begin with, increased span means more, not less, structural weight if structures employing the same structural principles are compared. However, each structural system has a certain range of operation, and a further increase of the span means a change of principle into one having a lower weight-to-span ratio.

If a large span really implies a more material-efficient system compared to that of a small span, we would expect the reduced weight to be visually observable.[107] Large, efficient structures ought therefore to look lighter than smaller structures. Moreover, visual lightness is addi-

2.69 A dramatic increase in scale forces structural openness to replace solidity. *The Bat Column* (1977), Chicago. Height 29.5 m, diameter 3 m. Sculptors Claes Oldenburg and Coosje van Bruggen.

2.70 *The Bat Column*. Detail.

tionally enhanced by an increase of the structural height that is often the result of a more material-efficient system, with a distribution of the reduced weight over a larger, structural area. An obvious example of this is a comparison of a steel truss and a rolled beam. To argue the point, we may consider a structural type commonly employed in large spans during the nineteenth century, where the scale called for the invention of a new, low-weight structural principle. The so-called Polonceau system, based on inverted roof trusses and forerunner to many contemporary light-weight structures, makes possible the construction of large, open spaces by way of light, structural elements.[108] The opening up of the structure achieved by a clever arrangement of several structural members also means that the structure ideally works by axial

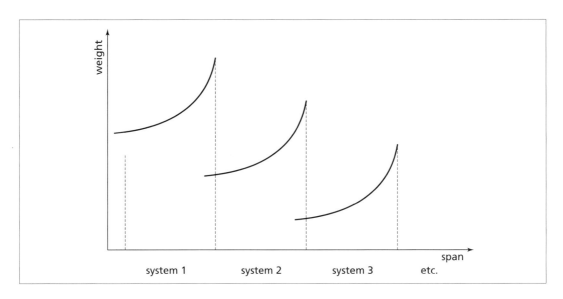

2.71 Schematic principle for the relationship between weight and span for different structural systems. System 3 is more efficient than system 2, system 2 more efficient than system 1.

forces rather than by bending and thus achieves a high bearing capacity with a minimum of materials. The Polonceau system was lighter than pre-existing systems, was easy to erect and also generated no horizontal thrusts.

The Gare Saint-Lazare in Paris (1841–52) is a typical example. The building was designed by engineer Eugène Flachat and architect Alfred Armand. Claude Monet has immortalised the interior in a number of oil paintings. Above the tracks are stretched a series of Polonceau trusses, spanning 40 m. The structure's tension rods are made of wrought iron, while the compression struts are of cast iron; all components are shaped in ways that make the different materials and manufacturing processes easily distinguishable. Large glass panels in the roof admit daylight into the hall, and the filigree character of the structure allows for much light to reach the tracks and platforms. The railway hall in the

2.72 Gare Saint-Lazare (1841–52), Paris. Architect Alfred Armand, engineer Eugène Flachat.

2.73 Gare d'Austerlitz (1865–9), Paris. Architect Louis Renaud, engineer M. Sévène.

Gare Saint-Lazare is a very large space with qualities that were appreciated in its day both by the public and Napoleon III.[109]

The same structural system is found in another Parisian railway station: the Gare d'Austerlitz, built between 1865 and 1869. This building was designed by architect Louis Renaud and engineer M. Sévène.[110] The structure has been described as 'one of the most beautiful Polonceau trusses that has ever been built'.[111] The free span of 51.2 m, one truss for every 10 m length, is significantly larger than the 40 m span of the Gare Saint-Lazare. At the time it was one of the largest uninterrupted spans for this type of building.[112] Although essentially similar to the structures of the Gare Saint-Lazare, there is a noteworthy difference caused by the increased span: the top member of the Polonceau structure has been transformed into a more complex trussed beam. Compared with the rolled profile of the Saint-Lazare it adds to the impression of lightness. The member is 0.75 m high and is subjected to both compression and bending stresses. The bending stresses stem from the system of continuous secondary beams with narrower spacing than the cast-iron compression struts of the Polonceau truss. The secondary beams elegantly divide the top member into four equal parts between the struts. The loads introduced, however, are not transferred directly into the system as axial forces, and the consequent need for a stiffer beam adds weight. Comparing the two stations, the Gare Saint-Lazare has a much less ordered relationship between the Polonceau system and the secondary beams. The beams are seemingly quite independent of the main bearing system, sometimes almost corresponding with the compression struts and sometimes totally out of reach. While this fact is visually experienced as a disturbing feature, weakening the impression of structural coherence, it does not reduce the overall impression of lightness and minimalism.

The reference to the Polonceau system here is just one example of a structural principle that, at a certain point in the history of structures

2.74 The influence of scale on some structural issues. As the scale increases, the tendency is towards higher structural efficiency, which also implies physically and visually lighter structures. Higher complexity is frequently an additional side-effect. On the other hand, increased scale reduces the number of structural options available.

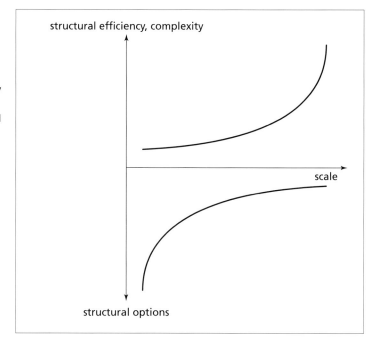

and in a particular functional context, was chosen for its effectiveness in reducing the weight of large-scale, load-bearing structures. Both these buildings illustrate the general tendency of large-scale structures towards higher structural efficiency and more complexity of structural form and of manufacturing processes. The opposite is generally the case for small ones. One aim of structural design is therefore to reach an *appropriate level* of structural efficiency for every structural scale.

A second architectural consequence of scale is linked to the first observation: *the necessity to search for lighter, more efficient structural forms at a larger scale means that structural conditions will dictate or at least influence architectural form and space to a larger degree than is the case at a smaller scale.*

A number of structural principles are not feasible at a large scale, where technological and static requirements become more substantial. The prize for ignoring or setting aside such requirements escalates when the scale goes up, both in terms of cost as well as of structural safety. Good historical examples of the relationship between (small) scale and a resulting (lack of) mechanical constraints are found in the roof structures of the glazed arcades or galleries of many European cities from about the beginning of the nineteenth century. The roof structures were usually built of cast or wrought iron, and their construction followed shortly after the development of iron structures in general. However, none of these arcades represents a *structural* development. Spans of about 3 to 5 m were obviously far too small to put structural principles to any kind of test. In principle, all formal and stylistic possibilities were

available. The spaces thus created were not really affected by structural requirements dictated by the relationship of load, form and force.

2.75 Passage Jouffroy (1836), Paris.

2.76 Passage du Caire (1799), Paris.

To illustrate the opposite outcome, we will take a look at a more recent structure. The Museum of History in Hamburg was designed and erected in only six months in 1989. The span of this structure ranges from 14 to 18 m, significantly longer compared to the old Parisian galleries. It is characteristic of the larger scale that the structural geometry and structural principles are more important for the overall design, especially where structural slenderness is favoured architecturally. Designed for stiffness and strength and with structural efficiency in mind, the visual result is light and lace-like. The softly curving and transparent membrane of steel and glass creates a new interior space while interfering as little as possible with the existing older building. It has been named 'a milestone in the development of large transparent urban roofs', and fully illustrates the interdependence that exists between the architectural space and concerns for efficient structural principles at a large scale.[113]

The exceptionally lightweight solution is based on two barrel-vaulted latticed shell structures meeting at right angles to one another by means of a transitional dome. Together these elements cover an L-shaped plan of about 1000 m². The shells are constructed on an orthogonal grid

2.77 Museum of History (1989), Hamburg. Architects von Gerkan, Marg and Partners, engineers Schlaich, Bergermann and Partner.

and measure 1.17 by 1.17 m of galvanised and painted solid (40 by 60 mm) steel sections. To ensure in-plane shear resistance, the grid is stiffened by cross-wise diagonal bracings of two 6 mm steel ropes, pre-stressed and then fixed to each structural node. Additional stiffness is introduced by a system of pre-stressed radial tie rods in three different vertical sections along the roof length. These help the structure work by compressive membrane forces rather than by bending, and are particularly important for asymmetrical snow and wind loads. The result of this optimised structural behaviour is a highly efficient shell structure that introduces very little physical and visual weight in the roof covering.

In the Messehalle 26 (1996) in Hannover the free span of the roof is about 55 m, long enough to demand a particularly efficient structural system if structural height and mass are to be kept at a reasonable level. An asymmetrical suspension structure was chosen for the span, three modules of which are connected along the length to make a continuous exhibition space of more than 25,000 m². At one end, the suspension structure is lifted up to admit light through the glazed façade created between the high and the low points of neighbouring modules, as well as to allow for natural ventilation. The funicular shape of the structure is constructed from flat ribbons of steel plates with a cross-section of 30 by 400 mm. Spaced at 5.5 m centres, the steel ribbons support wooden sandwich elements filled with sand which provide adequate dead load

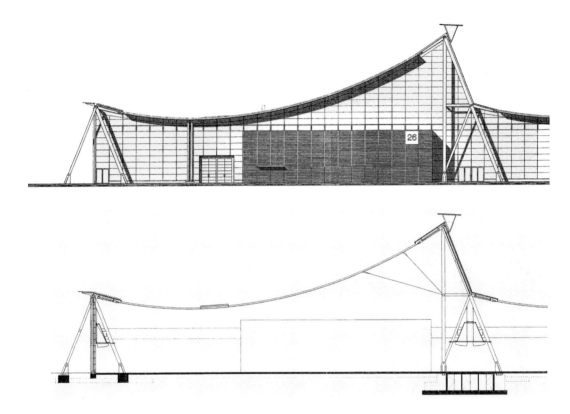

on the suspension structure. A-shaped frames at each end resist the horizontal tension forces as well as bringing the vertical forces down to the ground. This building shows a coming together of the mechanical and the spatial aspects of architectural construction, in which the conditions that apply to the former strongly influence the latter; inner space and outer form are in complete accord with the structural requirements of the large-scale structure. Span and space become a unity.

Of course there are also examples of buildings where the interior space does not derive its shape from the imprint of a dominating and efficient structural system. A large-scale structure may meet the mechanical requirements for external form without necessarily inverting this for the shape of the interior space. Nevertheless, the requirements of stiffness and strength that apply to large-scale structures *do* have architectural implications that can hardly be escaped. In one way or other they certainly put their mark on the architectural composition as a whole. The Burgo Paper Mill in Mantua (1961), designed by engineers Pier Luigi Nervi and Gino Covre, is an excellent example of this.[114] The enormous continuous-production machines required a column-free space of about 33 by 270 m and a structural system that could provide for a column-free future expansion on both sides. The building features a suspension structure system well known from bridge building; in the case of the paper mill the 'bridge deck' has become the suspended roof. In

2.78 Elevation. Architects Herzog + Partner, engineers Schlaich, Bergermann and Partner: Messehalle 26 (1996), Hannover, Germany.

2.79 Messehalle 26, section.

2.80 Burgo Paper Mill (1961), Mantua. Structural engineer Pier Luigi Nervi.

the long rectangular building volume the walls are consequently non-loadbearing, except for wind loads on the façades. The interior space of the building is shaped independently of the sweeping curve of the suspension structure, while on the exterior the two towers complete the structural system. Although not interfering with the shape and character of the interior space, the structure is nevertheless the dominating visual feature of the building.

Clearly, the structural concerns of large-scale buildings make the spatial and the mechanical aspects significantly more dependent on each other than is the case for small buildings. The exterior form or interior space will in some ways have to comply with an efficient structural type or system. For structures in architecture, a large scale will mean more severe mechanical constraints, which in turn means that considerations of structural behaviour and of manufacturing and construction necessarily become more important. This can perhaps be seen as diminishing one's freedom to design completely as one pleases. Another interesting interpretation, however, is the other side of the same coin: it is really the architectural scale that decides whether the mechanical requirements that apply to structures really need to act as guidelines for structural form – and hence for architectural expression. When designing for a smaller scale, the question will rather be *how* efficiently the structure should respond to the load pattern in a given situation. To put it differently: smaller structures can more easily and far more convincingly be shaped to comply with a different set of intentions for form. Architectural structures are designed with the particular intention of creating architectural spaces and are thus somewhat different from other kinds of structures. The highest possible efficiency may not necessarily be the aim, quite simply because an efficient structural form can easily conflict with other design priorities. At a smaller scale – possibly for most architectural works – we are not in a position of structural *necessity* but, rather, of *possibility*; we need not require structures to be perfectly light and efficient. Instead, some structures will make perfect sense because their design solves problems of space, which then sets other priorities. I will elaborate on this in Part 3.

There is yet another aspect of the scale problem: are there any mechanical reasons why one should also be careful with the *scaling down* of certain structural forms or systems that are invented for a larger scale? Looking at the roof structure covering the seats of a sports stand, it is quite clear that the trussed form of the cantilevered structure is well adapted to this particular scale, transforming the bending moment into axial forces in each member. Technologically, there is a certain complexity related to the manufacture of a truss, like the cutting of steel tubes and the assembly and welding of the structural members, which (as a large structure) is compensated for by the material savings. What about, then, a trussed cantilever the size of a chair? As a general principle this seems dubious. Neither the load nor the span can justify the extra amount of work necessary for the making of a truss where a

2.81 The cantilevering truss of Leppävaara sports stadium, Espoo, Finland (1985). Architects: the Building Design Department of the Technical Office of the City of Espoo/Pekka Kolari. At this scale there is no doubt that the structural principle balances both structural and technological efficiency criteria quite well.

2.82 A cantilevered seat at the Museum of Natural History, London. At this small scale, elaborate structural detailing rarely succeeds.

simple steel bracket could do the same job. A small scale expects – so to speak – structural simplicity. The arguments for this do not address problems of statics but, rather, problems of technology. The particular working processes needed to make trusses are generally not appropriate for this small scale, even if there would be some small savings in materials. With small structures and structural members, the making of joints will seem unduly complex and thus costly. The design choice is a question of economy, not purely in terms of finance but in a general awareness of what kind of technological level is best suited for each individual case and scale.[115] On the other hand, if efficient methods for the manufacture of very small trusses exist, a higher complexity of form may also be justified at this scale.

Clearly, cost influences the appropriate level of structural efficiency for different structural scales. The higher the cost of materials relative to the cost of labour, the more is gained by designing for high structural efficiency, and the smaller is the scale or span at which a shift to a more efficient (and also more complex) structural system is justified. In a highly industrialised culture, the reverse situation prevails: labour is expensive relative to material. When cost is decisive, then, there is an incentive to use easily built, inefficient forms of structural systems for small- to medium-scale structures; in most cases only larger structures will attempt greater complexity of form in order to minimise materials.

PART 3

AESTHETICS

An aesthetics of structures

What do we experience when we look at and think about a structure? What *kind* of experience do we have? When we look at structures, to enjoy them or dislike them do we need a well-developed feeling for form in general? How important are intellectual considerations? In what way do architectural and spatial intentions influence the way we experience the structural system? Such are the questions I would like to address, bearing in mind that the idea of this book is to discuss and understand structures in architecture in the broadest possible context.

In Part 2 we focused on mechanical matters, going into some detail to explain and interpret structures from the point of view of materials, efficiency concepts and the importance of structural scale – but not space. My aim therefore in Part 3 is to bring together the two main aspects of structures, the mechanical and the spatial. It is my belief that an aesthetic perspective is essential for experiencing structures as the multifaceted objects they are: both means and ends, both void and solid.[1] Aesthetics will quite simply help us to understand the whole picture.

An aesthetic qualification: the freedom to choose

Part 1's reflections on the various cognitive aspects of structures produced the hypothesis that structural form results from the careful interaction between the constraints of the mechanical *object* (governed by a set of scientific laws and technological rules) and the functional requirements serving the *space* (expressing intention or purpose). The two antitheses are both equally important, as an analysis restricted to only one would in many cases leave our understanding of structural form unclear or confused. By way of example, Anthony Webster remarks that Santiago Calatrava's bridge designs 'use principles of engineering mechanics as a springboard for formal expression',[2] thus contrasting and connecting these two equally necessary concepts of *mechanics* and *expression*.

The idea of developing an aesthetics of structures is to help us discriminate between different *aesthetic qualities* of structures.[3] I shall propose later a methodology that enables us to understand and articulate the *aesthetic experiences* we have when contemplating structures in architecture; essential parts of it have already been discussed. If we can *aesthetically* understand the structure's visual appearance, we will appreciate it fully, both with our intellect and all of our senses. It is important, therefore, that we look as broadly as possible at the context of any

structure, whether a roof or a bridge, judging them not just as mechanical objects prized for their structural efficiency or suitability for rational
production, but as three-dimensional objects that influence and are
influenced by architectural spaces.

It is taken for granted that the structural system or members are visually identifiable, that we can actually *see* the structure. In the case of
the structure being covered by, for example, non-loadbearing wall panelling or plaster, we can hardly have an aesthetic experience or make
a relevant aesthetic judgement. An aesthetic experience of a structure
presupposes an *exposed* structure.

In order to argue for the relevance of considering aesthetic issues of
structural form, it is not possible to define the design of, say, a roof structure as a *scientific* problem.[4] There is no causal relationship between
the conditions governing that span and a 'resulting' form of the roof
structure. A causal relationship would produce a single structural form
depending upon the climatic, functional and material conditions valid
for that particular problem, and this is obviously not the case. There are
numerous solutions to a structural problem which are all able to perform quite well mechanically and functionally, solutions that may also
be economically comparable. Structural mechanics, based on theories
rooted in mathematics and classical physics and dependent on causal
relationships, acts as a constraint on structural design, but obviously
needs a form to operate upon. Structural form is also a synthesis of a
number of other constraints, including technology and function conceived largely as the expression of intention or purpose. We *choose*
between several different proposals, making decisions according to
what we see as the best solution spatially and mechanically. These kinds
of decisions on structural form may be based (among other things) on
habit, preference and taste, and are therefore highly suitable topics for
analysis in any discussion of aesthetics. Many writers on this subject
support the idea of the designer's freedom to choose structural form,
thus opening up for reflection the concepts of intention and aesthetic
experiences of structures. Among the more noteworthy is Eduardo Torroja, who states that 'there is no method that enables us automatically
to discover the most adequate structural type to fit a specific problem,
as it is faced by the designer. The achievement of the final solution is
largely a matter of habit, intuition, imagination, common sense and
personal attitude.'[5] The term 'automatically' is surely another way of
expressing a cause–effect relationship. There certainly *are* causal factors involved in the load–form–force relationship, but such factors play
only a part. David Billington also seems to agree on the priority of form
over structural function, and introduces 'the idea that function follows
form, which means that the designer is free to set form rather than be
bound by some automatic application of scientific laws'.[6] In reality, the
relationship between form and structural function is probably not hierarchical – that one is a prerequisite of the other – but rather that they

relate interactively to each other. In any case, the freedom to set form that many writers refer to definitely underlines the relevance of aesthetic interest to structural form.[7]

Moreover, an interest in aesthetics is not the exclusive domain of the arts. Some writers have tried to establish structural design as a particular art form, wanting to emphasise how much individual choice and aesthetic considerations are involved.[8] We should, however, refrain from classifying structures as art objects, because of the strong mechanical and utility aspects that make structures different from sculptural 'constructions' or land art. Besides, the notion of art does not shed any new light on the issue of understanding and experiencing structures. On the contrary, things become more confused. When we meet titles like 'The Art of the Structural Engineer', or 'The Art in Structural Design', 'art' should therefore be taken in the more original meaning of skill in the making of things, rather than as a class of objects produced by artists.[9] An art form cannot have, as David Billington postulates, 'economy' and 'efficiency' as two basic characteristics and still claim artistic freedom to create 'elegance' – the only truly art term of the three fundamental aspects of a 'structural art' as defined by Billington. Elegance, whatever that is, might indeed be the result of a strictly pragmatic design concept; this could in fact constitute the programme of an artist. As the preconditions and requirements for an art form, however, economy and efficiency may easily contradict the very nature of art. Elegance can be created without any concern for economy; conversely, the extreme pursuit of efficiency may be costly. Structural design is thus neither a science nor an art. Scientific laws and technological requirements offer merely a set of minimum necessary requirements for structural form, and nothing more. Likewise, artistic concepts may inform the design, but cannot be its guiding principle. Yet, in the design of structures we apply *principles* from both science and art; indeed, Torroja strikes the right balance between instrumentalism and intentionality when he claims that 'artistic sensibility is as indispensable to the designer as technological skill'.[10] This is quite simply the defining feature of structural and other design forms: objects with utility and function we can also admire for the way they look. Aesthetics, however, does not presuppose art.

Aesthetics and structures

In the literature we come across two types of descriptions of aesthetic experiences and aesthetic judgements of structures: critiques of actual projects published in books and magazines, and more general reflections on the aesthetics of structures. However, in an architectural context, evaluations of specific structural achievements are relatively scarce, while general treatises on the subject are more common. There may be several reasons for this. Architects and architectural critics tend to avoid singling out the structure for detailed aesthetic evaluation – something which is frequently done with (for example) façades – even though in many projects this would have been highly relevant and rewarding. Besides, such critics on the whole do not necessarily possess the right knowledge and qualifications to offer professional opinions on matters involving the mechanical sciences and technology. On the other hand, engineers – also a profession that makes objects of potential aesthetic interest – seldom feel comfortable about discussing the aesthetic virtues (or otherwise) of the structures of buildings, although they frequently pay aesthetic attention to more visually dominant structures such as bridges.

Examples of more general reflections on the aesthetics of structures seem often to be undertaken by prominent engineers. After building up extensive design practices in civil engineering and architecture they seem to sum up their views on aesthetics based mainly upon their experience. Pier Luigi Nervi and Eduardo Torroja are well known, as are representatives from later generations like Fritz Leonhardt and Jörg Schlaich.[11] Nervi, however, did not confine his aesthetic criticism of structures to general observations. He was in fact a pioneer in making public appraisal of structures of individual projects, along with reflections on structural aesthetics on a more general basis. His four articles in *Casabella* in 1959 attempt to establish a critique of structures as a natural part of a more broadly defined architectural criticism, the first article being quite critical of aspects of Oscar Niemeyer's architecture for Brasilia.[12] His agenda is always to emphasise 'the correspondence between structural mechanics and aesthetics', claiming that 'the correct structural solutions [are] aesthetically the most satisfactory and, through a refinement of details, may possibly become a source of real architectonic beauty'.[13] Moreover, he also acknowledges the importance of 'considering the relationship between construction processes and the aesthetic result', and thus identifies both the scientific and the technological aspects of structures as potentially having aesthetic interest.[14] He sums up his aesthetic views in his Harvard lectures early in the 1960s by offering the conclusion that 'a technically perfect work can be aesthetically inexpressive but there does not exist, either in the past or the present, a work of architecture which is accepted and recognized as excellent from the aesthetic point of view which is not also excellent from a technical point of view. Good technology seems to be a necessary though not sufficient condition for good architecture.'[15]

In order to understand what Nervi actually means, we are left with the dubious task of defining the goodness of 'good technology'. Is this some property or quality intrinsic to itself, or does it depend on its context? In the latter case, 'good technology' would provide the best possible means for realising the architect's intentions, even at the expense of concepts such as 'efficiency' and 'optimisation'.

Towering engineers both, compared to Nervi, Eduardo Torroja is the better philosopher of structures. He articulates his views with far more subtlety and appears to be less of a purist or fundamentalist. Of course, both have to be understood in their historical context, a time when art and architecture kept strictly to minimalism and functionalism. Objects were supposed to be free from everything that could be seen as ornament, and ideas of 'honesty' and 'truth' dominated architectural discourse, if not always its practices. Yet, Torroja speaks of 'the beauty of structures', and legitimates his phrase by saying that 'structural design is concerned with much more than science and techniques: it is also very much concerned with art, common sense, sentiment, aptitude, and the enjoyment of the task of creating opportune outlines to which scientific calculations will add finishing touches, substantiating that the structure is sound and strong in accordance with the requirements'.[16] Since the designer has a choice, aesthetics is a real concern. Still, 'aesthetic evaluation of a building is seldom considered in relation to its basic structural design', Torroja says, explaining that perhaps 'the circle of people who can criticize constructively is smaller' than previously because of increasing specialisation. 'The fact that in this art and craft the state of stress must be integrated with the aesthetic effect implies that those who are sufficiently qualified to appreciate it constitute a relatively small group, who live in a highly academic environment.'[17] This is seen by Torroja as a hindrance to progress, since it excludes most people from participating in the open discussion he sees as a prerequisite for the gradual development of more refined structures, and thus better architecture.

How does Torroja look upon aesthetics in relation to structures? This is not straightforward: on the one hand, he seems to see aesthetics as 'a factor', something we should be able to point out and identify and which can be included (or not) in the design. For 'industrial buildings or utilitarian structures that are out of sight', Torroja says, 'the aesthetic factor can be neglected or omitted altogether'.[18] Furthermore, 'aesthetic considerations should be discussed separately because they have their special characteristics and specific relations with the finality of the construction'. Here, Torroja comes quite close to arguing that aesthetics are different from and relate to something else than an admiration for pragmatic structural design. Aesthetic experiences, according to this view, do not come from our appreciation of formal and spatial solutions to structural functions but from something further and additional. Hence, for Torroja, aesthetics 'can be sacrificed to factors of economy'. To experience a well-designed structure, then, you have to pay for it. The idea of a separate design for 'aesthetics', however, is not approved of in this book. It is also not true that a structure we experience as pleasing necessarily costs extra money: one of the most beautiful bridges of the twentieth century, Maillart's Salginatobel (1931) was the cheapest of all the entries, and yet it has become an icon. Maillart's achievement was to take to its logical conclusion a design based on the structural mechanics of 3-hinged arches, and to communicate visually a profound understanding of reinforced concrete as a structural material. Our aesthetic experience of the Salginatobel bridge stems largely from our enjoyment of how a well-adapted and appropriate structural system works mechanically.

On the other hand, rather than seeing aesthetics as an addition, Torroja also argues that 'the beauty of a structure is immanent in its structural form, and its strength properties exhibit a certain expressiveness of their own. Indeed, we think that if the work is essentially structural, its beauty must essentially reside in its structural quality'.[19] Mechanics is further tied to aesthetics by the way structural materials are employed. 'Consequently if the structural shape does not correspond to the materials of which it is made, there can be no aesthetic satisfaction'.[20] Torroja is, however, conscious of the anomalies, as he sees them, that may arise 'between artistic feeling and the strength requirements of an architectural work', and mentions the shape of the cupola of St Peter's as an example. This illustrates that 'the idea of truthfulness or sincerity was not pushed to the point of requiring that a work, to be beautiful, should adapt itself strictly to the optimum forms dictated by the strength requirements'.[21] Contrary to Nervi, he acknowledges 'that one should admit the intuition of forms aesthetically perfect' (meaning forms that might deviate from 'optimum forms'), but they should be constructed in versatile materials that can cope with the resulting stresses.

Refusing to speculate on the metaphysical aspects of aesthetics, 'not investigating the intimate causes of aesthetic feeling and expression', Torroja nevertheless makes the highly interesting remark that 'it is difficult to determine how far aesthetic exigencies are purely of a visual or of a sensible character and how much they are of an intellectual order'.[22] As we shall see later, this question becomes an important point in the discussion of the basis of our aesthetic experience of architecture and structures.

Other contributors to this discussion are the German engineers Fritz Leonhardt and Jörg Schlaich. Leonhardt is perhaps best known as a bridge designer, while Schlaich has engineered a wide range of impressive structures, often in collaboration with well-known architects. Since buildings or structures are erected for a purpose, Leonhardt states that primary requirement of 'aesthetic quality' is that 'the building must be designed so that it fulfils this purpose in an optimum way', and also that 'the structure should reveal itself in a pure, clear form and impart a feeling of stability'.[23] The first premise tries to link aesthetic quality with practical function; somehow aesthetic quality consists of the fulfilment of the structure's purpose in a particular manner, namely 'an optimum way'. This 'optimum way' is perhaps adequately interpreted as the best possible way, when all aspects of the structure's purpose are considered. This is about the same as stating that no structure can 'possess' aesthetic qualities unless the purpose or the practical function of that structure is solved in the best possible manner. The question arises: is this necessarily true? Does aesthetic quality in most cases depend upon an *optimum* solution to functional matters? We will let the questions go unanswered for now, but merely note this as one articulation of the view that 'beauty results from functional efficiency', as Alan Holgate puts it.[24]

Leonhardt's second point deals with how structures should appear, and what appropriate *feeling* should be conveyed. He then goes on to state other conditions, that of 'simplicity', and that the form of the structure 'must also correspond with the materials used'. Other important characteristics of structures of aesthetic merit are 'good, harmonious proportions' that 'should convey an impression of balance', either 'repetition of the same proportions' or 'contrasting proportions', as well as 'the principle of order' of which 'symmetry is a well-tried element'. Leonhardt also lists the importance of 'refining the form', 'integration into the environment', 'surface texture', 'colour', 'character', 'complexity' and the effects of 'natural beauty' – beauty as found in the nature. Two things are striking: first, Leonhardt's deep-rooted and almost classical assumption that aesthetic value is tantamount to 'harmony', 'symmetry' and 'balance'; secondly, Leonhardt sees aesthetic quality *as a result of* certain properties of the structural form: 'pure, clear form . . . impart[s] a feeling of stability', and 'good, harmonious proportions . . . convey an impression of balance'.

There seems to be, in Leonhardt's view, a *dependence* between aesthetic qualities and certain properties of the form. In this he agrees with the philosopher Frank Sibley, whose work has influenced aesthetics discourse since the 1960s.[25] What kind of dependence – whether characteristics such as 'good, harmonious proportions' *by necessity* convey the intended feeling, or whether there is some other instrumental causality – is a difficult question to answer, but we will presently return to it in a more general way. However, by formulating his ideals the way he does, Leonhardt touches upon the key issues in a discussion on aesthetic experience. Clearly, Leonhardt also holds aesthetic qualities to be objective qualities that exist or reside in the object itself.[26] This is a position that this book refutes; I will approach the reasons for aesthetic appeal in a different way.

While Leonhardt sets out to establish rules for aesthetic qualities, Jörg Schlaich declares that 'there are no general rules leading to aesthetic qualities of structures'.[27] Echoing Nervi, he makes the interesting remark that 'It is not true that a technically clean design will by itself look good, but the opposite is usually true. A poor design will not result in good aesthetics.' 'I find it difficult to imagine a building with structural deficits as being aesthetically good', Schlaich says.[28] It is not easy to be absolutely sure what is meant by expressions like 'structural deficits'. The same goes for 'a technically clean design' and terms like 'good' and 'poor', even though most engineers will probably agree on an interpretation in the general direction of simplicity and efficiency. To be able to say what significance these statements have, we need to ask if a 'technically clean design' also presupposes a high degree of mechanical efficiency, and if 'look good' means that the structure exhibits any aesthetic quality at all, or some aesthetic qualities, or whatever. One may probably imagine that a structure designed to be materially efficient to a very high degree would therefore also be experienced as having aesthetic qualities related to thinness and visual lightness; in other words, it would 'look good' from *that* point of view. This is no easy matter, and we need to elaborate on the nature of the aesthetic experience to be able to be more precise.

Schlaich also lists a number of aesthetic qualities or aesthetic terms relating to structures, some positive or 'more appealing' than others. He favours 'light', 'transparent', 'filigree', 'diversified', 'variegated' and 'harmonic' against the more negative 'heavy', 'bulky', 'clumsy', 'uniform', 'monotonous' and 'confused'. Apart from the problem of having a clear notion of what those terms actually mean, there are obvious difficulties in trying to identify specific aesthetic qualities without at the same time referring to the experience of a structure in a specific context.[29]

Bill Addis is a most interesting author who addresses the question of aesthetics of structures from an academic position. Writing of architecture, he claims that 'concern with aesthetics should be addressing what constitutes good and bad design and what it is to be a good structural engineer'.[30] Of course, 'good' and 'bad' are terms too wide and imprecise to illuminate the values we are searching for unless we describe or discuss, as Addis does, what they actually mean.[31] He offers quite extensive and no doubt widely shared views as to what constitutes good design in an engineering context, listing such virtues as 'economy of materials', 'elegance and simplicity in joints', 'skill and clarity with which structural actions are used and expressed (or hidden)', etc. Even though Addis's notion of 'good design' refers to a *mechanical* (operating within the sphere of structural mechanics and technology) view of structures, he makes clear that there are many ways of approaching the aesthetics of structures. He acknowledges that there are also other criteria for making judgements, among them 'criteria for judging structures as architecture and sculpture in the environment'.[32]

The relation of aesthetics to structures characteristically and necessarily involves the knowledge and theories of two professions, the engineer's as well as the architect's. This was, as we have seen, acknowledged by Torroja.[33] In my view, *we cannot adequately judge structures in architecture by considering them exclusively as the results of engineering, admittedly important as it is.* While engineering is no doubt a central activity in the process of planning and manufacturing structures, there are clearly other intentions involved in their design which must also be considered when trying to discriminate between successful and less successful results. If being 'a good structural engineer', to use Addis's expression, means (as it usually does) that he or she has the ability to produce efficient and economic designs, then 'good' engineering is not *necessarily* a more important contributor to the aesthetic qualities of structures than (for example) particular design requirements for the space, or any other architectural aims. Such considerations might be seen to bring in aesthetic qualities at the expense of some of the emphasis on efficiency and economy. Perhaps this is partly what Ove Arup meant by the notion of 'aesthetic accountancy', 'a balance between cost, efficiency and aesthetic values'. 'Aesthetic values' in this case probably refers to the visual appreciation of aspects of the structure other than the efficiency of the structural system.[34] On the other hand, the notion of 'good' engineering might also refer to the ambition of producing works of a high technological standard, even where an efficient and economic structure (for some reasons) is not possible. But the problem remains: even if a structure made the most out of a particular given situation, and even if it might be said (all things considered) to represent 'good engineering', then a structure of aesthetic merit would not automatically follow.

In Angus Macdonald's reflections on the notion of engineering he states that 'the principal objective of engineering design is to provide an object which will function satisfactorily with maximum economy of means'.[35] This means that a balance must be reached between the efficient use of materials (structural efficiency) and what I have called technological efficiency, meaning simplicity of production, erection and maintenance, as well as a predictable durability. According to these criteria, Macdonald argues that the standard portal frame shed that so often is used in warehouses and supermarkets 'would qualify as good engineering and the so-called "high-tech" supersheds which appeared in the architectural journals in the 1980s would not'.[36] Macdonald certainly has a point, but the structures of many of the latter buildings have given a lot of people valuable aesthetic experiences, and continue to do so, even though from a conventional point of view they do not strictly represent 'good' engineering. The reason why many such structures can, after all, offer aesthetic appeal is to be found in their *iconographic* and *contextual* qualities. Hence, an important observation to be extracted from this is that we make a grave mistake if we assume that structures not reckoned to be 'good' engineering cannot be objects of rewarding aesthetic experiences.

As a highly esteemed practitioner as well as an ideologist, engineer Cecil Balmond brings new perspectives to the discussion. Interestingly, he regards as unimportant the undeniable gain in technological efficiency resulting from repetition and an even distribution of structural elements. 'When structural elements have even distribution, the imagination has nothing to hold on to but the connection', Balmond says.[37] In espousing the importance of the imagination when designing structures Balmond speaks up for an aesthetic programme at the expense of such values as efficiency and rational manufacturing. With his concept of 'the informal', Balmond challenges traditional truths about 'good engineering' and makes a point of designing a structure that 'provokes its archetypes', as he says of the Kunsthal in Rotterdam.[38] With statements like 'the *informal* gives rise to ambiguity', which means 'interpretation and experiment as a natural course of events', Balmond is clearly aiming for a structural form that has a very different agenda than fulfilling the requisites of an optimum mechanical solution. 'Instead of solidity and certainty', Rem Koolhaas says, 'his structures express doubt, arbitrariness, mystery and even mysticism.'[39]

The matter is, as we might conclude from what the different writers have said, quite complicated: when considering structures aesthetically, there seems to be agreement that the evaluation of mechanical issues (such as structural performance) and the use of technology play an important part, but in judging *how* important those aspects are, views differ. In this book I maintain that the aesthetic appreciation of structural form should bring aspects of *both* the mechanical and the spatial functions into play. The aesthetics of structures becomes most interesting and rewarding when engineering criteria come together with those of architecture, and particularly when they clash. We can imagine a matrix of options. In some architectural works, we can imagine that the mechanical aspects of the structure are satisfactory and represent widely shared views on what constitutes 'good engineering', while on the other hand these structures do not give the overall impression of 'good architecture'. I am not really interested in this option, because my primary aim is to describe *architecture* of some merit, and how structures may contribute to this.[40] A second option is where both the engineering and architectural aspects qualify as 'good'. This is just fine, and should present no difficulty. Thirdly, and this is the core of the problem, some architectural works may perhaps have high architectural standards, while at the same time we may judge their structures to be the results of 'bad' – or at least not conventionally qualifying as 'good' – engineering. There are two possibilities here: firstly, bad engineering really does exist, and this will affect the aesthetic experience of the whole work, as judged by someone competent to identify structural flaws and blemishes. If these are sufficiently clear and indisputable, such buildings should be very rare. Secondly, structures that some engineers do not conventionally consider to represent 'good' engineering can in fact be considered as 'good' after all, because those structures help create architecture of merit. In such cases, we would have to allow for a different value system, in which economy and efficiency are not necessarily the main criteria for engineering success. We would certainly have to judge more strictly, however, that those structures really do contribute to the specific qualities of the space.

The reflections above also illustrate the problem of identifying mechanical aspects as being the concern of 'engineering', while spatial aspects are thought of as 'architecture'. It cannot constructively be conceived in this way, and we should preferably resent this way of thinking. The overall result is in reality what both professions should be concerned about.

Lastly, *how* should we understand an aesthetics of structures, and in what way should we make our viewpoints operative when making aesthetic judgements? This question will be discussed at length in the following section, but on the basis of the analysis so far, I offer the following formulation: given that aesthetic appreciation refers to *experiences*, 'aesthetics' should not be seen as an *aspect* of structures in the same way that we think of mechanical and spatial functions. We appreciate structural form not as 'things' added to a functional skeleton like so much ornament, separable from mechanical and spatial aspects, but as the pleasurable experience of appropriateness. We perceive that mechanical and spatial aspects of the form emphasise an expression of unity and intellectual coherence. To put it differently: *the aesthetic experience of structures is constituted through the basic concepts of the structure's mechanical and spatial functions.*

An example of aesthetic appreciation that clearly refers to the *mechanical* aspects of structural form can be deduced from another comment Webster makes about Calatrava. He remarks on Calatrava's bridge structures in general that 'they often derive their elegance from the direct expression of a structural type'.[41] This formulation implies several things: here the structural type, which is really a mechanical matter, is interesting not merely as a means of carrying loads but as a way of 'conveying' elegance. Thus the mechanical aspect of how the different bridge members are put together is interesting both as a way of 'doing' things, as a choice of structural performance and of manufacturing methods, and for its capacity to 'be' – in this case, to be elegant. Webster describes an aesthetic experience of the structure seen as a load-bearing system, and implies that the choice of structural type, and the form of that type, is 'responsible' in one way or other for the experience of a quality named elegance.[42]

An aesthetic description of the structures designed by Ron Arad and Alison Brooks for their 'One-Off' Studio in London (1992), makes things clearer. Focusing on the row of columns, Arad and Brooks make the observation that 'the columns might appear whimsical and calligraphic'.[43] Samantha Hardingham also speaks about the 'calligraphic shapes of the columns' that somehow recall the forms of the art of handwriting.[44] Statements like this clearly go beyond a mere description of observable form: they articulate an aesthetic experience by pointing out, in this case, the images most readily identified with the shape of the structures. The architects go on to explain the reason for this particular shape: 'They were actually designed around circular tracks to guide rotating windows, in addition to their role as triangulated props for the roof frames.'[45] The 'whimsical and calligraphic' shapes are never really

3.1 The 'One-Off' Studio and Showroom (1992), London. Architects Ron Arad and Alison Brooks, structural engineer Neil Thomas at Atelier One.

3.2 The 'One-Off' Studio and Showroom. Detail of column.

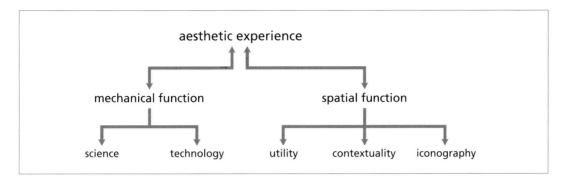

3.3 A taxonomy of the aesthetic experience in terms of the concepts of the structure's mechanical and spatial functions.

described, only the onlooker's experience of them. Arad and Brooks explain the reason why the structural form has become the way it is by referring to both functional and mechanical matters ('to guide rotating windows', 'their role as triangulated props'). When we are somehow made aware of the reasons for these particular shapes, they take on a certain meaning for us. We are thus helped to an understanding of the structural form and guided towards an aesthetic experience of its qualities.

In conclusion, our understanding that structures in architecture express both mechanical and spatial aspects is also instrumental in and a precondition for us being able to have substantive aesthetic experiences. Hence, our aesthetic experiences of structures depend on our consideration of specific concepts not only of technology and the natural sciences but also of the structure's spatial functions.

The aesthetic experience

The aim of reflecting on structures from an aesthetic point of view is to try *to understand the nature of the aesthetic experience*. Otherwise we will be quite lost when it comes to evaluating structures aesthetically. It is not, however, within the scope of this book to put forward opinions on aesthetic norms, how structures ought to look in order to arouse aesthetic pleasure. But even more important, it is seldom very convincing to lay down rules about how structures should be in order to look good. Take the often praised virtue of symmetry. It is not difficult to show that a symmetrical structure is appropriate in some cases but not in others. Hence, understanding the nature of aesthetic experience is more fundamental and should at least precede speculations on how to achieve structures of aesthetic merit. Consequently, and equally importantly, our aim is also to be able *to understand structures*, or structural form, in the light of our understanding of the nature of aesthetic experience. Fundamental to this book is a belief that we can not only appreciate the structures of architecture aesthetically but also know *why* we think some structures are attractive, and then recognise *the origins* of this appreciation. It must be possible to present generalisable arguments that analyse and articulate pleasing aesthetic experiences in order to communicate this understanding to others. The nature of aesthetic experience will perhaps depend on and be preconditioned by the nature of our arguments and analysis.

In order to understand the nature of aesthetic experience we need to distinguish between its different possible origins. This may take an analytical form commonly found in the literature on aesthetics. When combined with a 'rationalistic' approach inherited from Alexander Baumgarten, this analytical attitude is probably the reason why some call aesthetics 'the study or science of beauty'.[46] Theoretical aesthetics is a branch of philosophy, however, and is not classified as a science because philosophy 'does not investigate the causes of phenomena. It is an a priori or conceptual investigation, the underlying concern of which is to identify rather than to explain'[47]. Incidentally, the philosopher Ludwig Wittgenstein dismissed as 'ridiculous' the idea that aesthetics is 'a science telling us what's beautiful'.[48] What is also clear is that the philosophy of aesthetics is a highly specialised intellectual activity primarily for philosophers and art historians, and we can in this book only hope to know some basic concepts that will help when discussing the aesthetics of structures. Before reflecting further on the notions of aesthetic quality and the aesthetic experience in general, let us comment first on the concept of 'beauty'.[49] It seems clear that this term is only one of many characteristics that can be ascribed to the visual appreciation of form.[50] Ever since Plato and Aristotle 'beauty' had been considered the sole concern of aesthetics, a view challenged in 1757 in Edmund Burke's 'A Philosophical Enquiry into the Origin of Our Ideas of the Sublime and the Beautiful'. Here he introduced another aesthetic quality, the sublime, a term he mainly reserved for objects of vast size; beauty, in his opinion, only applied to comparatively small ones. 'Beautiful things must be light and delicate, sublime things solid and even massive.'[51] The important thing, however, is to notice what Hanfling calls 'the dethronement of beauty from its pre-eminent position in aesthetics', which means that an object of aesthetic value did not necessarily have to be described as being 'beautiful'.[52] The notion of beauty has also been attacked for being too vague or imprecise: Wittgenstein noted that terms like 'beautiful' are expressions of satisfaction and used as interjections, but since they do not say anything about *what kind of* satisfaction, they are quite inadequate as aesthetic terms.[53]

Historically, there seem to be two main lines of thinking about beauty or aesthetic qualities in general.[54] The 'classic' view holds that aesthetic quality is a quality or property of the object, and is *objective*; it inheres in the manner colour, line, matter, mass, etc. are visually organised. This might be expressed in terms of (for example) balance and proportion; it is, according to some, mathematically describable. An exponent of this view is, as we have seen, Fritz Leonhardt. In fact, this view seems to be the most common among writers in the field of structures and architecture. The second important viewpoint supports the idea that beauty or aesthetic quality 'is, or is to be identified by, a feeling experienced by the viewer' and is therefore referred to as 'subjectivist'.[55] This identification of aesthetic qualities with *feeling* was expressed by the philosopher David Hume, who questioned the objectivity of beauty and held that it could not be attributed to objects outside of the mind. According to this view, beauty was seen to depend on a feeling within the observer, and as such might vary from observer to observer because of the different dispositions of their perceptual organs, as well as differences in cultural orientation. There can be little doubt about the existence of a connection between feeling and the experience of aesthetic quality, the contemplation of an aesthetic object usually being an act of pleasure. In the view of Hume, however, 'beauty is itself feeling'.[56] One consequence of this view, now long abandoned, was that beauty could not exist in the absence of a person to perceive it.

As noted earlier, the contemporary discourse on aesthetics has been greatly influenced by the work of Frank Sibley, whose three or four early and most debated articles on the subject were published in the late 1950s and 60s. There has since been an enormous number of articles discussing his views. By way of summary, Sibley speaks of 'aesthetic words', 'aesthetic terms' and 'aesthetic concepts' as more or less synonymous, and gives examples such as unified, balanced, integrated, lifeless, serene, sombre, dynamic, powerful, vivid, delicate, moving, trite, sentimental, tragic. All of these terms can be used to describe 'aesthetic qualities', 'aesthetic features' or 'aesthetic properties' – also seemingly interchangeable.[57] Sibley also states that the application of such aesthetic concepts requires taste or perceptiveness, and that those 'aesthetic words apply ultimately because of, and aesthetic qualities ultimately depend upon, the presence of features' that are visible 'without any exercise of taste or sensibility'. Those are the *nonaesthetic qualities* or features, 'like curving or angular lines, colour contrasts, placing of masses', etc.[58] A central theme in Sibley's theory is the nature of the relationships between aesthetic and nonaesthetic properties or qualities. He makes the proposition that the nonaesthetic qualities of a thing determine its aesthetic qualities; aesthetic qualities are 'emergent'. Sibley also identifies different sorts of *aesthetic judgements*: some employ a characteristic aesthetic term ('graceful', 'balanced', 'gaudy') while others do not ('it's not pale enough', 'there are too many characters'). In addition to those two sorts are 'the purely evaluative judgements: whether things are aesthetically good or bad, excellent or mediocre, superior to others or inferior, and so on. Such judgements I shall call *verdicts*.'[59] What about, then, the possibility that aesthetic judgements can be true, 'that some works *are* graceful, others moving or balanced'?[60] This question addresses the problem of objectivity, that 'gracefulness' may really be an inherent quality of a particular object, and that anyone denying that such is the case would be in error. Sibley refers to the questions sometimes asked 'whether the [aesthetic] terms used connote "properties" or "objective characteristics" that are "in", "inherent in", or "intrinsic to" the object'.[61] Avoiding a direct answer by remarking that 'the philosophical uses of "property", "inherence" etc. are varied and often obscure', he seems inclined to admit 'that we manage with reasonable success to treat aesthetic concepts as objective'.[62] Sibley also states that 'in actual practice we do manage to give aesthetic terms a partial but not unsuccessful run as property terms', and that 'we will not need to abandon all claims to objectivity'.[63]

The question now arises whether Sibley's theory – that aesthetic qualities are emergent – can be a platform from which we can construct an aesthetic theory of structures. It is not hard to agree that the 'triggers' of aesthetic interest are the physical properties of objects, what Sibley calls 'nonaesthetic properties'. When talking about structures, however, the idea of *aesthetic* properties or qualities – identified by certain specified aesthetic terms – is infinitely more difficult. An obvious difficulty in applying aesthetic terms like 'elegant', 'delicate', etc., is that it is not altogether clear what those terms actually mean. Apart from being expressions of satisfaction, as Wittgenstein commented, they say nothing about the content of that satisfaction or about the possible reasons for it, and thus add no further understanding. Wittgenstein clearly disregarded the view that being 'beautiful' is a property or quality of the object.[64] To be beautiful is, rather, an expression of 'a relationship between the observer and the thing. Most often when we use the term "beautiful" in connection with an act, we mean that the act fits into its context.'[65] Hence there is in such a case an 'appropriate' relationship between the act or thing, ourselves as observers, and the situation in general. This is expressed in phrases such as 'this colour goes well with that colour' and 'these materials suit each other'.

A similar attitude is expressed by the philosopher Roger Scruton in his *The Aesthetics of Architecture* (1979).[66] Scruton's theories are of distinct interest here. The theoretical foundation for this particular work is his *Art and Imagination*, in which he presents a theory of aesthetic judgement and appreciation of works of art, though in the following analysis I shall focus on his work on architecture.[67] Scruton tries to avoid using specifically aesthetic terms; instead, inspired by Alberti, he proposes to use terminology that takes its meaning from a wider context. Rather than defining 'beauty' or any other aesthetic term, Scruton tries 'to expound aesthetic judgement by exploring the state of mind, and the mode of reasoning, in which it is based'.[68] He points out that an aesthetic experience is always an expression of a relationship between an experiencing subject and the object in question. Moreover, the experience is comprised of both feeling and thought: while the aesthetic experience is partly an experience of the senses, feelings are in aesthetics *intellectually processed*, and this processing is *part of* the aesthetic experience. When we evaluate an object, and when we communicate with others about the aesthetic experience, we do so by referring to what seems to be appropriate for that particular aesthetic object. Like Wittgenstein, Scruton regards the intellectual part of the aesthetic experience as the most important, the part that consists of our interpretation and understanding of the given object as an aesthetic entity. *Scruton's approach, partly resting as it is on Wittgenstein's philosophy, will be carefully considered for an inquiry into the aesthetics of structures.* I shall, contrary to the views of Sibley, try to avoid specifically aesthetic terms to describe what might be thought of as aesthetic qualities; instead, I shall express aesthetic experience and judgement by phrases such as 'the structure is not adequately open', 'the beam is too large', etc.[69] Scruton's theory, modified for thinking about architecture, brings us a long way in helping us to formulate our understanding of our aesthetic experience of artificial (but essentially non-artistic) objects of various kinds.

Let us pause briefly to think about the possibility of appreciating structures aesthetically in a way analogous to our appreciation of nature. When observing large structures in a landscape setting, such as bridges, dams, transmission towers, etc., we may reasonably ask whether we actually see those structures as parts of those landscapes, and thus we should appreciate them in much the same way. How, then, is nature appreciated aesthetically? We would expect to define an aesthetics of nature – nature being non-intentional and thus the opposite of artefacts and art objects – quite differently from an aesthetics of culture. Malcolm Budd states that the appreciation of nature 'must be *based* on the item's being natural'.[70] That is, the aesthetic appreciation should be 'free from a certain constraint of understanding, namely the understanding of its meaning *as art*'. We do not hear birdsong 'as intentionally determined by artistic considerations', Budd says, emphasising that nature should be experienced and appreciated as natural objects, whose forms are determined by their inner nature, their age, their habitat and the forces of nature. 'This enables the aesthetic observer to delight not only in the visual appearance of [nature's] blossoms, say, but in what they indicate, and so experience the flowering of the tree as a manifestation and beautiful expression of the resurgence of life triggered by the arrival of spring.'[71] While a hermeneutics of nature and natural objects would be highly speculative and certainly beyond the scope of this book, people-made structures are clearly designed and express human intention and agency; to borrow a highly relevant metaphor from discourse theory, structures are *constructed* – as such they, unlike natural objects, are open to analysis and interpretation. We experience and appreciate structures in a landscape as parts of that particular environment, but this is different from appreciating structures and nature in the same way. In such cases *structure-in-a-landscape* would be an adequate formulation; it might offer interesting conceptualisations of aesthetic experiences of structural forms relating to landscape forms, and supplement other concepts of structure. Acknowledging structures to be artificial objects, I shall therefore maintain that our aesthetic experience of structures is best understood along the lines Scruton has drawn up and made operational for architecture.

How, then, are we to understand our aesthetic experience of structures, and in what way may the manner in which we *think* about structures affect that experience? How, if at all, can *reasoning* help us communicate with other people who might share our aesthetic experience? To be able to answer those questions, I take as a point of departure that the aesthetic experience intimately relates to what the object actually is; in the case of artefacts, what the object might be for. Without some idea or *concept* of the object, it will probably be impossible to make any kind of aesthetic judgement – the aesthetic experience at the heart of an evaluation will be undermined by our lack of ideas or thoughts, thus preventing any reasonable aesthetic understanding of the perceived object. 'Our sense of the beauty of an object', Scruton says, 'is always dependent on a conception of that object.'[72] In experiencing (for example) a sports car aesthetically, we must bring to mind the intellectual concepts of speed and efficient movement so that our aesthetic experience of it shall be meaningful. The same is true in the field of architecture: it is *possible* to perceive structural form as independent of its material or its function as a load-bearing device, etc., but in such cases we do not see that form as a *structure*. It follows from this that we cannot discuss the aesthetic qualities of structures as if they were just another piece of 'fine art'. To be able to understand structures aesthetically, we must bring to our perception of them those conceptions that seem relevant. In fact, when aesthetics is concerned, our experience depends on how we think about the object, and those conceptions are very much part of our aesthetic experience of it.[73]

Part 1 introduced basic concepts of structures and discussed different ways of considering structures in an architectural context. The resulting schema identified those aspects vitally important for an understanding of structural matters in architecture: observation and reflection on the different functions relating to structural performance and spatial utility lead to a proper understanding and appreciation of structural form. Such considerations are *conceptions* of structures and must be present to consciousness when experiencing structures aesthetically.[74] We must therefore be sceptical when the aesthetics of structures is reduced to a question of 'good, harmonious proportions' – whether related to some proportional system like the golden mean or other well-known mathematically based systems – unless those notions are truly descriptive of meaningful conceptions of *structures*, and not just of any kind of object that can provide some sort of aesthetic experience.

Central to the evaluation of the aesthetic merits of structures is of course the aesthetic experience itself – what we actually *perceive* when we stand in front of them. And, moreover, this perception requires

some *conception* of what we are seeing. If we observe (for example) a structural frame in total isolation without having the faintest idea about what it is for, what it is made of, or how it is supposed to relate to the surrounding space, we will be aesthetically helpless; as perceiving subjects, we will have no significant clues to help us understand it. The ancient post and lintel structures of Stonehenge are a likely candidate for such a lack of aesthetic understanding. As soon as we realise, however, that the posts and lintels are elements in a circular composition that once connected each block of stone both visually and physically, we can see a meaning in the object, an order or a unity that may make us exclaim: 'Now I see!' All of a sudden, because of our conception of what is in front of our eyes, we can see this object as something meaningful. We have an *understanding* of it that results from our aesthetic experience and our interpretation of it; how the stones seem to us is a part of that experience.

3.4 Stonehenge, near Salisbury, England (c. 2200 BC).

What kind of perception in relation to aesthetic experiences are we talking about? Any active impression on consciousness via the senses: sight, hearing or smell. An aesthetic experience – rather than a purely sensory experience – requires that we perceive more than simple sense-data in order to arrive at aesthetic understanding.[75] The kind of perception I mean here presupposes thought and reflection, meaning that the necessary interpretation is not something that takes place after the experience, but simultaneously, as part of it. In fact, the active participation of the observer is required for the completion of the aesthetic experience. Perception and conception (thought, interpretation) are both part of the aesthetic experience. The experience we seek is one of pleasure, but not simply sensuous pleasure such as a loving embrace or the taste of a good wine. It is, rather, the experience of an *intellectual pleasure* that is 'not immediate in the manner of the pleasures of the senses, but is dependent upon, and affected by, processes of thought'.[76] Feeling is therefore a part of the experience, but (as Wittgenstein acknowledged) only as a 'raw material' subject to intellectual processing.[77] Experience and thought are therefore inseparable. Thought or interpretation has the ability to *modify* the aesthetic experience, because the perception depends upon having a conception of the work. If we interpret the work differently (having a different conception of it), we see it differently and the experience changes. This conceptualisation is made possible by our ability to *see* something *as* something; 'seeing as', according to Wittgenstein, is fundamental to our understanding of visual impressions.[78] We 'see it as we interpret it', says Wittgenstein. 'You can think now of *this* now of *this* as you look at it, can regard it now as *this* now as *this*, and then you will see it now *this* way, now *this*'.[79] 'Seeing' is the actual perception, while 'seeing as . . . is not part of perception', Wittgenstein says.[80] 'Seeing as' is interpretation. Yet, they depend on one another and they are both part of the aesthetic experience.

There is a quote from Mies van der Rohe that may exemplify these points: 'Once I understood how the George Washington Bridge works,' Mies is reported to have said, 'I realised that it is the most beautiful building in New York.'[81] When Mies understood the bridge and therefore thought about it differently, he saw it differently. We can say that the experience of a structure, a building or a bridge has an interpreted character. 'In perception,' Scruton says, 'experience and interpretation are inseparable.'[82] It is also clear that we are able to *change between different aspects* of the same work, which means that interpretation and perception imply the ability to choose. We can in fact choose between *ways of seeing*, and hence also between experiences. This choosing is not possible for ordinary or literal perceptions, where 'normally seeing is believing, and where knowledge is the fundamental aim'.[83] We cannot choose to see black and white as green and red, or zig-zag patterns as rectangles. By an act of will, however, we can really see the well-known ambiguous depiction of rabbit/duck as either rabbit or duck, but not rabbit and duck at the same time.[84] Each time we might think about and see the same picture differently, depending upon our

3.5 We can choose at will whether we see a rabbit or a duck.

preference. Typographical marks on a piece of paper can be seen as just that, or as meaningful words. It is much the same with architecture: different ways of seeing, and the ability to change between different aspects of form, make it possible for us to have an experience that leads to understanding. Moreover, the different ways add up to constitute an aesthetic whole.[85]

An architectural work displaying a quite distinct structure can serve to clarify how these ideas above may be of help. The Renault Distribution Centre in Swindon (1983) consists of a number of 24 by 24 m building modules each having a structural system that supports the roof from the top of four masts at the corners of the modules. The building height varies from 7.5 to 9.5 m. As a result the partly glazed façades are quite high and have to be supported against wind loads. The structural members of the façades, the mullions (visible in the glazed part of the building), are rolled steel profiles with circular perforations along the length. The structural rhythm of these profiles corresponds with that of the protruding steel beams of the roof structure: for each beam there is a mullion below. In perceiving this wall, we encounter a familiar problem often connected with the gable-wall of tall, one-storey buildings: we are aware that we might interpret the vertical profiles as columns supporting the roof, rather than local bracing of the tall façade against wind loads. By will, by imagination, we can see those profiles as members carrying vertical loads, and we thus have a different and opposite aesthetic experience of the roof and wall structures. We see them differently. When the vertical profiles are seen as columns, the end roof beam and underpinnings (as well as the masts themselves) lose their meaning. We quite simply do not understand their function. The aesthetic unity gets lost: the mullions look too slender, and the other structural members look too heavy. However, by changing to a different way of seeing them, to the one that sees those steel profiles for what they really are, we suddenly have a very different experience of aesthetic quality. We now experience unity of structural lines and an appropriateness of structural proportions.[86]

Because we can interpret the object in question differently ('seeing as'), and perceive form in different ways, and change between different experiences, all ways of seeing are not equally rewarding or even relevant. There is no relativism in this aesthetic theory that could delude us into believing that all aesthetic experiences are of the same value. On the contrary: Scruton argues that there are 'correct' ways of seeing buildings, not merely in the sense of the experience that is most satisfying, but in the sense of the experience that leads to understanding and appreciation.[87] Aesthetic competence shows in an ability to see the aesthetic object in the 'right' way, and by communication with other people to try to find those perceptions that reveal what is good or bad, or what is appropriate for the aesthetic object in question.[88]

In the case of the Renault Centre at Swindon, we can notice the

measures taken by the architect to prevent what Scruton might call a 'wrong' perception of the structures. If we are to see the mullions indeed as columns rather than local bracing we have to imagine their physical connection to the roof beams, a connection that, from the exterior, is hidden from us by a strip of neoprene.[89] This strip of neoprene acts functionally to prevent rain from penetrating the quite complicated structural connections that also have to allow for thermal movements, but its presence at that particular part of the structure make it appear less likely that forces could be transmitted between beam and imagined columns, forces that seemingly would have to be resisted by that very soft material. Still, it is quite possible to imagine those structural members being columns, especially when shadows fall on the top of the walls, but it is hardly a 'correct' way of seeing them, one that leads to aesthetic understanding and appreciation.

The Renault Centre perfectly illustrates the point that different ways of seeing lead to quite different aesthetic experiences. We can choose between them at will, but in this case one of those perceptions is more 'correct' than the other, because this is the one that leads to aesthetic appreciation. The architect has taken measures, by way of detailing, to make it easier for us to obtain that particular experience, an experience of a certain unity and intellectual coherence in the sense that it makes us understand why the structures look the way they do. The structures suddenly seem 'right' when those members are seen as mullions rather than columns, and this experience is one of pleasure. Pleasure then, to use the words of Scruton, 'is not so much an effect of its object, as a mode of understanding it'.[90]

There are, however, certain problems in describing aesthetic experiences as being 'correct' or 'right', alternatively 'incorrect' or 'wrong'. Those terms hint at a digitalised binarism where things are either 'on' or 'off'. They are better suited to characterise explanations of a causal nature and do not seem to fit descriptions of pleasurable or unpleasurable aesthetic experiences. Rather than speaking of 'correct' and 'wrong', I will propose terms like 'proper' and 'misleading'. To speak of 'proper ways of seeing buildings' (or 'misleading ways of seeing buildings') seems to allow that there might exist different degrees of attractiveness.

A French gothic cathedral may provide another example of our ability to see structures differently at will. Standing in the nave of the Rheims Cathedral, if we look at the piers and vault we can perceive the structures in at least two ways. Either we can choose to see each pier and the ribs of the vault that spring from it as parts of one entity, like the structure of a tree that reaches high up in the air and which barely touches the 'branches' of the 'tree' on the opposite side of the nave; or we can see the whole of the pointed vault as one structural element resting on two opposite piers. Each conception and accompanying perception implies a different aesthetic experience. The first experience, however, does not seem intellectually satisfactory: we are seeing only

3.6 The Renault Distribution Centre (1983), Swindon. Architects Foster Associates, engineers Ove Arup and Partners.

3.7 Rheims Cathedral, France
(thirteenth century). Interior.

one half of a 'tree', with the rest of the 'branches' missing. Also a recol-
lection of the system of flying buttresses that we noticed before stepping
inside – or a glimpse of them through the clerestory windows – will neg-
atively influence our experience: if we see a tree with cantilevering ribs
or 'branches', one of the main reasons for the buttresses (namely the
counteracting of the horizontal forces produced by the vaulting) comes
to nothing. We simply do not understand the structures of the nave in
relation to the structures on the outside. Thus, the 'tree' experience is
clearly misleading, and we move towards the other concept because
it looks more convincing. We seek by conception or interpretation
– in this example, of a system of forces – an intellectual grasp of the
structure in front of us. By changing between different ways of seeing

– ways that may be revealed through communication with others – different and perhaps conflicting aesthetic experiences will direct us towards the proper way of understanding and seeing. This, according to Scruton, is an experience of unity or *appropriateness*.[91] The structure somehow 'fits' into its context, and we should be able to persuade other people that this is in fact the case.

Scruton's preference for classicist architecture must not lead us to think that we should understand the notion of 'the appropriate' (termed 'decorum' in classical criticism) in a narrow sense, or in terms of the predictable, or the well adapted, or that which is to be expected. His philosophical aesthetics must be understood in a broader perspective. The sense of what is appropriate could just as well embrace contrast, surprise and deliberate opposites *if that is truly appropriate*. We might perceive a sense of unity or intellectual coherence in an object, or among objects that deliberately avoid adaptation to existing forms. The experience of unity, which is the mark of aesthetic understanding and appreciation, is not necessarily an experience of objects as 'being of the same kind' or 'arranged in the same way' or any such formula, but rather *the experience of some sort of attention to intellectual consistency*. Yet, the notion of the appropriate is impossible to define explicitly, as may be the case for other concepts or notions that articulate aesthetic response. Scruton thus makes a point of studying architectural detail in its proper context, not in order to claim that a 'sense of detail' comprises the whole of aesthetic understanding, but to emphasise that architecture is made of details and that by observing the relationship between the detail and the complete work we may have an aesthetic experience. 'The central operation of aesthetic taste', Scruton says, 'is the sense of detail.'[92] Attention to detail is therefore a key to a clarification of the notion of the appropriate, a notion that always implies a relationship between an object and a context. However, an aesthetic judgement is not exclusive: other details might have been equally appropriate. 'What is appropriate is not necessarily what is best. Our sense of the appropriate develops through recognizing multiple choices and through seeking a potential order among them.'[93] And this potential order represents an intellectual grasp of the objects in question, that we can see their significance as parts of a larger entity. The idea of the appropriate (elaborated on by Scruton and operationalised by directing our attention to a 'sense of detail') offers a strategy for properly understanding the aesthetic experience of structure and its relation to the architectural work as a whole. The structure itself constitutes a part or detail that (together with other building elements) comprises the complete architectural work.

So far, not much has been said about the status of an aesthetic judgement that seeks 'appropriateness' in all aspects. Is this a purely subjective enterprise, or can objective – or at least intersubjective – values apply? The binding together of the parts of a building in some relation of appropriateness enables us 'to see the existence of one part as providing a reason for the existence of another'.[94] But if we know the *reasons* for decisions on form will we necessarily enjoy or approve of them? Logic does not suggest that if we understand object so and so, then we must automatically come to like it. But, according to Scruton, we will probably 'feel a weight of reason in its favour'.[95] We would be able to give reasons for and against a certain way of seeing an object, and so be directed towards a positive experience. Moreover, we can perhaps make others see what we are seeing. Aesthetic reasoning is therefore what we do when we try to persuade others to share our aesthetic experiences. Scruton holds aesthetic reasoning to be an extrapolation of aesthetic choices.[96] Reasoning, however, does not have the capacity to change someone's aesthetic point of view *unless those reasons make the other person experience the object differently*. 'The point of view is the experience', Scruton says, thus making the end-point (so to speak) of a process of reasoning not a judgement but an experience.[97] This is perhaps a surprising observation, but preceding arguments provide cogent justification: since our experiences may be altered at will as products of our imagination (as with the Renault Centre at Swindon), those experiences are also part of the intellectual, reasoning activities of the mind. That is why a new experience may be the conclusion of an argument.

Thus, reasoning may change our aesthetic experience and hence our judgement.[98] The articulation of a point of view is reasoning because it aims at justification and not at explanation. We want to seek support from other people in order to justify our own experience, and this is possible because of the dynamic nature of the perceptual experience. Explanations, on the other hand, give *causes*, which is different from giving reasons. The possible objectivity of our reasoning is therefore different from the objectivity of deterministic explanations of causes and effects. We are not seeking to decide objectively what is true or false as we do in scientific explanations, but rather what informed individuals find *proper or misguided*. Scruton makes the question of an objective aesthetics into a question of ethics. When we give reasons to justify our experience, we involve ethical matters. Aesthetic reasoning and judgement reflect specific values about what is 'right' or 'wrong', and an aesthetics of structures should aim at helping us to decide, as objectively as possible, what is good and what is bad about architectural structures.

The notion of appropriateness of aesthetic objects indicates that if no 'proper' way of seeing the object in question can be found to lead to aesthetic understanding and intellectual pleasure, then it is therefore of no great aesthetic merit. But how can this judgement be considered objective? The distinction between the objective and the subjective is probably not so clear-cut as scientific thinking might have us believe. On the one hand, aesthetic judgement is 'the attempt to articulate an individual experience', whether good or bad.[99] In that sense the aesthetic judgement seems subjective. On the other hand, 'it aims to *justify* that experience, through presenting reasons that are valid for others besides oneself'. In that respect the judgement is objective, or at least intersubjective. However, there is still a difference between aiming at justification and achieving it. Often, we think of objectivity as a judgement (of something) that, independent of the nature of our experience of it, complies with a rule or a law, preferably of a scientific nature. By referring to rules we can decide what is true and what is false. Aesthetics, however, is intimately related to personal experience; each case is unique and must be argued for, persuasively and without compromising its singularity. It therefore seems that no critical conclusion can be reached by applying rules. Yet, the question arises whether a kind of objectivity is still possible, whose aim is not to separate truth from falseness, but good from bad? Scruton makes a comparison with moral judgements that, according to Kant, are imperatives, and hence cannot be true or false.[100] Our ability 'to recognize right actions partly stems from an ability to recognize good men', Scruton says; 'we can understand what is right and wrong not because we possess some catalogue of rules, but because we understand the motives and feelings of the man of virtue'.[101] In science, then, objectivity supposedly validates the discrimination between right and wrong. In aesthetics, objectivity can be considered to represent the ability to discriminate between good and bad. Thus the question will finally be whether or not an aesthetic experience can lead us to distinguish between what is good and what is bad. If this is the case, we may say that any judgement of a structure on the basis of an aesthetic experience implies the passing of an objective aesthetic verdict. This is particularly true because the aesthetic experience leads to *understanding* of what motivated the structural form, and also because the aesthetic experience has a dynamic nature and thus can be shared by many. I will conclude that what our aesthetic experiences do is precisely that of helping us to discriminate between good and bad, and that the nature of structures is such that this discrimination is not dependent upon our private inclinations or biases. We will therefore maintain that the simplistic view that aesthetic judgement is subjective quite obviously falls short of adequately describing the aesthetic experience because, to quote Alberti, in matters of aesthetic choice 'you do not follow mere fancy, but the workings of a reasoning faculty that is inborn in the mind'.[102]

Let us leave the philosophical question of objectivity versus subjectivity here. My main concern in this book is to reflect upon the aesthetic aspects of a particular class of objects, namely the structures of architecture, and to this end we needed to investigate some different definitions of the aesthetic experience as proposed in various works on aesthetics. In Part 1 the suggested concepts essayed the broadest possible understanding of architectural structures, but they are specific to load-bearing structures, and structures neither as sculptures nor any other piece of 'fine art'. We judge structures aesthetically by articulating our visual experience of their design and its reflection of the multifaceted functions 'assigned' to those structures. The notion of appropriateness implies that we aesthetically experience structures in a context, namely (broadly speaking) mechanical systems situated in and being part of the creation of architectural spaces. What this book proposes, then, is to create two primary *language games* (to use Wittgenstein's notion), a mechanical and a spatial, and to compare and contrast the ensuing similarities and differences of aesthetic experiences and judgements.

We also learned from Part 2 on pragmatics that it was illuminating to introduce another level of mechanical concepts, namely those of the properties of materials, of structural efficiency and of structural scale. The same can be said of the spatial functions. The concepts of utility, contextuality and iconography help us to bring more precision to our interpretations. Although I believe that the interpretations or conceptions of structures presented here are the most fundamental for a thorough critique of the structures of architecture, the inherent dynamism of aesthetic reflections in the tradition of Wittgenstein and Scruton might also permit the introduction of other relevant interpretative concepts that would mean yet further different experiences. What is, then, a different experience? Is there 'really something different there in me?' Wittgenstein asks. 'But how can I find out? – I *describe* what I am seeing differently.'[103] A characteristic of a different experience, resulting from a change of conception, is a change of thought accompanied by a different description of the aesthetic experience.

Let us proceed by applying, in the next two sections, this aesthetic theory of structures to specific problems of criticism. The idea is to articulate an aesthetic response to structures, describing the aesthetic experience as this changes depending on the conception in use.[104] The organising principle for discussing these problems is, firstly, to look at, interpret and seek an aesthetic experience from buildings chosen to be illustrative of the *mechanics* of structural form. The second part of the discussion will look at structures I consider to be informed, mostly but not exclusively, by the *spatial function*. Thus the difference in experiences specific to both interpretations and perceptions will become clear by comparison. It must be noted, however, that the decision to articulate a critique of structures in this way is based on methodological

3.8 A theoretical model, including both conception and perception, of our aesthetic experience of structures. We can change at will between different ways of seeing, and thus have different aesthetic experiences.

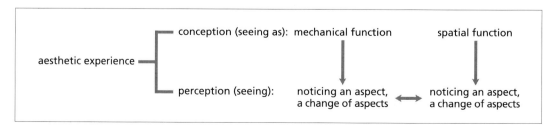

convenience and does not necessarily reflect our customary aesthetic experience of structures. The method seems to work well with the present examples, perhaps because they have been chosen particularly for their conceptual clarity. The reason for this procedural and literary choice is a wish to demonstrate how different interpretations work in relation to our experience of structural form. One possible consequence, however, is that the studied objects can be discussed from just a few – indeed important, if not the only – points of view. The following critiques will act as a testing ground for the validity of the classification of structural aspects in the previous parts of the book. We will see, then, how this way of looking at structures works when those initial assumptions are applied to actual aesthetic experiences of specific structures in architecture.

Aesthetics of the mechanical function

Virtually all theoretical reflections on the aesthetic merits of structures have been concerned with looking at structures from a purely mechanical point of view. This is not surprising; after all, the relationship between structural form and the concepts of strength, stiffness and stability – as well as actual manufacturing – is indeed a close relationship. Whatever the purpose of a structure, it supports loads. It is therefore a fundamental necessity that the structure safely and reliably can take on the physical burden of specified weights. Aesthetic evaluations will therefore quite naturally conceive or interpret a structure through the lens of our perception of its mechanical functions. While an excellent starting point, as I have already argued and will try to show in the next section, the mechanical point of view alone often cannot offer a route to a full aesthetic understanding.

Strategies for a critique of the mechanical

In many well-known texts that aim to shed light on the question of the aesthetic experience of structures, there is a tendency to list so many possible influences on the *design* of structures that they rarely inform us what might be the basic conditions for *experiencing* structures aesthetically in a proper way. There are, hence, good reasons for trying to sort out some issues here, acknowledging that some are far more important than others. I will therefore maintain that *to consider the aesthetics of structures from a mechanical point of view implies the appreciation of the capacity of materialised form to act structurally*. It also implies an appreciation of the visual results of the manufacturing and construction processes. Thus, an aesthetics of the mechanical function should embrace an aesthetics of materials and of scientific and technological processes (if applicable); it invokes the concepts of material properties, of mechanical efficiency and of structural scale. Since all structures

3.9 Musée d'Orsay, Paris (1986).
Architects Gae Aulenti and Act
Architecture.

must be capable of resisting the loads they are designed to support, the
focus of interest is naturally on how this is achieved.

Avoiding unduly normative proposals in the form of rules, a few possible strategies might guide aesthetic reflections related to the mechanical aspects of structures. The *negative* versions of those strategies
might read as follows. We should look out for:

1 structural form that ignores basic knowledge of the relationship
   between geometry and structural behaviour, the result being an inappropriate lack of structural efficiency;
2 structures that resolve unsatisfactorily the relationship between material properties and structural form. This applies to both the global
   and the local level of structural form, and may also involve questions
   of structural scale;
3 over-simplification of form in larger-scale structures, displaying less
   structural efficiency than is considered appropriate;
4 a complexity of form that seeks inappropriately high structural efficiency in a structure of a small scale, the result being a lack of technological efficiency.

Put the other way round, structures that avoid the above pitfalls may be
of aesthetic merit. On the other hand, if we can find non-mechanical
spatial concepts that can change our interpretation of the structural
form, and this conceptual change leads to a different perception, such
structures as otherwise violate the positive principles laid down above
might in some cases still be considered appropriate. This is the main
topic of the next section, 'Aesthetics of the spatial function'.

I refer here to 'small' and 'large' structures without defining precisely
what those terms mean. This reflects that there are no absolutes here.
The important thing is to see that such terms are relative to the material
and structural principle in use: a cable structure 30 m long, for instance,
is said to have a small span, while a beam the same length is thought to
be fairly long.

Let us illustrate these points with a few simple examples: the first
strategy addresses the relationship between structural geometry and
structural action. In the small bridge structure in the Musée d'Orsay
(1986) in Paris, the designers have deliberately omitted diagonal members in the centre of the span. Being basically a truss, obvious difficulties
with symmetry must have led to the decision to leave the middle part of
the beam open, inviting bending action rather than axial forces. Admittedly, even for asymmetrical loading, the shear forces or diagonal axial
forces in the truss are small at the centre, but a shift from one structural
principle to an altogether different way of transmitting loads leaves us
with a structure looking somewhat naked.

3.10 École d'Architecture de Lyon
(1987). Architects Jourda and
Perraudin.

The second point looks at the relationship of material, form and
scale. An example may be the openings at ground floor level of the École

3.11 Coutts Bank, London (1978). Architect Frederick Gibberd.

d'Architecture de Lyon (1987), made of reinforced concrete. The rather small and arched spans remind us of masonry, and only make sense from a mechanical point of view if we think of the concrete as unreinforced – that is, if we interpret the material as cast stone, a mono-directional material having compression strength only. Otherwise the particular global form of very small-span circular arches does not on first impression go well with the strong and versatile reinforced concrete. At the very least, the shape of the openings poses some interesting questions about the relationship between the material's structural potential and the actual design decisions.

An example of the violation of the third strategy is the roof structures of Coutts Bank (1978) in London. A fairly large-spanning steel structure supporting a glazed roof is made from welded plate girders of a considerable height. The sheer size of the I-shaped girders displays quite modest structural efficiency at both the global and local levels of structural form. A general awareness of the importance of structural scale seems to point to the need for a more open, sophisticated structure, as well as more spatial openness and the admission of daylight.

The fourth strategy for recognising inappropriateness of structural form involves the conflict between structural and technological efficiency. Quite a few candidates emerge from the hi-tech architecture movement in the 1980s and after. An architectural programme that seeks a richness of structural expression may fall into the trap of pre-

3.12 Sainsbury's, Camden, London (1988). Architect Nicholas Grimshaw.

senting overly articulated structures, resulting in a complexity of form that is less concerned with manufacturing and maintenance considerations. The structures for the Sainsbury's supermarket (1988) in Camden Town, London, may illustrate this point.

Materials, efficiency and scale

Let us now look at structures seemingly designed primarily to meet mechanical requirements, drawing freely on the four strategic points listed above. I shall start by commenting on a project that in some respects does not offer us an experience of structural appropriateness.

Softwood megalomania

A number of sports halls were built to house the indoor activities at the 1994 Winter Olympics in Lillehammer, Norway. Three of those feature large, free-spanning structures of laminated wood. The Hamar Olympic Amphitheatre (1993) was the venue for figure-skating and short-track speed skating. While both Hamar Olympic Hall, the so-called 'Viking Ship', a name derived from the structure's likeness to an overturned boat, and Håkons Hall are both arch structures, the Amphitheatre is spanned by large beams engineered by the manufacturer. Initially designed in steel, the architectural advisors to the Olympic Committee specifically asked for a structure in laminated wood.

3.13 Hamar Olympic Amphitheatre, Norway (1993). Architects HRTB, structural engineers Grøner AS. Section.

3.14 Hamar Olympic Amphitheatre. Plan.

The maximum span of 70.8 m is a very large span in an architectural

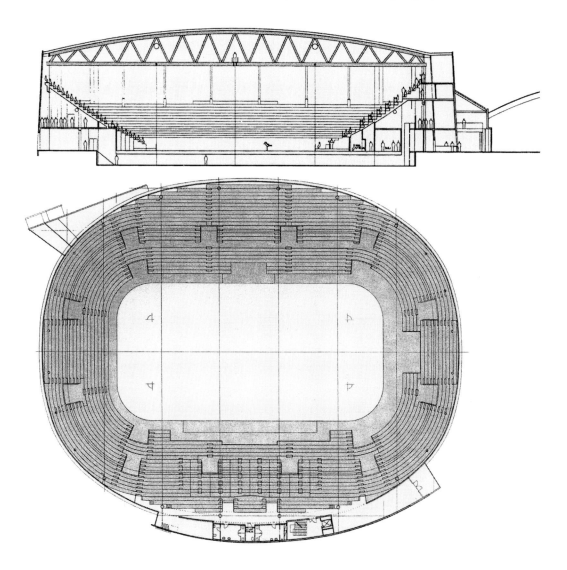

context. Since beams represent a relatively inefficient, global structural principle, this choice of structure is surprising from a mechanical point of view, even if the beams are trussed. The architects, however, explain their decision to rule out an arch structure because television cameras need a considerable roof height above the spectator level.[105] The trusses are manufactured in three parts and assembled at the site. The connections obviously have to provide for large bending moments. This is much simplified by the use of trusses, as bending moment stiffness is obtained by jointing the top and bottom chords axially to the corresponding chords of the neighbouring part of the beam, while the diagonals provide the shear stiffness. End-to-end connections of laminated wooden members are based on the insertion of a number of splice plates into the wood which are held in place by steel dowels. This system is an innovative, rational and technologically efficient solution. The trusses are of variable height and are repeated every 13.2 m; the centre one has the largest span, displaying a structural height at midspan of 6.5 m. At each end, huge pillars of reinforced concrete support the roof loads.

The tapering form of the large trusses is in accordance with the variation of the bending moment diagram, resulting in more or less constant compression and tension stresses in the chords along the beam length. Since manufacturing considerations and a common regard for a certain visual order do not permit a change of cross-sectional dimensions in the chords along the span, the tapering form of the truss seems to be a sensible decision aimed at achieving local efficiency: the material in the chords is evenly stressed. When seen from a point of view of local efficiency, this form also implies that the diagonals are gradually reduced in length as the truss approaches the supports. From the correspondence of the increasing forces in the diagonals with this reduction of member length, we may see the appropriateness of this particular design choice for the efficiency of the compression diagonals. However, knowing that the maximum bending moment that may occur in an arch amounts to only about 12–14% of the bending moment in a beam of the same span, the aesthetic problem of this structure is both to do with the relation of global structural form to structural efficiency, and (in particular) the relationship between the scale and the structural material.

Wood is indeed a most efficient structural material, measured by its strength- and elasticity-to-weight ratios. This was discussed in Part 2 on pragmatics. With a snow load of 2.5 kN/m^2, however, the longest truss supports a total snow load of about 2300 kN. This is a very substantial live load which reduces the importance of the favourable strength-to-weight ratio of the material. The maximum tension and compression forces in the chords are calculated to about 7000 kN each, with a maximum axial force in the diagonals of 2560 kN.[106] The result of those forces are cross-sectional dimensions of incredibly 630 mm by 600 mm in the top chord (b × h), 790 mm by 600 mm in the bottom chord and

3.15 Hamar Olympic Amphitheatre. Structural details.

630 by 300/400 mm in the diagonals. The visual result of those dimensions is a compactness of structural form not considered consistent with the general idea of a truss being an assemblage of members that are relatively quite slender.

Thus, when seen as a structural problem of a particular scale, the aesthetic experience is not one of undivided intellectual pleasure. Visually, the truss is quite simply too heavy. The material is too weak to cope properly with the chosen structural principle at that scale. Laminated wood cannot offer structural dimensions, and thus proportions, that correspond with our expectations of what a truss should look like. The aesthetic experience of the parts of the trusses near the supports is particularly disturbing, where there is an accumulation of material resulting from the gradually reduced distance between the top and bottom chords. Pressed in-between is the last diagonal, the one supporting the largest force. Owing to the amphitheatre-type arrangement of the seating, the spectators are quite close to these parts of the trusses, with a clear view of the inappropriateness of the structural proportions. If we translate the disappointing aesthetic experience into numbers, the slenderness ratio of the diagonals can be calculated to range from about 64 for the most 'slender' and down to 14 for the shortest one. An expected maximum slenderness in wooden structures according to internationally accepted codes of practice[107] would amount to a number in the area of 170.

In spite of a *local* structural form that, from the point of view of structural and technological efficiency, displays an understandable coherence between form, manufacturing and structural behaviour, we quickly notice aspects of it that present obvious aesthetic difficulties in terms of the relationship between the material properties and the scale. The structural span in the present case is so large that the wooden structure would probably have been aesthetically more satisfying if its *global* form followed a more efficient structural type.

Triangulated trusses for a terminal

In comparison with the Olympic Amphitheatre, this airport terminal building displays trussed structures that we experience quite differently, owing to a reduced span combined with a stronger material. The Fuhlsbüttel Airport in Hamburg (1993) is designed with seven curved and slightly tapered beam trusses spanning 62 m. The steel trusses have a triangular cross-section, each resting on two sets of inclined compression struts at both ends that take the load down to 12 pre-stressed

3.16 Fuhlsbüttel Airport, Hamburg (1993). Architects von Gerkan, Marg and Partners, structural engineers ARGE Kockjoy–Schwarz + Dr Weber. Interior of terminal building.

3.17 Fuhlsbüttel Airport. Detail of support structure.

concrete pillars cantilevering from the slabs of the lower floors. This arrangement also provides transversal and, with help from the secondary beams, longitudinal wind bracing.

The overall experience of this project is of well-adapted structural and technological solutions. Although being curved, the primary structure (of considerable span) still depends on not-too-efficient beam action. The V-shaped supports, however, apart from securing transversal stability, also provide rotational stiffness of the beam ends, which reduces the mid-span moment. This results in a reduced structural height than would otherwise have been the case. The small overhang also contributes slightly to that effect. The beams, obviously, are made locally efficient by trussing. Looking at the member profiles, we also acknowledge the contribution to local efficiency provided by the CHS (circular hollow section) tubes: as regards buckling, symmetrical cross-sections having a large Z/A ratio are favourable. When the structure is seen primarily as a mechanical system – and there are no clear alternatives to considering it otherwise – we also notice with pleasure the contribution to efficiency offered by the tapered form of the compression struts supporting the beams. Being quite large, the cigar-shaped struts add to the impression of a structure displaying an appropriate degree of efficiency.

Equally appropriate is the choice of material, given the scale and the overall structural context.

As regards the efficiency problem and a potential conflict between structural and technological efficiency, we experience this particular structure aesthetically as being highly appropriate. There is a coherence between global and local structural forms, and the structure reconciles quite well the two different efficiency criteria. The designers, however, have made a statement that partly disturbs this way of seeing the structure: 'The form and construction of the roof is based on the design theme of an aircraft wing.'[108] If we think about the structure in that way, we will quite certainly see it very differently. The only trace of such an iconographic reference might be on the exterior, and when looking at the building from above, where a superficial likeness to the shape of an aircraft wing can be seen. There is, however, not much supporting evidence from the appearance of the roof and structure on the interior. Neither the structural principle nor the articulation of the structural parts are anything like an aircraft wing. Rather than being arranged in discrete, one-way structural lines with a supported cladding on top, the structure of an aircraft wing is based on the stressed-skin principle that activates structurally both the interior ribs as well as the cladding. In this example, trying to see the structure this way is quite simply misleading. By bringing in the aircraft wing concept we fail to notice the merits of the structure, and the aesthetic experience becomes less understandable and intellectually coherent. This example shows that it might be misleading to rely on statements of the designer's intentions rather than trying to interpret the object at hand from what we can see for ourselves. The structures of the Hamburg terminal do not need iconographic references to be properly understood. On the contrary, in the

3.18 Fuhlsbüttel Airport. Transversal section.

3.19 Fuhlsbüttel Airport. Longitudinal section.

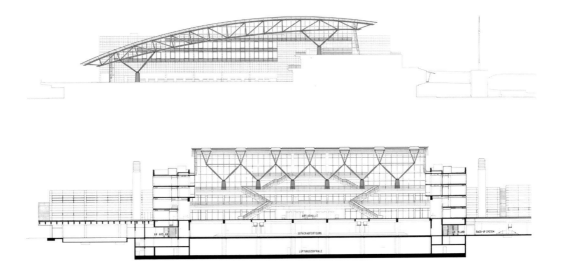

present case this interpretation disturbs the prospect of a pleasurable aesthetic experience.

There is, however, another aspect of this structure we perceive differently depending on which conception we choose: the secondary beams spanning continuously between the main girders or trusses. Rather than being cut off at the point where they reach the girders, they continue across the width of the girders' triangular cross-sections and move on to the next girder. When seen from a mechanical point of view, this seems quite correct: their static function is to brace the girders against overturning, to keep them from rotating about their bottom chords. Since the trussed girders are supported along their bottom chords only, it is necessary to devise some strategy – the bending stiffness of those secondary steel beams – to avoid rotation. We thus experience the design as being appropriate. On the other hand, however, we notice that the width of the trusses, where the secondary steel beams are continued uninterrupted, is also used to establish a strip of glazing to bring daylight into the deep terminal building. From the point of view of function, namely to allow the light to enter, this strip would have been better kept clear of as much structural material as possible. An interpretation of the structure in terms of its spatial function makes this structural detail seem less appropriately designed. When we change our conception and think about the structure differently, this makes us perceive it differently. Thinking about the secondary beams in terms of the light makes us see them less favourably, but we can change between the two different experiences at will.

The dome of cables

In spite of much controversy during the planning period, the Millennium Dome was designed and erected on schedule and within budget, and completed in late 1998. For several years subsequently it has been a landmark on the Greenwich Peninsula in eastern London. The Dome is generally thought of as a success, at least from the point of view of the engineering and design of a huge column-free space. Nevertheless, in terms of architecture that displays structural principles expressed in certain materials, a few points stand out for comment.

The global form of the spatial structure is close to that of a spherical cap. The reason why it is only nearly spherical is that the surface is broken up into a series of flat, fabric panels with distinct edges rather than having continuous curves. The structure of the Dome is comprised of 72 radially arranged cables that are supported from above by hangers fixed to the top of twelve masts; the cables are tied down by guys (indirectly) anchored to the ground. Circumferential cables complement the arrangement and keep the spacing between the radial cables in a correct position. The Dome covers an immense circular floor area of 320 m diameter and hovers a maximum of 48 m above the ground.

The question arises: is this building in fact a dome? From a structural point of view, it is not, even if it looks like one. A dome is commonly thought to be a shell structure with a surface produced by a rotated arch, characteristically carrying loads primarily by a combination of compressive 'arch' forces, or meridianal forces, and compressive or tensile ring forces, depending on the distance to the 'pole'. A dome is self-supportive and does not hang from an external support system of masts, cables and hangers. Because of its synclastic, double-curved surface shape, a dome is basically a compression structure. This 'dome' is a hybrid tension structure made of mono-directional materials and components that work only in tension. The name, however, is not really an issue here, but it does suggest a readily confusing way of experienc-

3.20 The Millennium Dome, Greenwich, London (1998). Architects Imagination Ltd and Richard Rogers Partnership, engineers Buro Happold. Aerial view.

ing the global form of the present structure. This 'dome' needs twelve masts 100 m high to stand up, masts which clearly perforate its surface. If we look at the structure, then, from the point of view of its global form and with a mind to the relationship between form and materials, the experience is certainly not one of appropriateness. The global shape of a spherical dome does not go well with the tensile materials we in fact observe, and the huge, protruding masts seem alien to the overall, dome-like shape. What looks like point-loading on the domed surface from those masts is particularly disturbing. A basic problem resulting from the choice of global, structural shape is also that the radial cables necessarily become straight between their points of support from hangers. Between each cable, the fabric surface is thus also straight. Hence both cables and glass-fibre fabric carry loads transversal to their natural line of forces, resulting in considerable deflection. Both cables and fabric need to deflect to be able to carry those loads. To restrict the deflection, the radial cables are pre-stressed by 400 kN, using up as much as 70% of their ultimate strength before external loads even act on the system.[109] This gives us a numerical expression of the difficulty of letting straight tension members form into what is fundamentally a compressive, global form.

   Is there really a problem here? That depends on what we are looking for. In terms of engineering success, measured by parameters like structural weight-to-span ratios, construction time and cost, the design decisions made for the Millennium Dome are probably both rational and appropriate. The Dome's chief claim to innovation, however, lies primarily in a structural strategy that seems to offer a rational construction of a huge space. The Dome's structural aesthetics in fact do not

3.21 The Millennium Dome. Isometric drawing of the cable net.

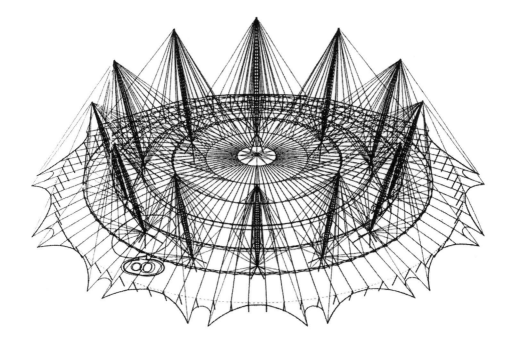

3.22 The Millennium Dome. Structural details.

3.23 The Millennium Dome. Cable net before the textile covering was put on.

deliver this promise, the visual conflicts intrinsic to this system being too obvious.

How should we set about appreciating the Dome, if this is at all possible? Is there a point of view, based on the notion of the structure as an efficient load-bearing system, that will make us see the whole concept differently? This is, admittedly, quite difficult, owing to the forceful and iconic image of a spherical dome. While the intellectual logic of the structure is relatively clear, the real problem is that we are hard put to find a way of actually seeing and appreciating it. A possible solution may be to shift our conception away from structural domes and look instead for the thinking behind the structure. Rather than staring blankly at the huge white spherical cap, we might seek out the structural lines that make this shape possible. There are two converging cable systems, one from above (represented by all the hangers) and one from below (represented by the radial cables). The hangers from opposite sides combine across the diameter to make up several hanging cable lines. They meet and connect with the inverted radial cables rising up from below. Together all the cables form a tensioned steel cable net, the cables from above and below mutually stiffening one another. Such a system needs masts to establish high points of support for the hanging cables. This is in fact what takes place in this complex structure; if we manage to think about it in this way, we might be able to see the structure differently. Even if it were perfectly rational from a functional point of view, the decision to let the fabric follow the inverted shape of the radial cables – taking the form of a dome – introduces the contradictions into our visual experience of the structure. This prevents real understanding and hence visual appreciation.

In the following section, we will turn our priorities upside down. We will now deliberately study structures that are seen to their best advantage if we regard their spatial functions as primary. Many of them have great visual qualities, *as structures*, even where they violate, to a lesser or greater degree, sound principles of structural mechanics or technology.

Aesthetics of the spatial function

Structures are made for a particular purpose. In architecture, this purpose is not *primarily* that of the support function. This is only a necessary result. The main purpose of the structure is to establish architectural spaces physically. It follows that the form or shape of structures must necessarily be, in most cases, heavily influenced by their spatial functions; an understanding and appreciation of structures hence needs to take this into account. The spatial utility functions – as well as the non-utility functions that influence structural form – may all serve as concepts or interpretations of structures that affect the aesthetic experience in various ways. The theory for this was discussed on pages 4–12 and 99–125. In the following analysis I will try to examine more closely, by discussing a number of cases, how such spatial aspects of structures may form the *primary* premises for imaginative perceptions that lead to aesthetic understanding. It is convenient to deal with one aspect at a time, starting with the utility functions. We will look – as two of the most important aspects – at how structures organise architectural spaces and influence incoming light. (Natural light is not only quantifiable and useful in a practical sense, however; it is also non-utilitarian and qualitative.) I will then discuss structures that are primarily the results of a spatial idea, where the reasons for the structural form cannot be understood without taking account of its particular spatial context. Lastly, we will look at structures that clearly have iconographic functions – we need to unveil their 'message' if we are to understand and appreciate them.

Utility vs. the mechanical

In this section we will look at three works of architecture. The design of all three structures is primarily and particularly concerned with spatial purposes of a practical nature. The first has column structures that have become more than load-bearing elements. The columns themselves make space for different functions, and also serve vertical communication in the building. The other two projects deal with beam structures that are actively designed to modulate the natural light coming into the respective buildings.

Thirteen latticed tubes

Let us start by considering the Sendai Mediatheque project (2000) in Japan, designed by Toyo Ito.[110] The programme called for a complex that combined an art gallery, library and audio-visual facility. The organisers of the competition signalled that they were looking for a proposal that was not bound by convention. Ito's answer is a large box clad in glass, 50 by 50 m square plans and, counting the ground floor, seven floors of varying height, the building reaching a total of 36 m above the ground. Besides the glass skin, there are only two basic elements forming the building's tectonics: square slabs made up of a sandwich of steel ribs and plates, and huge tubes of steel acting as vertical supports and – in the case of the four corner tubes – also as horizontal bracing.

The seven floors are organised very differently, depending on the activity. There is no visual partitioning other than the various facilities needed for the display of the art works, for the library and the coffee shop as well as the electronic media equipment. Hence the vertical structures feature very prominently in the interior; they are also the primary eyecatchers when looking at the building from the outside. The columns have different cross-sectional widths along their height, each one also having a uniquely different profile from the others; they are

3.24 Sendai Mediatheque, Japan
(2000). Architects Toyo Ito and
Associates, structural engineers
Sasaki Structural Consultants.
Exterior view.

also scattered around the plan semi-randomly. The tubes are made of
a number of steel CHSs, whose slenderness is a result of the application of thick-walled profiles. Their shape is that of hyperboloids of rev-
olution,[111] making it possible for the structures to be open and visually
light. The column structures provide space for various functions, and
their form must be interpreted accordingly. On their inside they provide for vertical circulation of people by stairs and elevators, as well as
containing ducts, pipes and wiring for the distribution of air, water and
electricity. They encase open 'wells' that run the whole height of the
building, penetrating each slab to open up 'a flow of natural and elec-

3.25 Sendai Mediatheque. Interior.

tronic energies'.[112] The function of the vertical structures is thus not merely to support the floor slabs and provide structural stability: their design, clearly, also relates directly to the building's infrastructure, both the transport of people and services needed to operate the building. When regarded from an aesthetic point of view, the most important conception of the structures therefore concerns their enclosing function, the serving spaces. The structures order the space by separating the serving and serviced spaces. Our aesthetic experience of those structures can be misleading unless we interpret them as functional tools for internal communication and transport.

This analysis implies that we will have a different kind of experience if we see the columns as having a support function only, as compared with when we include their spatial aspects in our interpretation. In the present case, it is clear that the sense of appropriate form we seek in order to appreciate the structures aesthetically relies on a conception of the structures as having a space-enclosing function. As we shall see, this interpretation leads to an experience of unity and coherence between what we actually observe and how we understand what we see. On the other hand, if we take the support function as the sole criterion our experience of aspects of the form will be fragmentary and incomprehensible.

How can we argue for this view? Starting with some purely mechanical issues: a non-ordered layout of the load-bearing columns – particularly combined with the marked differences in column widths – seems unjustifiable. Their placement and size do not correspond with the expected load to be carried by each column or tube, as represented by their share of the floor area. Some rather slender tubes carry more weight than some thicker or wider ones, so from the vertical support point of view, the sizes of the columns do not make much sense. The corner columns are triangulated and substantially wider because of their stability functions, but this does not alter the overall impression. There is also the peculiarity of 'inverted' columns. Some of the more slender tubes tend to be wider on the upper floors than they are on some of the lower, thus reversing the natural relationship between load and structural thickness. Yet, from the point of view of structural mechanics, these rather strange geometrical choices are probably insignificant. Since the same tubular steel sections pass through each cross-section along the column height, the same load-bearing capacity is present no matter the overall width of the column. Where the column tubes are not triangulated, the column width does not express its strength. This, however, does not explain or justify on mechanical grounds their inverted look and the differences of widths. We have to look elsewhere for a more tenable interpretation that makes us experience them differently. As suggested above, we must understand them aesthetically in terms of their spatial functions rather than their mechanics. In this case, the idea of spatial organisation and of architectural context is stronger and more reasonable than that of support, and should take priority.

It is when seeing the structures as vertical shafts or ducts for internal circulation that we begin to grasp their form intellectually. The reason why the tubes have different widths is that they provide spaces for different kinds of communication. While one tube contains the main stairs, another encloses a secondary, much smaller flight of stairs. One tube has a single elevator inside, another two, and so on. And then there is air, water and electricity. The width of each tube relates not to the amount of load to be supported but to its functional and spatial context. Similarly, the random distribution of tubes seems unjustifiable if we look

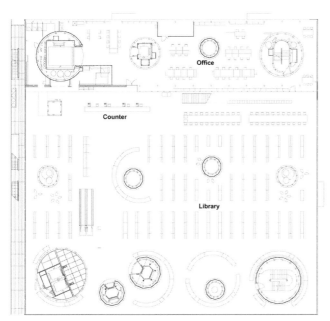

3.26 Sendai Mediatheque. Plan of third floor.

3.27 Sendai Mediatheque. Longitudinal section.

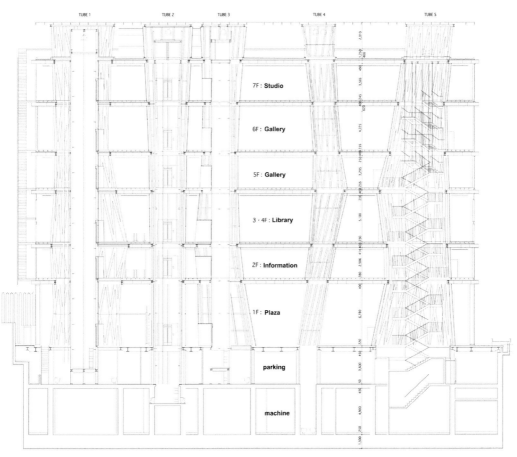

3.28 Sendai Mediatheque. Triangulated corner column providing lateral bracing.

upon the tubes solely as columns that provide support, but this lack of linear, structural order works quite well where the plan of each floor is organised differently and non-symmetrically. From the point of view of spatial function, there is in fact a close correspondence between what the structural form 'does' and what it looks like. If we see this we can then have an experience of appropriateness that is missing when we look at the structure solely from the point of view of mechanics.

The structure is nevertheless, when seen through the lens of structural mechanics and technology, not without visual appeal. Moving on from the previous analysis of structural order and column widths, it is noticeable that the area occupied by structural elements has consciously been expanded to provide usable spaces in themselves.[113] This is an alternative to the common strategy of trying to minimise structural footprints. This columnar expansion means a decentralisation of the structural mass, and the increased size results in a visually more open structure. Another pleasing aspect is that the hyperbolic shape of the tubes provides a shell structure of straight members where triangulated, and hence makes the manufacturing of the double-curved form less complex. Moreover, the structural principle also offers the right balance between strength and stiffness, the latter being particularly important in an area of seismic loads.

There is another aspect of the structural form in the present building not yet touched upon: the likeness of the structural tubes to gigantic tree trunks.[114] The use of hyperboloids enhances this effect by gradually and smoothly varying the widths – much like a tree – along the height of the columns. The experience of likeness to objects which are in actual fact not parts of the project, but solely constructs of the imagination, may nevertheless be a part of our aesthetic experience. In the present case, such an *iconographic* interpretation is certainly not unreasonable. Apart from physical likeness, the way these structural tubes serve the spaces by distributing water, air and electricity is similar to the internal water circulation system of a tree. Seeing this contributes to our experience of unity and intellectual coherence. I will give other examples of this kind of aesthetic experience later.

Beams of light

Architect Louis I. Kahn says of the direct relationship between the structure and the quality of light in architectural spaces that 'the structure is the maker of light', and 'the light of the vault is a choice out of structure. When you choose a vault you are already choosing the light. When you choose the column you are choosing a kind of light.'[115] In a way, we might say that Kahn looks upon light as a material. The structure is a tool for designing the rhythm and 'shape' of the light, for choosing its quantity, direction and colour. If, when observing architectural structures, we can think of structural form in this way, rather than as a medium for the support of loads, our aesthetic experience will change accordingly.

   Let us take a look at the museum (1983) designed by architect Renzo Piano housing the Menil Collection in Houston, Texas.[116] The structural engineers, Ove Arup and Partners, were partly responsible for the design of the most prominent structural feature of the museum: the roof beams made of iron truss elements acting compositely with curved, ferrocement shells.[117] The latter are frequently referred to as 'leaves'. The structures cover modules of about 6.6 by 13.2 m, each beam spanning about 12 m before resting on walls or transversal beams supported by free-standing columns. The composite beams hold up continuous glass skylights as well as the necessary drainage gutters. On the bottom edge of the 'leaves' are lighting tracks running their full length, providing artificial light that supplements the natural light reflected by the ferrocement part of the beams. Only a little outside light reaches the interior, and direct sunlight is totally excluded. To achieve the right amount of reflected light, the 'leaves' are made of marble sand and white cement. The amount of light – precisely specified by preservation conditions – is highly sensitive to the shape of the 'leaves' and the trussed iron members. The resulting form of the structures can be seen as a direct response to the constraints of using natural light for the displaying of works of art.

   There is a conflict of interpretations that drives our response: is the structural form to be understood as a supporting system or a provider of

3.29 Museum for the Menil Collection, Houston, Texas (1983). Architect Renzo Piano in collaboration with Fitzgerald Architects, structural engineers Ove Arup and Partners. Interior view.

the right conditions for natural light? In fact, the former (load-bearing) conception fails to lead on to a convincing aesthetic understanding. The idea of a curved and rotated lower part of a beam, swung aside from the axis of gravity to a position of locked-in energy and stress, seems absurd if interpreted on the basis of structural mechanics; our aesthetic experience is not one of undivided pleasure. It is as if we expect the web to swing back into a vertical, more effective position. However, the latter interpretation (the rationale of the structure is to control the admission of natural light) changes our perception, and the design starts to make sense. Overspanning the exhibition spaces, the structures have a lightness and a freshness about them that effectively contrast with the sombre darkness of the black-stained pine flooring. The lower edges form thin stripes of shadows in a roof structure that otherwise is perceived as quite homogeneous and light-filled (admittedly most so on a clear and sunny day). Even though the original design incorporated slightly thinner ferrocement elements that proved impossible to manufacture, the result is adequately 'delicate',

3.30 Museum for the Menil Collection. Composite structure of ferrocement and ductile iron.

and makes one think of white linen hung out to dry; a steady breeze gently pushes the textiles to one side and so admits the soft reflections of the sunlight.

By seeing the beams as designed for light, the roof plan seems to run just as naturally in the transversal direction as it does longitudinally – and we would expect the latter because of the load path. We perceive that one beam is connected to the adjacent one through light and reflection, and the two opposite surfaces form a meaningful relationship that helps our aesthetic understanding. In fact, it is almost impossible to perceive the 'leaves' as structurally active parts of load-bearing beams, even though we know they are. From the interior, most vistas obstruct the view of the upper part of the beams (the iron trusses that act compositely with the ferrocement 'leaves') and the transversal trusses. We can also see the gap between the 'leaves' in the longitudinal direction created by their connection to the transversal trusses. Both visual effects point to an interpretation of the 'leaves' as elements suspended from above rather than being structurally active in themselves.

3.31 Early sketch (1981) by Renzo Piano of the structure for the Menil Museum. Ink on paper.

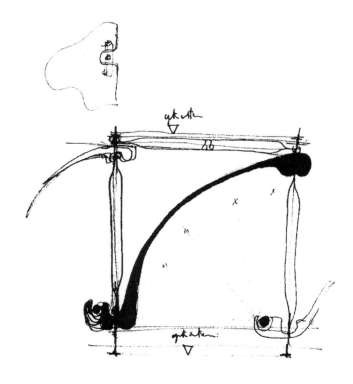

Hence the notion of louvres or 'leaves' seems to be very appropriate. Our enjoyment and aesthetic understanding of the structures thus depend on interpretations of them that (in this case) take into account their response to and control of natural light.

Why, then, are the 'leaves' structurally active at all? By being integral parts of the beams, the ferrocement 'leaves' reduce the stresses in the upper trussed parts, and thus reduce the required dimensions of the iron members. This makes a difference to the amount of light that filters through the roof structures, but it hardly explains the decision to make a composite beam. Other structural (and non-structural) solutions could probably also have provided the right light conditions. It is quite possible, therefore, that our aesthetic experience might have been enhanced if we could more easily perceive the structures as being *both* load-bearing *and* devices for controlling the quality of light of the interior spaces. As it is, the design almost excludes the experience of the former, and thus restricts the imaginative perception that might have helped us to see the structures more clearly in both roles. The conceptual ambiguity that exists could have enriched our aesthetic experience if it had been expressed visually more assertively.

It is interesting to study the sketches made by Piano at the beginning of the design process: he envisaged a space frame in which ferrocement louvres were integrated into the structure as shear elements that replace the usual diagonals. The design – with its possible structural problems –

was in fact rejected on the grounds that it would not meet the light specification. However, there is in this proposal a more readily understandable expression both of the structure's differing intentions and the means of bringing them to fruition.

A matrix of illumination

About twenty years before the Menil Museum, architect Sverre Fehn designed the Nordic Pavilion for the Venice Biennale (1962).[118] In many ways the two art galleries deal with similar issues regarding the relationship between the form of the structures and the assignation of functions. For us to have an aesthetic experience of both buildings that leads to

3.32 The Nordic Pavilion, Venice (1962). Architect Sverre Fehn, structural engineer Arne Neegård.

understanding, we also need consider how each structure manipulates natural light. 'Building a museum for the visual arts', Fehn says, 'is the story of the struggle with light.'[119]

The Nordic Pavilion is essentially a room of about 470 m² for displaying different kinds of art works. The room is without any intermediate support. On two adjacent sides there are concrete walls closing off a more or less square plan, while the other two permit an almost invisible transition between the interior and the exterior. This is achieved by sliding floor-to-ceiling glazing. This openness visually brings the surrounding park inside the building, the only element pointing out the boundary being the floor covering of slate tiles.

Again, one of the basic ideas of the roof structure design is to protect the paintings from direct sunlight. This is done by devising a structure of two orthogonal layers, consisting of narrowly spaced, thin concrete girders that create an atmosphere of diffused light that recalls the light of 'the shadowless world of the Nordic countries'.[120] The art works are thus exhibited in an environment of light supposed to resemble that of the countries in which they were made. To keep as much of the intensity of the light as possible, the concrete is cast in a mixture of white cement, white sand and crushed white marble. The girders follow a structural module of 523 mm (an ancient Egyptian module, according to Fehn), while their height and thickness are 1000 by 60 mm. These figures relate exactly to the trajectory of the sun at the Venetian summer sol-

3.33 The Nordic Pavilion. Plan.

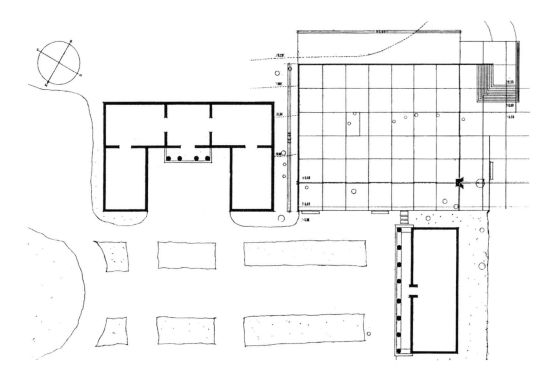

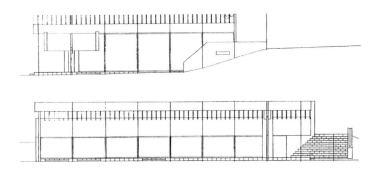

stice (64 degrees), and ensure the blocking out of direct light. The span of the bottom layer girders is about 18 m, not counting the 4+ m cantilevering part. In between the upper layer of girders are hung translucent gutters of glass fibre reinforced plastic sheets.

The quality of the light is thus the key to our aesthetic appreciation of the structure. The spacing, heights and remarkably small thicknesses of the girders derive from the manipulation of the light. If such a conception escapes us, we will experience the structure differently; if mechanical constraints alone were decisive, the proportions and the structural module will not seem appropriate in relation to the span and the choice of material. We will wonder why a primary tier of girders is as narrowly spaced as the secondary tier of purlins. If we conceive the roof structure as a two-way grid of beams, we will question why the grid is made by placing one layer of beams or girders on top of the other (making a total structural height of 2 m). This would be a quite unusual solution when seeking two-way structural action, especially when constructing in reinforced concrete.

There are, then, different possible interpretations as well as a number of different perceptions, but not all of them induce an experience of intellectual coherence or appropriateness. A grasp of the relevant concept when experiencing structures (as well as other objects of aesthetic interest) is very important. In this case, the idea of the control of light very nearly (but not entirely) dominates the concept and hence the experience. Another factor informing the choice of structure and determining how that choice is experienced was the need to protect the trees on the site from being cut down, trees that are part of the only park in Venice. The highly appropriate two-way beam system controlling the interior light also seems right and fitting for making room for the trees. The trees actually penetrate the roof level by way of openings in the structure; this is made possible by the two-way structural action. From a mechanical, load-bearing point of view, then, the openings for the trees legitimate the structural system to a certain degree, although that particular two-layered form is not necessary for achieving this. Hence a richness of aesthetic experiences is possible because different ways of seeing sometimes harmonise and strengthen the feeling

3.35 The Nordic Pavilion. Two-layered structure filters the light and allows trees to grow through the roof.

of appropriateness; sometimes they clash and make us wonder. Ambiguity – when a structure looks right from one point of view and strange from another – reveals the complexity of the work and thus contributes to our intellectual enjoyment.

The real highlight of our aesthetic attention is the areas around the openings. Here the experience of the structure and the light reaches a particular intensity, where the diffused light reflected by the surfaces of the girders mingles with the direct light that reaches us through the openings for the trees. These areas are 'packed' with perceptual tension related to the different possible ways of seeing the load path of the structure: the lower tier of girders (generally experienced as supporting the tier above) is in some places abruptly cut off to give room for the trees. Seemingly without support, the girders read as hovering in the air. We can enjoy the fascination of choosing between ways of seeing: lower tier as supporting, or lower tier as suspended from above. The two ends of the girders in question introduce additional ambiguity because they are very differently designed, with the opposite end from the openings firmly underpinned. Even if we know that the orthogonally directed upper girders relieve the cut-off lower ones in these areas by 'pulling' the load upwards, a support from underneath is definitely easier to grasp perceptually than a device for suspending them from above.

The Nordic Pavilion by Sverre Fehn shows with great clarity the value of considering structures not merely as mechanical assemblages but also, as in the present case, as architectural compositions that affect natural light and thus qualitatively influence our experience of the structure and the architectural work as a whole. In a wider perspective, the discussion concerns the relationship between architectural tectonics and the corresponding architectural spaces, and our experience of enjoyment when confronted by both. Kenneth Frampton understands this relationship when he says of the Pavilion that 'the architectonic form of the structure was once more to reinforce the spatial system'.[121]

Contextuality vs. the mechanical

Leaving the particular relationship that exists between structural form and the practical requirements of the architectonic space, let us now study three structures primarily given form and shape by the prevailing design idea. Without necessarily being assigned certain utility functions relating to the space, those structures support not only loads but also the weight of the architectural concept. The structure may directly follow up on the shape of the building, describing the lines of its volumes; more abstractly, the structure is designed to support or strengthen the visual character intended for the building. In both cases, in order to reach understanding we will have to consider the structure in a context of the fundamental design decisions for the whole work.

Viennese liberality

This extension of a law firm's offices in Vienna was designed by Coop-Himmelb(l)au and engineered by Oskar Graf. The roof-top remodelling was finished in 1988. Rather than being based on rational (from a mechanical point of view) structural decisions, the present work deconstructs commonly accepted ideas of structural organisation and efficiency (and architectural criticism) and puts them to the test. One striking feature of the exterior of this building, and indeed of a number of other deconstructivist buildings, is the absence of a geometrical order; this also applies to the structure. From a load-bearing point of view this can be problematic. For want of such an order, it is necessary to uncover a geometrical coherence where, as in the present case, no real *system* exists. Instead, we have to seek a geometry that has the potential for being employed structurally. Linguistically, a system is 'a group of related parts which work together forming a whole', indicating that any group of parts can be thought of a system if those parts work together in some way. By a *structural* system, however, we usually mean a system that comprises one or more structural types. Those basic types typically include trusses, arches, frames, beams, etc., which also represent clear structural actions. According to this definition it is difficult to think of the structural configuration of this particular building as a structural system. It is, rather, a *composition of elements having*

3.36 Roof-top remodelling, Falkestrasse, Vienna (1988). Architects Coop-Himmelb(l)au, structural engineer Oskar Graf. Early sketch.

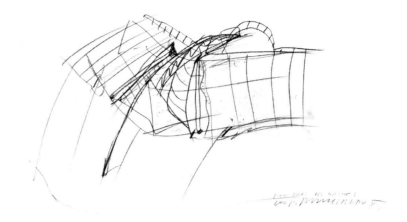

certain structural properties. In reality, then, the existence of a structural *system* is not a fundamental prerequisite for supporting and 'transmitting' loads. Loads use what material and geometries are at hand; the results are deformations and stresses according to the available load-paths and the properties of the materials. In fact, geometrically simple structural systems need not at all be the best way for loads to generate minimum force reactions. If set free in matter, loads will create load-paths that commonly have a much more complicated pattern than those we usually force them to take. Yet, to be able to confirm and trust the stability and strength of a supporting structure by doing a structural analysis, some geometrical coherence is a necessity. However, a preference for lucid and relatively simple structural geometries is not as important as it was in the age before the computer.

Deconstructivist architecture often employs what look like structural elements as objects to help constitute the architectural space, establishing spatial relationships and architectural expressions by a collage of steel profiles, folding plates, curved members, projecting slabs, etc. We should look for the structural potential of form in general, rather than expect the application of easily surveyed structural systems, when approaching architectural works of this kind. Hence, one strategy when trying to make sense of deconstructivist architecture from a structural point of view is to look for connections between the bits and the parts that may offer a structural geometry. This, incidentally, is a true de-construction of form, with the aim of making it possible for us to perceive and articulate a coherent understanding of the structure.

In the case of the present building, we quickly spot what might be termed a spine, an assemblage of steel profiles in a skewed plane that cuts right through the project, forming a line of symmetry – well, something that resembles symmetry. This is obviously a structural element. In hierarchical terms it is a primary structural element, acting as support for a series of secondary steel beams. The most spectacular feature of this structural spine is the thin curving line formed by a steel rod that binds

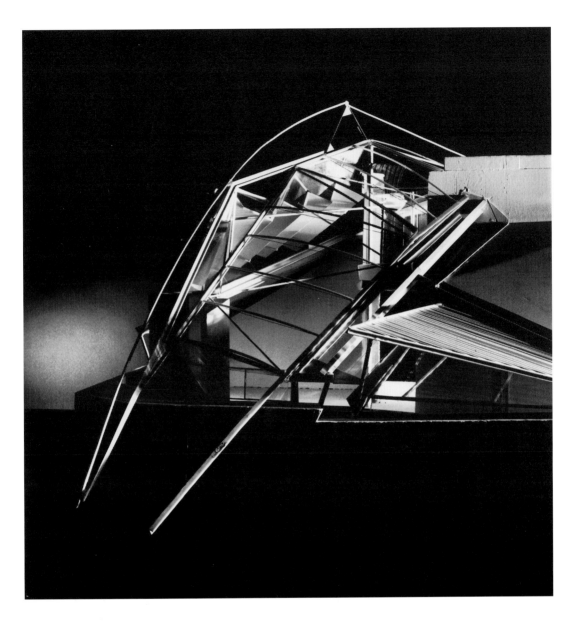

the different members together. However, when trying to see this composition of steel members from a point of view of structural mechanics,
the experience is confusing. One aspect of the curved rod is that it can
definitely be seen as load-bearing. As a top member of a beam or a
truss it looks familiar and yet, in the present case, also strange. At that
particular position in a truss we would expect the member to be in
compression, but its curvature and slenderness prohibit such an interpretation. It would quite simply not support significant loads. Well over
the 'ridge', the member straightens out and reads suddenly more like
a tension rod with a turnbuckle, and being properly fixed at the end.

3.37 Roof-top remodelling,
Falkestrasse, Vienna. Model of roof
structures.

Midway, however, the rod is intercepted by another thin steel member, the thinness hinting at tension, but taking its shortness into account this particular member reads as a compression strut supporting the dead-load of the straight part of the rod above.

Disregarding any possible supporting function of the curved top member of the composition of steel profiles, we seek some sort of coherence of structural lines in the remaining assemblage. We can work out a configuration that might form a truss, but as this truss approaches the left side of the 'ridge', which also represents a line of support, the triangulation of the truss ends abruptly and is supplemented by a piece of coupled steel profiles, suddenly introducing bending. If seen as one truss spanning from the edge of the roof onto the central column, this absence of triangulation is quite meaningless. There is another interpretation or conceptualisation, however, that will help us to see a coherence among possible structural lines, and the key to it is the inserted double profile. This is in fact where one structural unit stops and another takes over. The truss spanning from the edge of the roof is supported by a cantilevering bracket, formed as a triangle, projecting out from the top of the central column.[122] This is the reason for the presence of the straight tension rod described above; it is resisting the tension force generated by the cantilevering bracket. The thicker profile beneath this rod is the corresponding compression part of this load-bearing arrangement. The double profile of the inserted piece suddenly starts to make sense as providing the necessary cross-sectional thickness to cope with the shear force at work. A structural logic among the different profiles can now be established: most of the 'spine' elements seem to have a load-bearing function except for the thin, curving rod that draws a demarcation line around the whole structural composition. The rod also projects out from the edge of the roof, hovering over the street below as it connects with other steel profiles to bring the composition to an end.

We might ask: is the complexity of structural pathways and the absence of a structural system visually disturbing? Does this prevent us from appreciating the composition as a structure? The answer is no, and the reason for this is that both the great intensity of the lines and the ambiguous character of the structure add to the experience of a 'high-energy' work of architecture. Wolf Prix once said that 'structures, although metaphors for forces, follow another force, not of weight, but of energy'.[123] We experience the structure here, distorted as it is, as being highly appropriate for an equally distorted spatial configuration. A regular, geometrically simpler structure, if at all possible, would probably have weakened that particular spatial quality. The particularities of this structure relate to its spatial function, namely that its form is intended to express a specific conception of the space. In the words of the engineer Oskar Graf: 'The structure follows the architectural requirements, and if the structure is good, it supports the statement made by the architecture.'[124] We should thus interpret the structure as

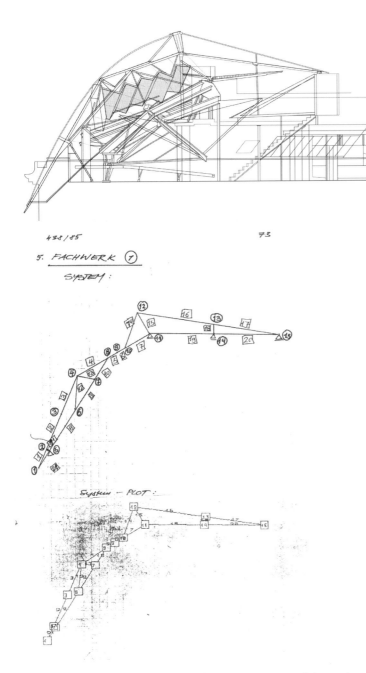

3.38 Roof-top remodelling, Falkestrasse, Vienna. Section showing the thin arc as a prominent part of the structural composition.

3.39 Roof-top remodelling, Falkestrasse, Vienna. Analysis by Oskar Graf of the main structure. Even though it is part of the structural configuration, the arc has no structural function.

being part of an integrated design where we cannot explain, understand or therefore appreciate structural form without recognising its strong co-dependence with the particular character of the architectonic space. Our perception of coherence in the congruence of the structure to the particularities of the architectonic space offers a pleasurable aesthetic experience. The structure's contextuality (adaptation to context), like its iconographic ambitions, exists *solely* to be aesthetically

3.40 Roof-top remodelling,
Falkestrasse, Vienna. Interior view.

experienced. It has no practical function, but nevertheless offers a concept whereby we can understand structural form.

What is the real significance of those structures? Geoffrey Broadbent,
commenting on this building as well as on other Coop-Himmelb(l)au
projects, suggests that 'what is being "deconstructed" in terms of
structures is nothing more nor less than the desiccated precision of
High-Tech'.[125] It is, however, more profound than that. These structures challenge the very paradigm of mechanical efficiency, the ideal
that sees structural and technological efficiency as intrinsic to quality
of structural form and thus to architectural quality. High-Tech architecture tends to emphasise structural efficiency, minimum weight, at the
expense of the more balanced and wholesome concept of mechanical efficiency, which posits the idea of an *appropriate* technological
level. *The structures of the present building, however, disregard both
aspects of efficiency, turning structural form into a question of spatial composition.* Still, the frivolity of the structural form might have its
own logic resulting from the properties of the material it uses: if it reinforces the architectonic idea, why not take advantage of the potential
of some structural materials to adapt to 'almost any form'? This, as I

mentioned earlier (page 47), is a property of bi-directional materials, which can (in principle) resist all kinds of force reactions. In such a case, throwing structural and technological efficiency to the wind, all that remains are questions of stable geometrical configurations and structural dimensions. This offers a particular freedom of structural form, where complexity and ambiguity are seen as desirable.[126] We may think of it as a shift of concerns from *structural systems* to *structural compositions*. This can be an especially interesting option when the structural scale is relatively small.

BMW branding

Like many international corporations, car manufacturers BMW see the potential of architecture as an important means of promoting their brand. In order for a building to act as a huge advertisement for the qualities BMW wish car buyers to think are intrinsic to their cars, they have tentatively tried to translate their values, competence and visions into three-dimensional structures, commissioning ABB Architekten with Bernhard Franken to design several exhibition pavilions. The IAA 2001 pavilion in Frankfurt, named Dynaform and engineered by Bollinger + Grohmann, features a long, curved building that aims to express movement and 'the joy of driving'. The basic geometry of the building attempts to visualise the Doppler effect associated with our experiences of the sound of cars approaching or retreating.[127] A computer-generated form based on sound waves as a physical phenomenon is perhaps somewhat obscure. Can the resulting geometry readily cope with the functional and structural requirements?

The roof has an interesting undulating form which immediately reads as a roof structure making use of shell action. This is noticeable in the digitally rendered volume drawings as well as the finished building. The wave-like roof very clearly hints that structural stiffness is created by the curved shapes, if made in a suitable material. Even more importantly, having an undulating structure with ridges running along the length of the building will be expressive of the architectural idea and strengthening our experience of movement through the space. This will make the structure seem part of the same visual context as the architectural space. In the present building, however, this is unfortunately not the case. The structure actually cuts transversally through the computer-generated building shape, forming so-called 'dynaframes' – heavy, irregular Vierendeel structures clad on the outside in white, fibreglass fabric. Rather than emphasising longitudinal movement, the structure seems to obstruct it. 'Our focus is on the spatial rather the details', says Bernhard Franken, 'and where possible, all traces of structure are hidden.'[128] In the present case the opposite is true, as the structure attracts considerable visual attention.

Designing the structure to follow the particularly irregular shape of

3.41 IAA pavilion 'Dynaform' (2001), Frankfurt. ABB Architects with Bernhard Franken, structural engineers Bollinger + Grohmann.

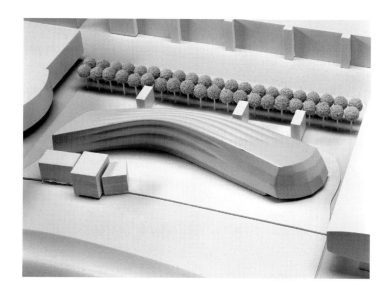

3.42 IAA pavilion 'Dynaform'. Detail of the structure.

the building section also creates complexity that greatly complicates its manufacture. Vierendeel frames are not particularly efficient, resisting loads by structural members being subjected to bending rather than axial forces, as is the case with a truss. An awareness of structural or technological efficiency, however, has clearly not informed the design

3.43 IAA pavilion 'Dynaform'. Interior view.

decisions. Acknowledging that spanning longitudinally by way of shell action might have proved difficult, and that intermediate supports at appropriate intervals would have been called for, the present solution is still quite problematic. The technological dilemmas resulting from the high complexity of form have been to a certain extent diminished by advanced manufacturing methods, as the structural sections were welded together from pieces machined out of steel plate by computer-controlled cutters. Still, a design method that derives architectural form from a rather abstract 'free form' generated by computer drawings is likely to discover that the process of form-finding itself does not feed adequate information back to help create an efficient structure. The design method is not likely to be iterative but depends entirely on some concept or idea unrelated to either utility or support functions.

In the case of the BMW pavilion, the resulting structure may not appear particularly pleasing. If our starting conception of the structure is that it is designed for support, it is quite impossible to see the qualities of the rather awkward shape and profile of the frames. We cannot understand and appreciate the structural design decisions from that point of view, because the form does not correspond with a reasonably efficient geometry for 'transmitting' forces. Instead, the structural form in this case closely follows the shape generated to express a particular spatial idea, and we should best consider the structure from this point of view. And here arises the real problem: we might be happy with a structure that is fundamentally inefficient *if this serves other architectural purposes*. This is unfortunately not the case here. It is not easy to see what qualities the structure offers the space, or in what way the structure expresses or reinforces broader architectural aims. The scale is quite simply too large to prevent the transversal frames from hindering the visual movement. Thus the intention of a fluid and dynamic space suffers from the choice of structure. In the present building there is a conflict between the spatial and the mechanical aspects.

Unlike the BMW project, even if designers of structures ignore conventional (pro efficiency) wisdom, we shall see that 'free-form' architecture can still convincingly mix and integrate the parameters of space, structure and exterior shape to express the same underlying idea. The Chemnitz Stadium project is an illustration of this, although our response will have to be based on drawings and models only, since it has not yet been built. So how can we aesthetically experience a building not perceived spatially at full scale? Anyone who is engaged in the design and construction of buildings knows that the finished job can give us one or two surprises, compared to what we might anticipate from the design material. However, it is from this material that design decisions are made, and those decisions are reached by using whatever ability we might have to imagine and empathise. A discussion of aesthetic matters based on *representations* of an actual work is of course standard among practising architects as well as teachers and students of architecture (and readers of architectural books). There can be, therefore, no major objections to the principle of analysing our experience of the *design material*, bearing in mind that our experience will not necessarily be the same as when we look at or walk around the finished building.

The Chemnitz lessons

For anyone who is interested in an occasional liberation of structure forms from the paradigms of mechanical efficiency and of minimal solutions, the Chemnitz Stadium project (competition 1997) is well worth a close look. It is a formidable lesson in how highly skilled architects and engineers can help us question our deep-rooted belief that visual quality somehow is intrinsic to and results only from highly efficient structural designs, and then substitute a set of quite different design criteria. The result is a compelling experience of architectural enjoyment and aesthetic satisfaction. In this project we should indeed look at structural form in terms of its architectural context, and not as a manifestation of the dogma of 'forces following the shortest route to the ground'. The structure contributes along very particular lines to the development of the space; we should therefore seek to understand and appreciate how it does so, and not necessarily judge it on mechanical performance.

'The focus of our work', Königs Architects say, 'is to find a powerful combination of architectural theory and practice' – as illustrated in their prize-winning work on the Chemnitz Stadium competition.[129] For a project where 'forms have developed in an evolutionary process, both from an architectural and a structural point of view', there could be no more suitable engineer than Cecil Balmond.[130] With him, architects Peter Kulka and Ulrich Königs created a well-considered synthesis of

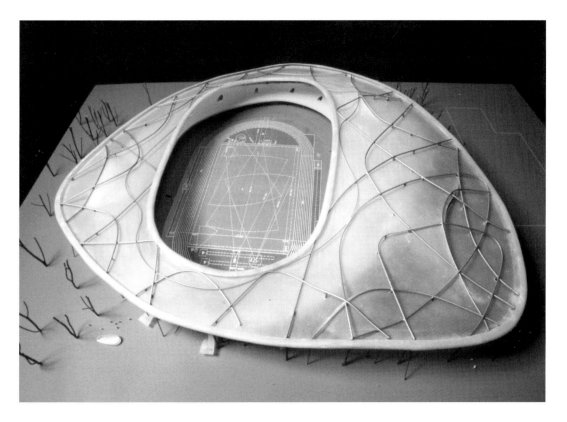

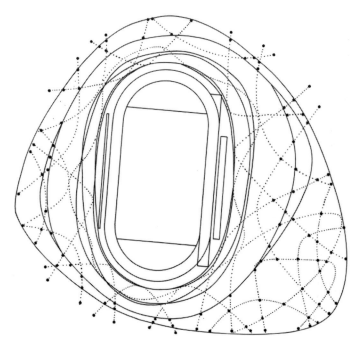

3.44 Chemnitz Stadium project, Germany (competition 1997), Chemnitz, Germany. Peter Kulka Architektur and Königs Architects, structural engineer Cecil Balmond. Model: roof structure with curved beams.

3.45 Chemnitz Stadium project. Plan.

3.46 Chemnitz Stadium project.
Sketches by Cecil Balmond analysing
structural options and structural
behaviour.

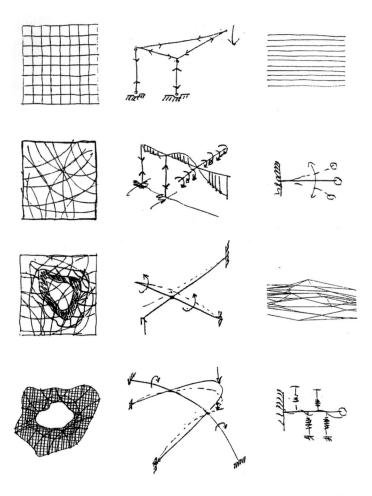

structures and architectural spaces, arranged in a topology of different layers. A point of theoretical reference for the relationship between structure and space is Balmond's influential book on the 'informal'.[131] Although it had not yet been published in 1997, his theories were no doubt well developed in his own mind and must have influenced the solution presented for the Chemnitz Stadium. Indeed, in *informal* Balmond gives an account of the design process and points out the attitudes and beliefs that were the guiding principles for his decisions on structures and structural form. The project is very clearly anchored in Balmond's theoretical reflections that guide the 'evolutionary process' of the design in a definite direction.

This poses an interesting problem for us as observers. All the published theories and commentary (including the designers' own verbal explanations and presentation of their aims) concerning this project – or at least the structural issues it addresses – will no doubt influence those observers familiar with it when they make their own interpretation of what they see. We are directed what to look for and how we should understand what we see. Is this an asset or a problem? The present case is an example of how theoretical statements about the design become part of the existing project documentation. Such statements obviously cast light on the designer's intentions, but in most cases such statements just do not exist; or if they do, they are not necessarily adequate or explanatory. For a long while there has been a debate – still ongoing – about the role of intention in the interpretation of art works.[132] Although we are not dealing with works of art here, the position articulated by Wittgenstein is very à propos when he says that 'an intention is embedded in its situation, in human customs and institutions', and thereby points out that the notion of intention should not necessarily be tied up with the private wishes of an individual practitioner.[133] 'Intention' can mean at least two things. To distinguish one from the other, the latter has been called 'private intentions', while 'intention' as Wittgenstein refers to it is called 'institutional intentions'.[134] Wittgenstein uses the terms 'practice', 'custom' and 'institution' interchangeably. Familiarity with the relevant practice, 'including the concepts which help to constitute the practice, is a necessary condition for the possibility of experiencing objects of art'.[135] If this notion of intention is aesthetically relevant for the arts, then it probably equally applies to the visual appreciation of structures. Intention in Wittgenstein's sense is rather institutional than private: that is, it may be 'uncovered' by interpretation of the actual work without the observer having to find out the designer's wishes. In principle, all the observer needs to know is the situation or practice of which the work is a part, which as always in this book means familiarity with structures and architecture. In the specific case of the Chemnitz Stadium I will therefore try to base my analysis on the visual material present, the architectural project itself, rather than leaning too heavily on written statements. I will look for 'institutional intentions' and make my interpretations from what we can actually see. The designers' factual descriptions of what is actually taking place in the project are helpful, though, as we can only access it through the project material.

The three main elements comprising the stadium architecture are the track with the lower seating, the main tier and the 'free-form' roof. The elements appear as layered rings having different functions. A large number of scattered columns connect these elements visually, but they do not really belong to either of them. In an early phase of the design process, the elements were metaphorically thought of as the Earth, 'the floating object' and the Cloud, with a Forest of columns growing in-between. The design strategy has sought to maintain the geometric and visual independence of each element, the project appearing to be the result of a seemingly random overlay of the different elements. Concentrating on the roof and its support, we notice that some of the numerous columns are vertical, some are inclined. Since the roof is undulating, the columns have somewhat different lengths, but it is more important that their thicknesses seem to vary greatly in proportion to the loads each

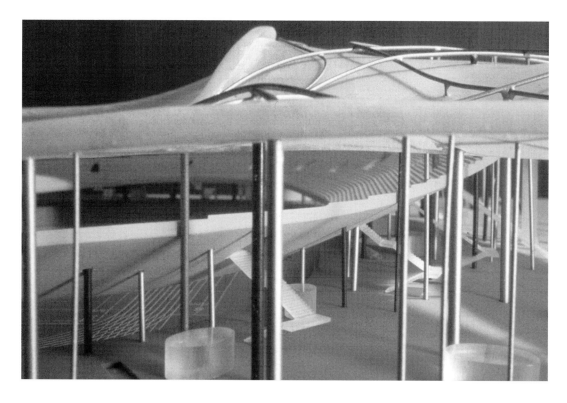

3.47 Chemnitz Stadium project. Model: roof structure supported on slender columns.

supports. This might reflect the differences of the intervals between the columns or, more probably, differences of compression forces acting as a result of their supporting continuous roof beams in bending.

If we consider the columns as solely the result of a design informed by scientific and technological concepts they will be difficult for us to appreciate, because efficiency is the essence of mechanical matters, and this is hardly a dominant feature of the columns here. The columns' scattered positioning, varying inclinations and thicknesses make the project much more complex. The columns also inform us of a far from straightforward roof structure above. The key to our interest and appreciation of these things, then, is for us to see and understand the columns' contribution to the apparent randomness of the overall design.[136] We can see that the columns play an important part in maintaining and strengthening the visual freedom and independence of the three rings. The column structures share in the same freedom as the primary spatial elements in order to prevent them from stiffly regulating the space by dividing it into equal compartments. This would ruin the effect of a floating, free-form composition. Instead, the structures seem equally as arbitrary as the spatial volumes. Once we are aware of this, we can see them in a different light. No longer restricted to bearing witness to an optimum solution, the column structures join forces with other architectural elements to create a stunning and dynamic sequence of interwoven spaces.

And yet, all the columns relate directly to fixed points in the ground as well as to points in the peculiar roof structure. As a pattern, the columns' footprints are invisible. Connecting the foundations with the points of roof support, no regular column grid is apparent. Balmond tells us there is an order, but the eye cannot trace it. Studying the roof structure, the reason for the differences in intervals between the columns becomes perceptible. The highly irregular network of curving roof beams is supported where thought necessary, and no fixed distance between points of support appears as a logical outcome of the network geometry. The overriding idea is obviously to provide support so that each curved beam becomes continuous and can span from the outer perimeter to the inner before curving back to a new position. The beams follow what resemble overlapping ballistic paths, although in more or less horizontal movements. This is an ingenious way of covering the roof surface with beams that only occasionally need to be supported by columns resting on the main tier, thus resulting in a possible obstruction of the view, while still maintaining the stiffness and strength necessary to carry loads. From a structural point of view, we appreciate the logic behind this design and admire its functional qualities. The design concept solves a practical problem. It comes at a cost, however, in terms of mechanical efficiency. The curved shapes of the tubular beams no doubt result in substantial bending and torsion, adding weight to the roof structure as a whole. Besides, the manufacturing of the tubes with spatial curvature, as well as the actual construction work, points to less technological efficiency than would be thought appropriate for similar buildings. Seen as a large-scale structural system from a mechanical point of view, the relatively low structural efficiency (bending and torsion) as well as the geometrical complexity of the roof structure are not overly appropriate.

Again, structural form and design in this case is more a matter of architectural context. If we want to appreciate and really understand the structure we should see the structure from this point of view. The disposition of the curved roof beams is, up to a point, akin to Nervi's beams in the Palace of Labour that follow isostatic lines. Rather than following optimum force paths, though, the roof structure of the Chemnitz Stadium follows another logic and thereby solves a visual problem in addition to providing support: the undulating, irregular plane of the roof surface calls for a structure with the same character. More than simply adapting to a given form, the structure draws lines along the surface which in some areas actually define its movements and help us to perceive better its spatiality. In other words, the structure seems most appropriate for purpose when looked at from the point of view of its spatial function.

The Chemnitz project introduces the metaphors of earth, forest and cloud as ways of explaining the basic design concept; clearly, too, they gave focus to the development of the design. Metaphors can also help observers of architecture to understand certain aspects of the structures they see, or to imagine things that are not really there. Architects also sometimes deliberately shape structural elements so as to *resemble* objects that are not present in reality.

Iconography vs. the mechanical

How does a structural form act representationally? In what way can we see that the structural form stands for, or represents, something outside of itself? This is obviously not a part of the structure's mechanical or spatial utility functions. While not motivated by reasons of utility, its representationality can still be thought of as a *function* coexistent with functions of a more pragmatic nature.

From a semiotic point of view, we might perceive and interpret all aspects of structural form as signs of some kind of function. One example would be the gradual decrease of the beam height of a cantilever towards its outer end, which we might see as a sign, or rather an index, of a particular stress condition. Another, as we have seen, is that the best interpretation of the shape of beams at the Menil Collection takes account of the conditions for natural light. I will not, however, discuss semiotic theories in order to describe aspects of our aesthetic experiences of structural form: I want to avoid another level of abstraction that could make an understanding of structures less easily accessible.

In this section I want to address the *intentional likeness* of a structural form (or part of it) *to another object or phenomenon*, without which the structure is unintelligible. This structural aspect therefore differs from others through the absence of any direct, existential connection with that which generates the form. The connection is purely representational, and the representation is by way of likeness. What, then, is meant by 'likeness', and what are the implications of likeness for aesthetic experience? The structure must have a sufficiently similar form or shape as that other thing to enable us to see the structure as a representation of it. In such a case we may speak of the structure as an icon. Imitation or copying, Scruton says, is different from representation, but imitation 'becomes representational when knowledge of the thing imitated is an essential part of true architectural understanding'.[137] There are certainly examples of architectural structures where an aesthetic understanding is quite simply not possible *unless* we have a knowledge of an object or a phenomenon outside of the structure, which the structure can be seen to represent, and which constitutes the concept through which the structure must be seen in order to be aesthetically appreciated. This might apply when mechanical or utility aspects alone do not seem to make sense visually. Even if representation in such cases is not the *only* route to aesthetic understanding, a conception of the structure as representing something outside of or beyond itself may enrich and deepen our experience. This is the case for the structures of the Concert Hall

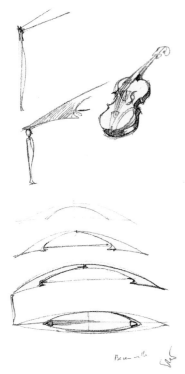

3.48 Community Centre (1988), Suhr, Switzerland. Architect and engineer Santiago Calatrava. Structures for the concert hall.

in the Community Centre of Suhr, Switzerland, by Santiago Calatrava (1988). Here, mechanical aspects have partly become subordinate to formal concerns of another kind: the softly curving shapes of the steel box girders, together with chromium-plated steel cables, create an image of the roof structures as huge stringed instruments. In the words of Calatrava: 'The roof should echo something musical.'[138] We cannot appreciate all aspects of the structural form unless we can see the structures as Calatrava suggests. That the representation is not 'complete', to use Scruton's term, should not be an argument to exclude the idea of representation: we are not fooled into believing that the structure *becomes* 'the mask which it tries to wear'.[139] Such credulity is not a prerequisite for our ability to 'see something *as* something'; on the contrary, imaginative conception allows for a virtual reality.

Before entering into a longer discussion of a structure, I would like to make clear the difference between conceptions that are either *iconographic* (our ability to see something as something else owing to its marked likeness to that other thing) or merely *associative*. Association is not restricted to likeness: we may associate motorways with cars, even though there is no likeness of form or shape, but the mental operation needed to see something as something which it is not – invoking iconography as a concept for understanding structures – demands that likeness.

Stuttgart's white forest

Entering the Terminal 1 building (1991) of Stuttgart Airport is like coming into a forest of artificial trees. The steel columns of the building (by architects von Gerkan and Marg) branch out while stretching up to reach the roof. Resting on the tree structures, the roof is a sloping steel grid of beams which rises towards the departure level and creates roof heights for a number of staggered floors in the hall. In the main hall there are 12 huge structural 'trees', each supporting a part of the roof separated by glass skylights.

The idea of modelling structures and other architectural elements on forms found in nature is not new. For structures in particular, the usual purpose of mimicking natural forms is to achieve the same efficiency as do objects whose shapes grow naturally. We know that nature makes use of its materials to the best advantage of the particular functions of each genus, and by copying its forms we might try to obtain the same optimum results. Rarely, however, will we find instances where nature presents us with models whose functional requirements are similar to those of structures. Take trees as an example: trees have forms and dimensions that allow them to sway in the wind, and the lack of rigidity is not considered a disadvantage. On the contrary: by being flexible, trees can resist high windloads. For structures in architecture, however, stiffness is of utmost importance in most cases, as excessive deflections

3.49 Stuttgart Airport Terminal 1 (1991). Architects von Gerkan, Marg and Partners, structural engineers Weidleplan Consulting. Interior.

will harm materials and secondary elements, besides severely limiting their use. Also the structure of natural trees does not support loads other than its own, and its purpose is to position the leaves to receive as much sunlight as possible. Hence the uppermost branches can be very thin and swing freely, even in a light wind. The artificial tree structures we meet in architecture, on the other hand, usually support heavy roof loads that affect the top struts or branches more or less the same way as they do the lower sets of supporting elements. Besides, structural trees are not the results of natural growth, but take great effort to mould, assemble or construct. The requirements for trees and tree structures are hence very different, and we cannot expect to obtain the same mechanical efficiency. 'In its more intelligent form', Alan Holgate says, 'the nature analogy simply proposes natural forms as a source of inspiration', by which it might be possible to 'recognize some correspondence between the purposes of a biological structure' and our own aims for a structure.[140] In such a case, the likeness need not be superfluous because both may express a particular principle or idea that structures and nature may have in common. Still, structures that mimic natural trees are not infrequent in architecture, and it makes sense to discuss their merits.

What can we say about our aesthetic experiences of structures shaped as trees? In Stuttgart Airport Terminal 1, they are so dominating that it is impossible to experience the space without being acutely aware of their distinctive shape. As always, when perceiving structures we need to see them as such; this means that they have a supporting function to fulfil. It is easy to understand and appreciate that a fundamental requirement of the tree structures is that they support the huge roof while at the same time allowing clear passage for busy pedestrian traffic and the many other activities at floor level. The tree 'trunk' collects the loads from many 'branches', reducing the number of potentially obstructive supporting structures. Conversely, the roof is supported by a large number of structural members, thus reducing the free span of the roof structures. The result is a pleasing two-way grid of beams with quite modest structural dimensions. While the ends are admirable, from a mechanical point of view we must question the means. As the tubular compression struts branch out in many directions and increase in number, both structural and technological efficiency are reduced. Many struts mean more material, and the increasing angle by which they tilt as they branch out means larger forces to be carried. In fact, the outer struts carry the largest forces at the point where they are supposed to represent the thinnest, most fragile branches. Their length is also greater than the others because they need to reach out the farthest. This aspect of the structural form, then, is a case where the mechanical function does not fit very well with the tree analogy, and we are conscious of a certain lack of coherence between form and mechanical content. Besides, the large number of compression struts connecting at varying angles calls for an equally large number of structural connections of complex geometries, making the use of technology also less efficient. In the present case, those connections are specially made cast steel joints welded to the tubes at both ends.

3.50 Stuttgart airport, Terminal 1. Column-to-roof connections.

3.51 Stuttgart airport, Terminal 1.
Detail of cast steel joint.

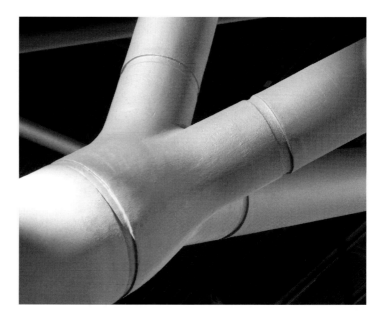

The roof beams obviously also act as tension members connecting the upper set of 'branches' horizontally. This establishes triangular structural forms and renders those struts axially loaded. At lower levels, however, the struts hover in the air without horizontal support, and bending is introduced. There are ways this might have been avoided, involving a form of trussing, but this would have meant dispensing with the tree iconography. If we accept the tree as a premise of the design we will have to bear the reduced-efficiency consequences, a design not entirely satisfactory from a mechanical point of view.

It is, on the other hand, perfectly legitimate to perceive these particular structures from another point of view and still see them as structures. They certainly meet their mechanical requirements, but they should also be seen as spatial elements that contribute to the qualities of the space. It is when we *think* of the structures as trees that their qualities are most obvious, even though the two ways of seeing them (mechanical/spatial) are partly contradictory and make the structures ambiguous. Seen as trees, we enjoy how naturally the thickness of the branches decreases as they seem to reach up to the roof. They quite simply resemble trees to a degree that we fully accept, and seeing them filtering the sunlight completes the impression of an artificial, pleasant forest. The material and the colour are different from real trees and help to prevent us getting the impression that we are being deceived, that we are being fooled into believing that we are actually looking at real trees. Yet, even though the roof is structurally quite slender it still represents a huge visual mass in the treetops. Perhaps structural trees are even better-suited to situations where they support a glass roof, in which case the likeness to nature will be more striking.

3.52 Stuttgart Airport, Terminal 1.
The tree structure.

3.53 Lofoten Aquarium (1989), Lofoten, Norway. Architects Blå Strek, structural engineers Fossum. View of the location.

Vernacular representation: roof structures with a local flavour

In our last example, any discussion of our aesthetic experience requires, above all, that we see its mechanical and representational aspects in confrontation. As I will try to show, a contemporary understanding of rational structural behaviour makes this structure quite incomprehensible. We can only aesthetically understand it iconographically, as a reference to a local and historical building tradition.

This aquarium building is located in the archipelago of Lofoten, in the north of Norway, a group of islands that stretches far out from the mainland into the Norwegian Sea.[141] This is an area of extremely rich fisheries, and has been so since prehistoric times. The aquarium (1989) houses an ample collection of fishes and sea animals from the northern cold waters. Central to the overall concept is the inspiration of 'the built image of Lofoten',[142] with its wharf structures as well as the structures used to hang up fish and dry fishing nets. There are two distinct volumes that form the main parts of the aquarium: a flat-roofed, curved volume containing the fish tanks, and a higher volume dominated by a double-pitched, wooden roof structure of a quite modest span. This part contains the entrance hall, a cafeteria and the circulation area. The roof covers a width of slightly less than 7 m, and is also supported by a central row of columns. This roof structure is the main object of our interest.

When we look at it, we see numerous wooden members crisscross-ing the span, all running at different angles between the vertical and the horizontal. The members all have more or less the same dimensions, and it is hard to identify an order whereby some have a more signifi-cant supporting function than the others. In fact, the structure does not read as a system, nor indeed as *one* system: seeing the structure as a mechanical device for the 'transmission' of forces is a confusing experi-ence. The apparent absence of a hierarchical structural order makes it difficult to see and understand the load path. Statically speaking, it is only when we realise that we are not confronting a system but rather what Tom F. Peters calls an 'overlay' that the structure begins to make sense mechanically.[143] We can identify, by deconstructing elements that seem to coact, at least five different principles that, if taken separately, should be able to overspan the actual width with a slight modifica-tion of the dimensions of the members.[144] Hence the structure is highly redundant. As a first reaction it comes as a surprise, from a mechani-cal point of view, that the architects and engineers should deliberately want to introduce that kind of disorderliness. It seems inappropriate for the rather simple job it has to do.

There might be a reason, however, for that particular structural form: the roof resembles the traditional local structures used for the fisheries. Seeing this, we can have a different aesthetic experience. The struc-ture's reference to vernacular construction methods helps us to see that it represents a tradition, not in an abstract way, but as an icono-graphic representation of a traditional building structure used for the drying of fish and fishing nets.[145] These sheds or buildings were quite common in the coastal areas of Norway. The aquarium structure might very well 'stand for' or represent the complex, additive character, as well as a double-pitched form, of those traditional building structures. They quite often feature a somewhat haphazard cluster of architectural components, where structural members of the roof structure, members meant for horizontal bracing as well as the cladding material all mix up in a rich but confusing composition of elements. Such vernacular

3.54 Lofoten Aquarium. Elevation facing the sea.

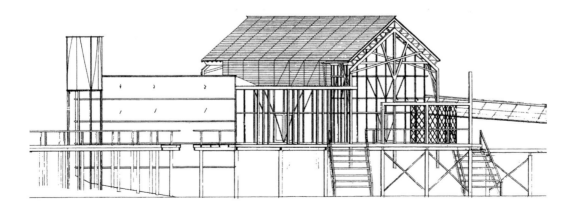

3.55 Lofoten Aquarium. Analytical drawing of the main roof structure.

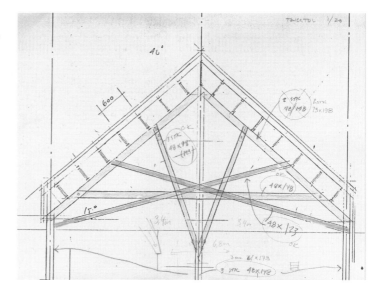

building structures will over time often become even more disorderly as the original materials and components are damaged and replaced by new and different ones. In the present case, an image of linear complexity is re-created, although in a modified form that applies only to the roof structure. Without seeing the structure as a representation of this traditional type of building structure, it makes little sense and its virtues go unnoticed.

In a wider historical and cultural context, we might notice a conceptual likeness of the present structure to certain historic structures erected without the aid of scientific verification methods. Such structures may show a striking lack of rational and efficient *system* thinking. Load-bearing capacity may instead be provided by an overlay of several supporting principles. Tom F. Peters writes of the principle of overlay that 'before the advent of modern statics, the traditional method

3.56 *(near left)* Lofoten Aquarium. Possible structural systems within the existing overlay. *All* might function separately.

3.57 *(far right)* The Knudsen shed, Haugesund, Norway. A structure for the drying of fish and fishing nets. Structure and cladding combine to convey an image of informal pragmatism that also suggests that appearances will change over time.

 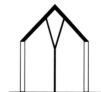

3.58 An old boat shed, Asker, Norway. A hotchpotch of elements from the main roof structure and bracing produce the richness and chaos of the visual language of this vernacular structure.

of creating ever-larger spans of greater loading capacity was to take a successful simple structure and overlay it with other, known simple structures'.[146] This is a useful piece of information that helps us to adjust our conception of the structural principles involved. Even if this particular structure is quite small, this piece of historical information may enable us to see it differently. Seen as an iconographic representation of a vernacular structure based on overlaying structural principles, the mechanical aspects of the structure also start to make some sense. Rather than seeing the structure as a meaningless hotchpotch of elements, we realise the need to identify the various structural principles involved. When we see those principles, our aesthetic experience of the structure's mechanical aspects will also change, and the roof structure can be aesthetically understood and appreciated.

Notes

Part 1 Philosophy: fundamental aspects of structures

1 'The primary functions of all structure' are 'to enclose space
   and to protect it from the natural elements'. 'Then too, every
   structure has a resistant function'. Eduardo Torroja, *Philosophy
   of Structures*, Berkeley and Los Angeles: University of California
   Press, 1958, p. 3.
2 Daniel L. Schodek, *Structures*, 2nd edn, Upper Saddle River, NJ:
   Prentice Hall, 1992, pp. 2, 3.
3 Angus Macdonald, *Structure and Architecture*, Oxford:
   Butterworth Architecture, 1994, p. 1.
4 See Bård Helland, 'Forholdet mellom konstruksjon og uttrykk i en
   fremtidig arkitektur', *Byggekunst*, no. 4, 2004.
5 Patrick Hodgkinson, 'An English Sensibility: The Making of an
   Architectural Technology' in Colin Davies, *Hopkins*, London:
   Phaidon, 1993, p. 163.
6 The idea of a duality of structures, called by different names, is
   not a new observation. Gottfried Semper stresses the technical
   and the symbolic aspects of construction, rephrased by Kenneth
   Frampton as ontological and representational aspects of tectonic
   form. The 'tectonic', admittedly, encompasses a wider range of
   architectural components than the load-bearing structure. See
   Kenneth Frampton, *Studies in Tectonic Culture: The Poetics of
   Construction in Nineteenth and Twentieth Century Architecture*,
   Cambridge, MA: MIT Press, 1995, pp. 16–19.
7 See *Architectural Review*, April 1988, no. 1094; *Domus*, May
   1987, no. 683; *Technique et Architecture*, Dec. 1988–Jan. 1989,
   no. 381.
8 Virginia Fairweather, *Expressing Structure: The Technology of
   Large-Scale Buildings*, Basel: Birkhäuser, 2004, p. 6.
9 Simon Unwin, *Analysing Architecture*, 2nd edn, London:
   Routledge, 2003, p. 161.
10 The application of statics, of theory, to structures is not an exact
   science, but depends on how well the actual structure correlates
   with the static model or mathematical model used. Bill Addis
   makes this very relevant point, and draws, somewhat surprisingly,
   the conclusion that statics is a branch of mathematics rather than
   a branch of the natural sciences. Bill Addis, *Structural Engineering:
   The Nature of Theory and Design*, Chichester: Ellis Horwood 1990,
   p. 59.

11 'In a building, an architect might wish to evoke something by association – a floor structure similar to the jack-arch structures ubiquitous in 19th century warehouses and mills, or a Roman barrel vault – with no intention that it should work structurally in the original manner.' Bill Addis, *The Art of the Structural Engineer*, London: Artemis, 1994, p. 10.

12 Iconography, from the Greek *eikon*, meaning 'likeness', and *graphein*, to reproduce in lines, to write or to describe. The term is used here in a meaning similar to the one employed by art historians, where iconography deals with the different meaning content that might be attributed or programmed into art works by the use of certain recognisable visual features. The American philosopher C. S. Peirce also employs the notion of the 'icon' as one of three different categories of 'signs', namely the symbol, the index and the icon. The last is defined as a sign which has a likeness to or similar characteristics to the object to which it refers. See Justus Buchler, *Philosophical Writings of Peirce*, New York: Dover Publications, 1955, p. 102.

13 Robert Mark and David Billington, 'Structural Imperative and the Origin of New Form' in *Technology and Culture*, vol. 30, no. 2, April 1989.

14 Macdonald, *op. cit.*, p. ix.

15 Bill Addis, 'Free Will and Determinism in the Conception of Structures' in *Journal of the International Association for Shell and Spatial Structures*, vol. 38, no. 2, 1997, p. 83.

16 Macdonald, *op. cit.*, p. ix.

17 D. Billington, *The Tower and the Bridge: The New Art of Structural Engineering*, New York: Basic Books, 1983, pp. 5, 16.

18 A particularly interesting example in this respect is Alexander Baxandall's reflections on Benjamin Baker's Forth Bridge, where the point of departure is precisely that of seeing the bridge as a *historical* object. Alexander Baxandall, *Patterns of Intention: On the Historical Explanation of Pictures*, New Haven, CT: Yale University Press, 1985, pp. 12–36.

19 Well-known examples are Newton's first, second and third laws of dynamics.

20 G. H. von Wright, *Explanation and Understanding*, London: Routledge and Kegan Paul, 1971 (1975).

21 Billington, *op. cit.*, p. 9.

22 A view of the interaction between different ways of understanding technology is expressed by Hans Siggard Jensen: 'The difference between art's relationship to nature and technology's is that the artist and the work of art can be understood completely within the frameworks of intentional systems; technology and the technologist, however, necessarily share in an interaction with material systems. Such systems cannot be understood in

terms of intentionality, as tools at the service of a pure creation of the spirit, but precisely as tools *qua* (for instance) causality and functionality, and therefore in opposition to human intentionality.' H. Siggard Jensen, 'Formålenes rige Rige: Om teknologi og natur' in *Philosophia*, no. 3–4, 1991, pp. 65–79 (author's translation). This view stresses the causal and functional aspects of material systems, while tuning down the intentional aspects which are also present in the making of artefacts by technological means.

23 Tom F. Peters, 'How Creative Engineers Think' in *Civil Engineering*, March 1998, p. 48.

24 That the actual purpose may seem obvious to us is another matter. But then we are, after all, relying on our initial (and perhaps unconscious) interpretation.

Part 2 Pragmatics: structural form and some mechanical problems

1 The *Cambridge Encyclopedia of Philosophy*'s entry for *form* says this: 'Aristotle agreed that forms are closely tied to intelligibility, but denied their separate existence. Aristotle explains change and generation through a distinction between the form and matter of substances. A lump of bronze (matter) become a statue through its being molded into a certain shape (form).' Cambridge: Cambridge University Press, 1995, p. 271.

2 From the 'Dictionnaire', vol. 9, cited in Barry Bergdoll (introduction), *The Foundations of Architecture: Selections from the Dictionnaire raisonné*, New York: George Braziller, 1990, p. 28.

3 Ibid., p. 105.

4 Ibid., p. 33. Viollet-le-Duc's italics.

5 Ibid., p. 242.

6 Viollet-le-Duc, *Lectures on Architecture*, Vol. 2, New York: Dover Publications, 1987, p. 71.

7 Viollet-le-Duc in Bergdoll, *op. cit.*, p. 106.

8 Viollet-le-Duc, *Lectures on Architecture*, Vol. 1, New York: Dover Publications, 1987, p. 448.

9 Viollet-le-Duc in Bergdoll, *op. cit.*, p. 242.

10 Viollet-le-Duc, *Lectures*, Vol. 1, *op. cit.*, p. 459.

11 Viollet-le-Duc, *Lectures*, Vol. 2, *op. cit.*, plate VVi, pp. 64–5.

12 Viollet-le-Duc in Bergdoll, *op. cit.*, pp. 242, 243.

13 Ibid., p. 106.

14 Viollet-le-Duc, *Lectures*, Vol. 1, *op. cit.*, p. 452.

15 Edward R. Ford, *The Details of Modern Architecture, Vol. 2, 1928–1988*, Cambridge, MA: MIT Press, 1996, p. 1.

16 F. L. Wright, 'In the Cause of Architecture', first printed in *The Architectural Record*, March 1908. Reprinted in the book by the

same title, ed. Frederick Gutheim, New York: Architectural Record
Books, 1975, p. 55.

17 F. L. Wright, 'In the Cause of Architecture: The Meaning of
Materials' in *The Architectural Record*, 1928. Reprint in *op. cit.*,
pp. 171, 172.

18 Terry Patterson, *Frank Lloyd Wright and the Meaning of Materials*,
New York: Van Nostrand Reinhold, 1994, p. 240.

19 Wright, *op. cit.*, p. 198.

20 John Lobell, *Between Silence and Light: Spirit in the Architecture
of Louis I. Kahn*, Boston, MA: Shambhala Publications, 1979,
p. 40.

21 Ibid., p. 63.

22 Ibid., p. 40.

23 Arthur Schopenhauer, *The World as Will and Representation*, Vol.
1, New York: Dover Publications, 1966, p. 215.

24 Pier Luigi Nervi, *Aesthetics and Technology in Building*,
Cambridge, MA: Harvard University Press, 1965.

25 Ibid., p. 2.

26 Pier Luigi Nervi, *Structures*, New York: F. W. Dodge, 1956.

27 Nervi, *op. cit.* (1965), p. 3.

28 Ibid., p. 22.

29 Ibid., p. 185.

30 Ibid., p. 187.

31 Ford, *op. cit.*, p. 423.

32 This is particularly evident for synthetic composite materials, which
(at least in theory) may be manipulated at a molecular level to have
precisely the most suitable characteristics.

33 Bernard Tschumi, *Architecture and Disjunction*, Cambridge, MA
and London: MIT Press, 1994, p. 110.

34 Ibid., p. 252.

35 Ibid., p. 252.

36 Wolf Prix, 'On the Edge' in Peter Noever (ed.), *Architecture
in Transition: Between Deconstruction and New Modernism*,
Munich: Prestel Verlag, 1991, p. 20. Prix's italic.

37 Ibid., p. 19.

38 Ibid., p. 20.

39 Ibid., p. 18.

40 Wolf Prix in a conversation with the author, September 1996 in
Vienna.

41 Prix, *op. cit.*, p. 23.

42 Ibid., p. 24.

43 From a conversation with the author, September 1996 in Vienna.

44 B. Lindsey, *Digital Gehry: Material Resistance/Digital Construction*,
Basel, Boston, Berlin: Birkhäuser, 2001, p. 37.

45 Bernard Charles quoted in M. Friedman (ed.), *Gehry Talks:
Architecture + Process*, New York: Universe Publishing, 2002, p. 50.

46 J. Gilbert-Rolfe with F. Gehry, *Frank Gehry: The City and Music*, London and New York: Routledge, 2001, p. 13.

47 Significantly, one of the most influential thinkers on the philosophy of structures in architecture today, the engineer Cecil Balmond, hardly mentions materials at all as a basic requirement for structures. Indeed, he is very little concerned about structural form as such but investigates the creation of attitudes and approaches to the structure–architecture relationship. Still, the realisation of his ideas takes for granted materials with characteristics that enable 'a generating line of structure' to 'crank, flex or branch' or even where 'the idea of line disappears' and 'zones and surfaces take over'. Quoted from Cecil Balmond, *informal*, Munich, Berlin, London, New York: Prestel Verlag, 2002, p. 388.

48 'The unity of art and technology', says Curt Siegel, 'ought to be characteristic of contemporary architecture. Forms born of this union, with features derived from modern techniques of construction, are what we shall call "structural forms".' Siegel here includes some subjective requirements in his 'definition' of the term which I think are best avoided. See Curt Siegel, *Structure and Form in Modern Architecture*, Huntington, NY: Robert E. Krieger, 1975 (1962), p. 7.

49 See Macdonald, *op. cit.*, pp. 37, 38. Heinrich Engel first introduced the notion of form-active structures in his book *Structure Systems*, London: Iliffe Books, 1967.

50 Semi- and non-form-active structures will comprise what Engel calls 'vector-active' (i.e. trusses), 'bulk-active' (i.e. beams, frames) and 'surface-active' (i.e. shell) structures.

51 Heinrich Engel discriminates between 'structure systems' and 'structures' by denoting the former term 'orders and hence design PRINCIPLES' and the latter 'examples and hence design IMPLEMENTS'. See Engel, *op. cit.*

52 Ford, *op. cit.*, p. 21.

53 In the Tokyo project the engineers were anxious to avoid frames with excessive stiffness because of the earthquake risk. Adequate flexibility was achieved by the use of eccentrically braced frames.

54 For wood, this applies vis-à-vis stress and strength in the direction of the fibres.

55 See C. Davies and I. Lambot, *Century Tower: Foster Associates Build in Japan*, Berlin: Ernst and Sohn, 1992.

56 For the purpose of discussing material properties versus form, the idea of structural and technological properties seems to work well. In more common engineering taxonomy, terms like 'mechanical' (i.e. strength, ductility) and 'physical' (i.e. thermal, elastic) properties of materials are used. I have moved the classifications around a bit and also introduced new terms to clarify certain points.

57   See J. A. Charles and F. A. A. Crane, *Selection and Use of Engineering Materials*, 2nd edn, Oxford: Butterworth-Heinemann, 1989, p. 2.

58   I have chosen the term 'directional' rather than 'axial' because we are primarily interested in the material having, or not having, properties that enable it to resist tensile and/or compressive stresses along at least one axis, like wood. This means that it could just as well resist stresses along both axes, like textiles. The difference is really between a material that can resist stresses directed either out from it or in towards it, and one that can resist stresses acting both outwards and inwards. Bill Addis refers to materials that have only compression or tension strength as 'another way' of being 'non-linear'. See Addis, *op. cit.* (1994), p. 11.

59   In practical design, both the actual strength capacity and the elasticity of the material obviously influence the structural scale and dimensions, and may also affect the possibilities for structural form. Large, thin shells, for instance, or very slender columns are difficult to construct from materials having a low Young's modulus which greatly reduces the buckling capacity, even when the compressive strength is adequate.

60   Here we encounter a logical problem in that we are not necessarily speaking about materials as such, but *particular products* of basic materials. For those, the materials have already been given a certain form in the manufacturing process, and the resulting products have thus been assigned particular strength and stiffness properties. In this particular context (and with acknowledgements to Galileo for his important distinction between materials and structures/products made from a material), thinking about some products in the same way as we think about materials 'in themselves' is no more than a practical way of categorising certain products that frequently appear as ready components with characteristic structural properties.

61   Charles and Crane, *op. cit.*, p. 3.

62   See also Schodek, *op. cit.*, p. 4.

63   Bill Addis observes that 'some structures or structural forms will simply not work, or will work in some materials but not in others'. He discusses structural engineering as a conflict between determinism and free will, two concepts that hold a particular meaning when related to the two main groups of structural materials identified here. Addis, *op. cit.* (1997), p. 83.

64   *Architectural Review*, Sept. 1987, no. 1087, pp. 40–9.

65   Peter Rice, *An Engineer Imagines*, London: Artemis, 1993, p. 119.

66   Ibid., pp. 121–2.

67   David Billington made a study of this structure in D. Billington, *Robert Maillart and the Art of Reinforced Concrete*, Zurich and Munich: Artemis, 1990, pp. 28–31.

68 R. Collovà, 'Una piazza coperta' in Pierluigi Nicolin (ed.), *Lotus International*, no. 99, 1998, pp. 6–22.

69 Compare this structure with the roof structure of the terminal building for the Dulles Airport (1962), Virginia, by Eero Saarinen.

70 Probably a similar observation has led Tom Peters to suggest that 'the manufacturing criteria of materials' should replace the traditional 'material constraints' as the 'criteria that influenced the appearance of engineering structures', and thus also form the premises for a new 'aesthetics of process'. Tom Peters, '"Bridging the Gap": Point of Contact between the Architect and Engineer' in *Architronic*, vol. 9, 1992.

71 Addis, *op. cit.* (1997), pp. 83–9.

72 E. Partridge, *Origins: An Etymological Dictionary of Modern English*, London: Routledge and Kegan Paul, (1958) 1990.

73 Balmond, *op. cit.*, p. 122.

74 Christian Norberg-Schulz, *Meaning in Western Architecture*, New York: Rizzoli Publications, 1980, p. 24.

75 The stiffness-to-weight ratio is also clearly an expression of efficiency.

76 H. Seymour Howard Jr., *Structure: An Architect's Approach*, New York: McGraw Hill, 1966, p. 277.

77 P. R. Head, 'Construction Materials and Technology: A Look at the Future' in *Proceedings of the Institution of Civil Engineers* (online), vol. 144, 2001.

78 See M. F. Ashby, *Materials Selection in Mechanical Design*, Oxford: Pergamon Press, 1992, pp. 56 ff.; J. E. Gordon, *The Science of Structures and Materials*, New York: Scientific American Books, 1988, p. 51.

79 Considering this theoretically and comparing relative numbers, we ignore safety factors. ρ is (mass) density and σ_y is failure strength.

80 A spectacular exception is the titanium cladding of the Guggenheim Museum in Bilbao, Spain (1997) by architect Frank Gehry and engineers Skidmore, Owings and Merrill. This was due to an abrupt, and timely, fall in the price of titanium on the world market.

81 This principle is discussed in detail by Erik Reitzel in his *Fra brud til form: Om minimering og ressourceøkonomi*, Copenhagen: Polyteknisk Forlag, 1979.

82 The columns, however, are on their part quite efficient structural elements since the forces are primarily axial.

83 The notion of 'local efficiency' corresponds to what Macdonald calls 'the concept of "improved" cross-sections'. Macdonald, *op. cit.*, p. 39.

84 That the weight is strictly proportional to the beam height presupposes a rectangular cross-section with a constant width.

For a steel profile with flanges this may not be correct, but the tendency is obviously the same: less beam height means less weight.

85 These reflections do not take *deflections* into account as a problem that will influence the relative differences of weight between the beams.

86 The calculations require some simple integration of parabolic curves that is not shown here.

87 Ole Vangaard and Duelund Mortensen (eds), *Le Ricolais: Visions and Paradox*, Copenhagen: Kunstakademiets Arkitektskole, 1998, p. 28.

88 Heinrich Engel calls such structures 'vector-active' structures. H. Engel, *op. cit.*

89 Ariel Hanaor, *Principles of Structures*, Oxford: Blackwell Science, 1998, p. 110.

90 The arguments for this are quite similar to the explanations for indeterminate structures being susceptible to additional stresses as a result of (for example) uneven settlements of the supports, which is not the case for statically determinate structures. In order to pre-stress the system, there has to be redundancy.

91 Vangaard and Duelund Mortensen (eds), *op. cit.*, p. 24.

92 W. d'Arcy Thompson, *On Growth and Form*, Cambridge: Cambridge University Press, 1961, p. 17.

93 Such as 'large-scale housing development', 'human scale', etc. See C. Moore and G. Allen, *Dimensions*, New York: Architectural Record Books, 1976.

94 The actual proportion, however, can be such that the beam will have either adequate or inadequate strength and stiffness.

95 Examples are the wooden trusses that were designed for the structures of the Lillehammer Winter Olympics in 1994, where innovative jointing made it possible for a trussed wooden beam to span about 70 m.

96 See Robert Mark, *Light, Wind and Structure: The Mystery of the Master Builders*, Cambridge, MA: MIT Press, 1990.

97 Galileo Galilei, *Dialogues Concerning Two New Sciences*, New York: Dover Publications, 1954, pp. 123–32.

98 Andrea Palladio, *The Four Books of Architecture*, New York: Dover Publications, 1965, p. 67.

99 If we also consider the deflection of the beam, we will find that increasing all dimensions n times will result in a deflection n^2 times larger.

100 Galilei, *op. cit.*, p. 131.

101 In addition to the effect of increased stresses from dead weight in the larger scale, experiments show that the actual failure strength of materials decreases in inverse proportion to the scale of the structures (and hence section thicknesses).

102 The dynamic response of the structure also changes when the scale changes.

103 Schodek, *op. cit.*

104 Tom F. Peters, *Transitions in Engineering: Guillaume Henri Dufour and the Early 19th Century Cable Suspension Bridges*, Basel and Boston, MA: Birkhäuser Verlag, 1987, pp. 9–11.

105 After Jacob Leupold (1726), in ibid.

106 F. dal Co and K. W. Forster, *Frank O. Gehry: The Complete Works*, Milan: Electa Architecture, Phaidon Press, (1998) 2003.

107 There are no absolutes here. The eye is often fooled by the visual perception of weight and mass. A rectangular hollow section of steel can, for example, look heavier than a rolled I-beam of the same weight because of the assembled character of the flanges and web of the latter.

108 Named after the French engineer Camille Polonceau (1813–59), who suggested this type of system in 1840.

109 See P. Chemetov and B. Marrey, *Architectures à Paris 1848–1914*, Paris: Dunod, 1984, p. 188.

110 Two reference sources differ on this information: this is from Chemetov and Marrey, *op. cit.*; G. Behnisch and G. Hartung, *Eisenkonstruktionen des 19. Jahrhunderts*, Munich: Schirmer-Mosel, 1983, p. 106, states as designer Leonce Reynaud, engineer.

111 From Chemetov and Marrey, *op. cit.*, p. 48.

112 See Behnisch and Hartung, *op. cit.*, p. 106. The largest was probably the arched span of St Pancras station in London by Barlow and Ordish, built about the same time, with a free span of 73 m.

113 *Domus*, Sept. 1990, no. 719, pp. 66 ff.

114 Pier Luigi Nervi, *op. cit.* (1965), pp. 35, 36 and 90–6.

115 To distinguish between scientific and technological arguments, Alexander Zannos introduces the notion of the 'construction scale', and talks about correct and incorrect construction scales. See Alexander Zannos, *Form and Structure in Architecture: The Role of Statical Function*, New York: Van Nostrand Reinhold, 1987, pp. 123 ff.

Part 3 Aesthetics: an aesthetics of structures

1 'We put thirty spokes together and call it a wheel; / But it is on the space where there is nothing that the usefulness of the wheel depends. / We turn clay to make a vessel; / But it is on the space where there is nothing that the usefulness of the vessel depends. / We pierce doors and windows to make a house; / And it is on these spaces where there is nothing that the usefulness of the house depends. / Therefore just as we take advantage of what

is, we should recognize the usefulness of what is not.' Lao Tzu, tr. Arthur Waley, in *The Way and Its Power: A Study of the Tao Te Ching and Its Place in Chinese Thought*, London: Allen and Unwin, 1934, ch. 11.

2 Anthony C. Webster, 'Utility, Technology and Expression' in *Architectural Review*, Nov. 1992, p. 69.

3 The concept of 'aesthetic qualities' is widely but not universally accepted in aesthetics.

4 For a lengthy discussion of the differences between science and design, see Addis, *op. cit.* (1990).

5 Quoted in Addis, *op. cit.* (1994).

6 Billington, *op. cit.* (1983), p. 266.

7 See also Alan Holgate, *Aesthetics of Built Form*, New York: Oxford University Press, 1992.

8 The most notable being David Billington, *op. cit.* (1983). In fact, Eduardo Torroja coined the term 'structural art' in *Philosophy of Structures*, Berkeley and Los Angeles: University of California Press, 1958, p. 279.

9 For the titles referred to, see W. Addis, *The Art of the Structural Engineer*, London: Artemis, 1994, and A. Holgate, *The Art in Structural Design*, Oxford: Clarendon Press, 1986.

10 Torroja, *op. cit.* (1958), p. 268.

11 Fritz Leonhardt, *Bridges: Aesthetics and Design*, 3rd edn, Stuttgart: Deutsche Verlags-Anstalt, 1990, pp. 26 ff. Also Jörg Schlaich, 'The Excellence of Structural Design' in *Publication 139*, Dec. 1993, Stockholm: Stålbyggnadsinstitutet.

12 Pier Luigi Nervi, 'Critica delle strutture' in *Casabella*, no. 223, 1959; 'Cinque ponti' in *Casabella*, no. 224, 1959; 'Rapporti tra ingegneria e architettura' in *Casabella*, no. 225, 1959; 'Modello e imitazione' in *Casabella*, no. 227, 1959.

13 Nervi, *op. cit. Casabella*, 224, p. 54.

14 Ibid., 227, p. 51.

15 Nervi, *op. cit.* (1965), p. 2.

16 Torroja, *op. cit.* (1958), p. 1.

17 Ibid., p. 271.

18 Ibid., p. 5.

19 Ibid., p. 287.

20 Ibid., p. 282.

21 Ibid., p. 272.

22 Ibid., pp. 268 and 5.

23 Leonhardt, *op. cit.* (1990), pp. 26 ff.

24 Holgate, *op. cit.* (1992), notes this view as one of a number of other views of the aesthetics of structures.

25 See F. N. Sibley, 'Aesthetic and Nonaesthetic' in *The Philosophical Review*, no. 74, 1965, pp. 135–59.

26 Leonhardt, *op. cit.* (1990), p. 12.

27 Schlaich, *op. cit.* (1993), p. 37.

28 J. Schlaich and R. Bergermann, *Leicht Weit, Light Structures*, Munich: Prestel, 2003, p. 9.

29 Cf. Wittgenstein: 'In order to get clear about aesthetic words you have to describe ways of living, e.g. "this is a fine dress".' Ludwig Wittgenstein, *Lectures and Conversations on Aesthetics, Psychology and Religious Belief*, Oxford: Basil Blackwell, (1966) 1970, p. 11.

30 Addis, *op. cit.* (1994), p. 18.

31 Sibley calls aesthetic judgements of this kind 'verdicts'. Sibley, *op. cit.*, p. 136.

32 Bill Addis, 'Structural Criticism and the Aesthetics of Structures' in *Proceedings of IABSE Congress*, Copenhagen, 1996.

33 An author who has specifically confined his reflections on the aesthetics of structures to include the role solely played by statics is Alexander Zannos. See Zannos, *op. cit.*

34 See Holgate, *op. cit.* (1992), p. 241.

35 Macdonald, *op. cit.*, p. 68.

36 Ibid., pp. 68, 69.

37 Balmond, *op. cit.*, p. 122.

38 Ibid., p. 106.

39 Ibid., p. 9.

40 The 'bad'/'bad' option is ruled out for obvious reasons!

41 Webster, *op. cit.*, p. 69.

42 Formulations like 'conveying elegance', 'derive their elegance', etc. are not unproblematic. The aesthetic views implicit in such formulations are clearly debateable, and will be further discussed in the next section. At this stage, however, they will have to do.

43 R. Arad and A. Brooks, *One Off Three*, London, Zurich, Munich: Artemis, 1993, p. 13.

44 S. Hardingham, *London: A Guide to Recent Architecture*, London: Artemis, 1993, p. 156.

45 Arad and Brooks, *op. cit.*, p. 13.

46 See *Longman Dictionary of Contemporary English*, Harlow: Longman, 1987. Baumgarten's 'Reflections on Poetry' (1735) set out to study aesthetics in mathematical terms.

47 'Aesthetics' in *Encyclopedia Britannica*, 15th edn, 1991.

48 Wittgenstein, *op. cit.* (1966) 1970, p. 11.

49 It seems that the idea of the existence of 'aesthetic qualities' is recognised primarily among philosophers (Sibley et al.) who support the view that these are qualities of the objects. I will in any case use the term, for the time being, to express a meaning that is valid independently of the position taken regarding the question of objectivity versus subjectivity. In the latter case, so-called aesthetic qualities like 'elegance', 'charm' and 'beauty' may be taken as *particular articulations* of a certain aesthetic experience.

50 The most common aesthetic term employed in connection with
    structures is probably 'elegant'. Numerous others are in use, like
    'delicate', 'vital', 'harmonic', etc.

51 Cited in Oswald Hanfling (ed.), *Philosophical Aesthetics: An
    Introduction*, Oxford: Blackwell Publishers, 1992, p. 44.

52 Ibid., p. 44.

53 Wittgenstein, *op. cit.* (1966) 1970, pp. 1–11.

54 Hanfling, *op. cit.*, p. ix.

55 Ibid., p. ix.

56 Ibid., p. 46.

57 F. N. Sibley, 'Aesthetic Concepts' in *The Philosophical Review*, no.
    68, 1959, pp. 421–50.

58 Ibid., p. 424.

59 Ibid., pp. 135–6.

60 F. N. Sibley, 'Objectivity and Aesthetics' in *Proceedings of the
    Aristotelian Society*, suppl. vol. 42, 1968, p. 32.

61 Ibid., p. 32.

62 Ibid., p. 44.

63 Ibid., p. 53.

64 L. Wittgenstein, *Philosophical Investigations*, Oxford: Basil
    Blackwell, (1953) 1989, p. 212.

65 J. Lundequist, *Designteoriens kunnskapsteoretiska och estetiska
    utgångspunkter*, Stockholm: KTH, 1992, p. 14.

66 Roger Scruton, *The Aesthetics of Architecture*, London: Methuen,
    1979.

67 Roger Scruton, *Art and Imagination*, London: Methuen, 1974.

68 Scruton, *op. cit.* (1979), p. 234.

69 Incidentally, articulations like these are acknowledged also by
    Sibley as being representative of a sort of aesthetic judgement.
    Sibley, *op. cit.* (1965), pp. 135, 136.

70 Malcolm Budd, 'The Aesthetic Appreciation of Nature' in *British
    Journal of Aesthetics*, vol. 36, no. 3, July 1996, p. 211.

71 Ibid., p. 215.

72 Scruton, *op. cit.* (1979), p. 10.

73 Bill Addis makes more or less the same point: 'While anyone can
    perceive a structure, it starts to get interesting when we look
    at who is perceiving it and how they think and talk about the
    perception, and how they remember it or store it in the form of
    knowledge. Perceiving a structure is an active process and utterly
    dependent on the eye and brain of the person involved.' Addis,
    op. cit. (1994), p. 10.

74 The importance of this is made clear by Scruton throughout his text:
    'The value of a building', he says, 'simply cannot be understood
    independently of its utility.' Scruton, *op. cit.* (1979), p. 7.

75 Scruton calls this kind of perception 'imaginary perception', as
    opposed to 'literal' or ordinary perception. Ibid., p. 78.

76 Ibid., p. 72.

77 Lundequist, *op. cit.*, p. 17.

78 Wittgenstein, *op. cit.* (1953) 1989, pp. 193–227.

79 Ibid., pp. 193, 200.

80 Ibid., p. 197.

81 Recalled from memory by engineer Horst Berger from an LP recording made in the 1960s. From a conversation with the author.

82 Scruton, *op. cit.* (1979), p. 75.

83 Ibid., p. 87.

84 See Joseph Jastrow, *Fact and Fable in Psychology*, Freeport, NY: Books for Library Press, 1971.

85 'Architect and engineer think about form and structure in different ways', Addis says. 'They interpret what they see in a structure differently and the differences are not superficial. The very concepts in terms of which architect and engineer think of structures are different and this affects the very thoughts and ideas they are likely to have.' Addis, *op. cit.* (1997), p. 3.

86 'In general terms, the main consequence of the notion of "seeing as" is that the whole attitude of someone contemplating an actual or projected engineering structure can be utterly different from the attitude of another, apparently doing the same.' Addis, *op. cit.* (1990), p. 66.

87 Scruton, *op. cit.* (1979), p. 92.

88 See Lundequist, *op. cit.*, p. 27.

89 'Norman Foster: 1964–1987' in *Architecture and Urbanism: 1988 Extra Edition*. Tokyo: a+u Publishing, 1988.

90 Scruton, *op. cit.* (1979), p. 112.

91 Ibid., p. 101.

92 Ibid., p. 205.

93 Ibid., p. 227.

94 Ibid., p. 225.

95 Ibid., p. 119.

96 Ibid., p. 134.

97 Ibid., p. 110.

98 See Colin Lyas, 'The Evaluation of Art' in Hanfling (ed.), *op. cit.*, pp. 357 ff. Lyas disputes the relevance of reason to aesthetic criticism. 'The critic cannot reason me into seeing that something has a certain property by giving me propositions from which it follows that I will see that it has.' Scruton, however, by focusing on the aesthetic experience rather than the postulation of certain aesthetic 'properties', and by admitting intellectual activities as parts of the aesthetic experience, very convincingly argues for the possibility of changing, by reasoning, another person's point of view. This takes place neither by way of deduction nor of induction, but by opening up new imaginings that also imply a change of the aesthetic experience.

99 Scruton, *op. cit.* (1979), p. 237.

100 Ibid., p. 238.

101 Ibid., p. 239.

102 Leon Battista Alberti, *The Art of Building in Ten Books*, book no. 9. Translation of 'De re aedificatoria', Cambridge, MA: MIT Press, 1988, p. 302.

103 Wittgenstein, *op. cit.* (1953) 1989, p. 202.

104 The criticism of structures is, as might be understood from the discussion so far, no easy matter. 'To criticize the overall design of structures is at once more interesting and more foolhardy than to concentrate solely on the engineering. However, if it is done well it is certainly more meaningful', says Holgate, *op. cit.* (1986), p. 272.

105 Ola Mowé, 'Hamar Olympic Amphitheatre' in *Byggekunst*, no. 5–6, 1993, p. 329.

106 According to information supplied by the manufacturer. By comparison, the corresponding axial forces in the Hamar Olympic Hall, an arch structure of 30% longer span, amount to a 'modest' 4900 kN and 740 kN.

107 All industrialised nations used to have their own 'codes of practice' setting out rules for how you should calculate and construct in wood, steel, concrete, etc. These have now been replaced by European codes, American codes, etc.

108 See John Zukowsky (ed.), *The Architecture of von Gerkan, Marg + Partners*, Munich and New York: Prestel, 1997, p. 171.

109 Ian Liddell and Paul Westbury, 'Design and Construction of the Millennium Dome' in *Structural Engineering International*, vol. 9, no. 3, Aug. 1999.

110 See 'The Third Reality/Japan Today '95 Exhibition' in *The Japan Architect* vol. 19, no. 3, 1995; 'Toyo Ito, Sendai Mediatheque Competition' in *GA Document*, no. 43, 1995; and Sophie Roulet, 'Au-delà du visible: Médiathèque de Sendai, Miyagi, Japon' in *Architecture et Technique*, Nov. 1995.

111 The surface is made by rotating a hyperbola about a fixed axis. Through every point on the surface pass two straight lines contained entirely within the surface, a characteristic that makes the shape easier to construct.

112 Sophie Roulet, *op. cit.*, p. 61.

113 A column-free span of about 48 m would be in the same range as that of (for instance) the Centre Georges Pompidou in Paris.

114 Ito himself likens the structure to floating seaweed. See also Ron Witte (ed.), *Toyo Ito: Sendai Mediatheque*. New York: Prestel Publishing, 2002.

115 Jan Digerud, Per Olaf Fjeld and Christian Norberg-Schulz, *Louis I. Kahn: Speech at OAF 1964*, Oslo: Arkitektnytt, 1982.

116 See Peter Rice, *An Engineer Imagines*, London: Artemis, 1994, pp. 87 ff.; Deborah Gans (ed.), *Bridging the Gap*, New York: Van

Nostrand Reinhold, 1991, pp. 90–3; John Pastier, 'Simplicity of Form, Ingenuity in the Use of Daylight' in *AIA Journal*, May 1987, pp. 84–90; Peter Davey, 'Menil Museum' in *Architectural Review*, March 1987, pp. 36–42.

117 The iron is actually what is called 'ductile iron', in which the carbon occurs in formations of spheroidal form. This reduces the brittleness characteristic of normal cast iron, and results in an iron with higher strength and ductility. Compared to and unlike cast steel, which has to be re-heated after casting, ductile iron can be made into finer and more delicate shapes.

118 See Per Olaf Fjeld, *Sverre Fehn: The Thought of Construction*, New York: Rizzoli, 1983; *Progressive Architecture*, vol. 75, Feb. 1994; *l'Architecture d'aujourd'hui*, no. 287, June 1993.

119 Sverre Fehn, 'Nordisk paviljong ved Biennalen i Venezia' in *Byggekunst*, no. 6, 1962, p. 145 (author's translation).

120 Ibid., p. 145.

121 Per Olaf Fjeld, *op. cit.*, p. 11.

122 Oskar Graf, the engineer, calls the structure a 'Gerber Fachwerkträger', indicating the existence of a theoretical pin-joint along the piece of steel where the truss meets the bracket. A 'Gerber Fachwerkträger' is a continuous trussed beam made statically determinate by inserting pin-joints at appropriate places along the spans. Oskar Graf, 'Die Statik, die Konstruktion und der Dekonstruktivismus' in *Bauwelt*, no. 26, 1989, p. 1259.

123 From a conversation with the author, Sept. 1996 in Vienna.

124 Oskar Graf, *op. cit.*, p. 1260. ('Die Struktur folgt dem architektonischen Anspruch, und wenn sie gut ist, unterstutzt sie die architektonische Aussage.')

125 Geoffrey Broadbent, *Deconstruction: A Student Guide*, London: Academy Editions, 1991, p. 91.

126 Cecil Balmond, describing his structures for the Rotterdam 'Kunsthalle', expresses similar thoughts when he asks: 'Why should structure be comprehensible and explicit? Structure need not advertise itself.' And: 'I prefer structure *as trace rather than skeleton*, with pathways that attempt to interpret space.' Cecil Balmond, 'New Structure and the Informal' in *Lotus International*, no. 98, 1997, pp. 76–83.

127 See Peter Cachola Schmal (ed.), *Workflow: Architecture-Engineering, Klaus Bollinger + Manfred Grohmann*, Basel: Birkhäuser, 2004.

128 Bernhard Franken, 'Utstillingshall for presentasjon av biler' in *Byggekunst*, no. 7, 2002, p. 32.

129 Königs Architekten, www.archilab.org/public/1999.

130 Peter Kulka and Ulrich Königs in Y. Förster and I. Flagge (eds), *Peter Kulka: Minimalism and Sensuality*, catalogue, Frankfurt-am-Main: Deutsche Architekturmuseum, Edition Axel Menges, 2005, p. 257.

131 Cecil Balmond, *op. cit.* (2002).

132 A good summing up of this debate preceding the 1990s is
Gary Iseminger, *Intention and Interpretation*, Philadelphia, PA:
Temple University Press, 1992. Later contributions have not been
sufficiently illuminating to be of much help for the present book.

133 Wittgenstein, *op. cit.* (1953) 1989, § 337.

134 Tore Nordenstam, 'Intention in Art' in K. S. Johannesen and
T. Nordenstam, *Wittgenstein: Aesthetics and Trancendental
Philosophy*, Vienna: Verlag Hølder-Pichler-Tempsky, 1981, p. 129.

135 Ibid., p. 131.

136 Incidentally, Balmond refers to this free-floating and apparent
random form as the opposite of a 'coherent, uniform Cartesian
logic'. He is not alone in criticising dull, rectangular and ordered
systems as products of Cartesian thinking. This is very peculiar.
If something resembling chaos is to be mimicked at all in built
forms, we have no better way of precisely defining that form than
with the help of Descartes's wonderful instrument for combining
geometry and algebra. Descartes's observation from his sick-
bed of the complex, random tracks made by a fly in his room
led to his genial conclusion that these seemingly chaotic paths
could be fixed as a graph if an adequate number of its positions
in space were related to their distances from the three surfaces
meeting in a corner. That 'Cartesian logic' should come to refer
to his rectangular system of axes, rather than to its wonderful
consequence of enabling us to map any geometry, is a mystery as
well as a case of grave injustice . . .

137 Scruton, *op. cit.* (1979), p. 183.

138 Werner Blaser (ed.), *Santiago Calatrava: Engineering Architecture*,
Basel, Boston, Berlin: Birkhaüser Verlag, 1990, p. 42.

139 Scruton, *op. cit.* (1979), p. 183.

140 Holgate, *op. cit.* (1986), p. 261.

141 See *Byggekunst*, no. 5/6, 1990, p. 269; *Byggekunst*, no. 7,
1990, pp. 409–11; *Architectural Review*, vol. 1122, Aug. 1990,
pp. 49–51.

142 *Byggekunst*, no. 5/6, 1990, p. 269 (author's translation).

143 Peters, *op. cit.* (1987), p. 9.

144 In reality, the engineers calculated the structure by considering
the rafters to be supported by the three columns, as well as by the
forked compression struts that reduce the span. The horizontal tie-
beam acts as a local bracing for the struts, reducing their effective
length.

145 This likeness is, in the present case, clearly intended. The architects
speak about the structure as referring to 'the complex structures
of the rig for the drying of fishing nets'. *Byggekunst*, no. 7, 1990,
pp. 410, 411 (author's translation).

146 Peters, *op. cit.* (1987), p. 10.

Bibliographical references

Addis, Bill, *Structural Engineering: The Nature of Theory and Design*, Chichester: Ellis Horwood, 1990.

Addis, Bill, *The Art of the Structural Engineer*, London: Artemis, 1994.

Addis, Bill, 'Structural Criticism and the Aesthetics of Structures' in *Proceedings of IABSE Congress*, Copenhagen, 1996.

Addis, Bill, 'Free Will and Determinism in the Conception of Structures' in *Journal of the International Association for Shell and Spatial Structures*, vol. 38, no. 2, 1997.

Alberti, Leon Battista, *The Art of Building in Ten Books*. Translation of 'De re aedificatoria', Cambridge, MA: MIT Press, 1988.

Anscombe, G. E. M., *Intention*, 2nd edn, Oxford: Oxford University Press, 1963.

Arad, Ron and Brooks, Alison, *One Off Three*, London, Zurich, Munich: Artemis, 1993.

Architectural Review, no. 1087, Sept. 1987.

Architectural Review, no. 1094, April 1988.

Architectural Review, no. 1122, Aug. 1990.

Architecture and Urbanism, 1988 extra edition: 'Norman Foster: 1964–1987', Tokyo: a+u Publishing, 1988.

l'Architecture d'aujourd'hui, no. 287, Jun. 1993.

Ashby, M. F., *Materials Selection in Mechanical Design*, Oxford: Pergamon Press, 1992.

Balmond, Cecil, 'New Structure and the Informal' in *Lotus International*, no. 98, 1997.

Balmond, Cecil, *informal*, Munich, Berlin, London, New York: Prestel Verlag, 2002.

Baxandall, Alexander, *Patterns of Intention: On the Historical Explanation of Pictures*, New Haven, CT: Yale University Press, 1985.

Behnisch, Günter and Hartung, Giselher, *Eisenkonstruktionen des 19. Jahrhunderts*, Munich: Schirmer-Mosel, 1983.

Bergdoll, Barry, *The Foundations of Architecture: Selections from the Dictionnaire raisonné*, New York: George Braziller, 1990.

Billington, David, *Robert Maillart and the Art of Reinforced Concrete*, Zurich and Munich: Artemis, 1990.

Billington, David, *The Tower and the Bridge: The New Art of Structural Engineering*, New York: Basic Books, 1983.

Blaser, Werner (ed.), *Santiago Calatrava: Engineering Architecture*, Basel, Boston, Berlin: Birkhaüser Verlag, 1990.

Broadbent, Geoffrey, *Deconstruction: A Student Guide*, London: Academy Editions, 1991.

Buchler, Justus, *Philosophical Writings of Peirce*, New York: Dover Publications, 1955.

Budd, Malcolm, 'The Aesthetic Appreciation of Nature' in *British Journal of Aesthetics*, vol. 36, no. 3, Jul. 1996.

Byggekunst, no. 5/6, 1990.

Byggekunst, no. 7, 1990.

Cambridge Encyclopedia of Philosophy, Robert Audi (ed.), Cambridge: Cambridge University Press, 1995.

Carlson, Allen, *Aesthetics and the Environment: The Appreciation of Nature, Art and Architecture*, London: Routledge, 2000.

Charles, J. A. and Crane, F. A. A., *Selection and Use of Engineering Materials*, 2nd edn, Oxford: Butterworth-Heinemann, 1989.

Chemetov, Paul and Marrey, Bernard, *Architectures à Paris 1848–1914*, Paris: Dunod, 1984.

Choay, Françoise, *The Rule and the Model: On the Theory of Architecture and Urbanism*, Cambridge, MA and London: MIT Press, 1997.

Collovà, Roberto, 'Una piazza coperta' in Pierluigi Nicolin (ed.) *Lotus International*, no. 99, 1998.

Davey, Peter, 'Menil Museum' in *Architectural Review*, Mar. 1987.

Davies, Colin and Lambot, Ian, *Century Tower: Foster Associates Build in Japan*, Berlin: Ernst and Sohn, 1992.

Dickie, George, *Art and the Aesthetic: An Institutional Analysis*, Ithaca, NY: Cornell University Press, 1974.

Digerud, Jan, Fjeld, Per Olaf and Norberg-Schulz, Christian, *Louis I. Kahn: Speech at OAF 1964*, Oslo: Arkitektnytt, 1982.

Domus, no. 683, May 1987.

Domus, no. 719, Sept. 1990.

Dunin-Woyseth, Halina and Noschis, Kaj (eds), 'Architecture and Teaching. Epistemological Foundations' in *Transactions on Architectural Education*, no. 02, Lausanne: Comportements and Authors, 1998.

Eggen, A. and Sandaker, B., *Steel, Structure and Architecture*, New York: Whitney Library of Design, 1995.

Eiler Rasmussen, Steen, *Experiencing Architecture*, Cambridge, MA: MIT Press, 1959.

Ejnar Wåhlin (ed.), *BYGG: Handbok för hus, -väg och vattenbyggnad*, vol. 1, 2nd edn, Stockholm: Tidsskriften Byggmästarens Förlag, 1959.

Encyclopedia Britannica, 15th edn, 1991.

Engel, Heinrich, *Structure Systems*, London: Iliffe Books, 1967.

Fehn, Sverre, 'Nordisk paviljong ved Biennalen i Venezia' in *Byggekunst*, no. 6, 1962.

Fjeld, Per Olaf, *Sverre Fehn: The Thought of Construction*, New York: Rizzoli, 1983.

Ford, Edward R., *The Details of Modern Architecture*, Cambridge, MA: MIT Press, 1990.

Ford, Edward R., *The Details of Modern Architecture, Vol. 2, 1928–1988*, Cambridge, MA: MIT Press, 1996.

Förster, Y. and Flagge, I. (ed.), *Peter Kulka: Minimalism and Sensuality*, catalogue, Frankfurt-am-Main: Deutsche Architekturmuseum, Edition Axel Menges, 2005.

Frampton, Kenneth, *Studies in Tectonic Culture: The Poetics of Construction in Nineteenth and Twentieth Century Architecture*, Cambridge, MA: MIT Press, 1995.

Friedman, Mildred (ed.), *Gehry Talks: Architecture + Process*, New York: Universe Publishing, 2002.

GA Document, no. 43, 1995.

Galilei, Galileo, *Dialogues Concerning Two New Sciences*, New York: Dover Publications, 1954.

Gans, Deborah (ed.), *Bridging the Gap: Rethinking the Relationship of Architect and Engineer*, New York: Van Nostrand Reinhold, 1991.

Geist, J. F., *Arcades*, Cambridge, MA: MIT Press, 1983.

Gilbert-Rolfe, J. with F. Gehry, *Frank Gehry: The City and Music*, London and New York: Routledge, 2001.

Gordon, J. E., *The Science of Structures and Materials*, New York: Scientific American Books, 1988.

Graf, Oskar, 'Die Statik, die Konstruktion und der Dekonstruktivismus' in *Bauwelt*, no. 26, 1989.

Hanaor, Ariel, *Principles of Structures*, Oxford: Blackwell Science, 1998.

Hanfling, Oswald (ed.), *Philosophical Aesthetics: An Introduction*, Oxford: Blackwell Publishers, 1992.

Hardingham, Samantha, *London: A Guide to Recent Architecture*, London: Artemis, 1993.

Harris, J. B. and Li, K. Pui-K., *Masted Structures in Architecture*, Oxford: Butterworth Architecture, 1996.

Helland, Bård, 'Forholdet mellom konstruksjon og uttrykk i en fremtidig arkitektur' in *Byggekunst*, no. 4, 2004.

Hermerén, Göran, *The Nature of Aesthetic Qualities*, Lund: Lund University Press, 1988.

Holgate, Alan, *Aesthetics of Built Form*, New York: Oxford University Press, 1992.

Holgate, Alan, *The Art in Structural Design*, Oxford: Clarendon Press, 1986.

Hubbard, Bill, *A Theory for Practice: Architecture in Three Discourses*, Cambridge: MIT Press, 1995.

Iseminger, Gary, *Intention and Interpretation*, Philadelphia, PA: Temple University Press, 1992.

The Japan Architect, vol. 19, no. 3, 1995.

Jastrow, Joseph, *Fact and Fable in Psychology*, Freeport, NY: Books for Library Press, 1971.

Kemp, Peter, 'Teknologifilosofi: En kropsontologi' in *Philosophia*, no. 3–4, 1991.

Leonhardt, Fritz, *Bridges: Aesthetics and Design*, 3rd. edn, Stuttgart: Deutsche Verlags-Anstalt, 1990.

Liddell, Ian and Westbury, Paul, 'Design and Construction of the Millennium Dome' in *Structural Engineering International*, vol. 9, no. 3, Aug. 1999.

Lindsey, Bruce, *Digital Gehry: Material Resistance/Digital Construction*, Basel, Boston, Berlin: Birkhäuser, 2001.

Lobell, John, *Between Silence and Light: Spirit in the Architecture of Louis I. Kahn*, Boston, MA: Shambhala Publications, 1979.

Longman Dictionary of Contemporary English, Harlow: Longman, 1987.

Lundequist, Jerker, *Designteoriens kunskapsteoretiska och estetiska utgångspunkter*, Stockholm: KTH, 1992.

Macdonald, Angus, *Structure and Architecture*, Oxford: Butterworth Architecture, 1994.

Mark, Robert, *Light, Wind and Structure: The Mystery of the Master Builders*, Cambridge, MA: MIT Press, 1990.

Moore, C. and Allen, G., *Dimensions*, New York: Architectural Record Books, 1976.

Mowé, Ola, 'Hamar Olympic Amphitheatre' in *Byggekunst*, no. 5–6, 1993.

Nervi, Pier Luigi, *Aesthetics and Technology in Building*, Cambridge, MA: Harvard University Press, 1965.

Nervi, Pier Luigi, *Structures*, New York: F. W. Dodge, 1956.

Norberg-Schulz, Christian, 'The Paustian House' in *Arkitektur DK*, no. 8, 1989.

Norberg-Schulz, Christian, *Meaning in Western Architecture*, New York: Rizzoli Publications, 1980.

Nordenstam, Tore, 'Intention in Art' in Kjell S. Johannesen and Tore Nordenstam, *Wittgenstein: Aesthetics and Transcendental Philosophy*, Vienna: Verlag Hølder-Pichler-Tempsky, 1981.

Palladio, Andrea, *The Four Books of Architecture*, New York: Dover Publications, 1965.

Partridge, Eric, *Origins: An Etymological Dictionary of Modern English*, London: Routledge and Kegan Paul, (1958) 1990.

Pastier, John, 'Simplicity of Form, Ingenuity in the Use of Daylight' in *AIA Journal*, May 1987.

Patterson, Terry, *Frank Lloyd Wright and the Meaning of Materials*, New York: Van Nostrand Reinhold, 1994.

Perez-Gomez, Alberto, *Architecture and the Crisis of Modern Science*, Cambridge, MA: MIT Press, 1983.

Peters, Tom F., *Transitions in Engineering: Guillaume Henri Dufour and the Early 19th Century Cable Suspension Bridges*, Basel and Boston, MA: Birkhäuser Verlag, 1987.

Peters, Tom, '"Bridging the Gap": Point of Contact between the Architect and Engineer' in *Architronic*, vol. 9, 1992.

Prix, Wolf D., 'On the Edge' in Peter Noever (ed.), *Architecture in Transition: Between Deconstruction and New Modernism*, Munich: Prestel Verlag, 1991.

Progressive Architecture, vol. 75, Feb. 1994.

Reitzel, Erik, *Fra brud til form: Om minimering og ressourceøkonomi*, Copenhagen: Polyteknisk Forlag, 1979.

Rice, Peter, *An Engineer Imagines*, London: Artemis, 1993.

Roulet, Sophie, 'Au-delà du visible: Médiathèque de Sendai, Miyagi, Japon' in *Architecture et Technique*, Nov. 1995.

Saarinen, Aline (ed.), *Eero Saarinen on His Work*, New Haven, CT: Yale University Press, 1968.

Sandaker, Bjørn N. and Eggen, Arne P., *The Structural Basis of Architecture*, New York: The Whitney Library of Design, 1992.

Schlaich, Jörg, 'The Excellence of Structural Design' in *Publication 139*, Dec. 1993, Stockholm: Stålbyggnadsinstitutet.

Schlaich, J. and Bergermann, R., *Leicht Weit, Light Structures*, Munich: Prestel, 2003.

Schmal, Peter Cachola (ed.), *Workflow: Architecture-Engineering, Klaus Bollinger + Manfred Grohmann*, Basel: Birkhäuser, 2004.

Schodek, Daniel L., *Structure in Sculpture*, Cambridge, MA: MIT Press, 1993.

Schodek, Daniel L., *Structures*, 2nd edn, Upper Saddle River, NJ: Prentice Hall, 1992.

Schön, Donald A. and Rein, Martin, *Frame Reflection: Toward the Resolution of Untractable Policy Controversies*, New York: University Press of America, 1999.

Schopenhauer, Arthur, *The World as Will and Representation*, Vol. 1, New York: Dover Publications, 1966.

Scruton, Roger, *Art and Imagination*, London: Methuen, 1974.

Scruton, Roger, *The Aesthetics of Architecture*, London: Methuen, 1979.

Searle, John, *The Construction of Social Reality*, London: Allen Lane, 1995.

Seymour Howard Jr., H., *Structure: An Architect's Approach*, New York: McGraw Hill, 1966.

Sibley, F. N., 'Aesthetic and Nonaesthetic' in *The Philosophical Review*, no. 74, 1965.

Sibley, F. N., 'Aesthetic Concepts' in *The Philosophical Review*, no. 68, 1959.

Sibley, F. N., 'Objectivity and Aesthetics' in *Proceedings of the Aristotelian Society*, suppl. vol. 42, 1968.

Siegel, Curt, *Structure and Form in Modern Architecture*, Huntington, NY: Robert E. Krieger, (1962) 1975.

Siggard Jensen, Hans, 'Formålenes rige Rige: Om teknologi og natur' in *Philosophia*, no. 3–4, 1991.

Simon, Herbert, *The Sciences of the Artificial*, Cambridge, MA: MIT Press, 1969.

Sinding-Larsen, Ståle, *Arkitekturteori og bygningsanalyse*, Trondheim: Tapir Forlag, 1994.

Stål Håndbok (Norwegian), forenklet nytrykk, Del 1, utg. 3. 1983.

Technique et Architecture, no. 381, Dec. 1988–Jan. 1989.

Thompson, W. d'Arcy, *On Growth and Form*, Cambridge: Cambridge University Press, 1961.

Torroja, Edouardo, *Philosophy of Structures*, Berkeley and Los Angeles: University of California Press, 1958.

Tschumi, Bernard, *Architecture and Disjunction*, Cambridge, MA and London: MIT Press, 1994.

Vangaard, Ole and Mortensen, Duelund (eds), *Le Ricolais: Visions and Paradox*, Copenhagen: Kunstakademiets Arkitektskole, 1998.

Viollet-le-Duc, Eugène-Emmanuel, *Lectures on Architecture* (*Entretiens sur l'architecture*), Vols 1 and 2, New York: Dover Publications, 1987.

von Wright, Georg Henrik, *Explanation and Understanding*, London: Routledge and Kegan Paul, 1971 (1975).

Waley, Arthur (tr.), *The Way and Its Power: A Study of the Tao Te Ching and Its Place in Chinese Thought*, London: Allen and Unwin, 1934.

Webster, Anthony C., 'Utility, Technology and Expression' in *Architectural Review*, Nov. 1992.

Wilkinson, C., *Supersheds: The Architecture of Long-Span, Large-Volume Buildings*, Oxford: Butterworth-Architecture, 1991.

Witte, Ron (ed.), *Toyo Ito: Sendai Mediatheque*, New York: Prestel Publishing, 2002.

Wittgenstein, Ludwig, *Lectures and Conversations on Aesthetics, Psychology and Religious Belief*, Oxford: Basil Blackwell, (1966) 1970.

Wittgenstein, Ludwig, *Philosophical Investigations*, Oxford: Basil Blackwell, (1953) 1989.

Wormnæs, Odd, *Vitenskapsfilosofi*, 2nd edn, Oslo: Gyldendal Norsk Forlag, (1987) 1991.

Wright, Frank Lloyd, 'In the Cause of Architecture: The Meaning of Materials' in *The Architectural Record* 1928. Reprint.

Wright, Frank Lloyd, 'In the Cause of Architecture', first printed in *The Architectural Record*, Mar., 1908. Reprinted in the book by the same title, ed. Frederick Gutheim, New York: Architectural Record Books, 1975.

Zannos, Alexander, *Form and Structure in Architecture: The Role of Statical Function*, New York: Van Nostrand Reinhold, 1987.

Zukowsky, John (ed.), *The Architecture of von Gerkan, Marg + Partners*, Munich and New York: Prestel, 1997.

Index

Note: page numbers in *italic* refer to illustrations.